Dynamic Macroeconomic Models in Emerging Market Economies

Daniel Lukui Jia

Dynamic Macroeconomic Models in Emerging Market Economies

DSGE Modelling with Financial and Housing Sectors

palgrave
macmillan

Daniel Lukui Jia
Beijing, China

ISBN 978-981-15-4587-0 ISBN 978-981-15-4588-7 (eBook)
https://doi.org/10.1007/978-981-15-4588-7

This Palgrave Macmillan imprint is published by the registered company Springer Nature Singapore Pte Ltd.
The registered company address is: 152 Beach Road, #21-01/04 Gateway East, Singapore 189721, Singapore

Foreword

The evolution of economics is a process of reviewing, rethinking, developing and empirically examining it. After the sad experience of the Global Financial Crisis (GFC), relevant rethinking emerged in terms of the relevant experience with monetary and other policies and their role in terms of their effects on the GFC. Scholars turned their attention to the modern mainstream macroeconomics, especially on the theoretical basis of the policy of the majority of central banks. This book examines the development of modern mainstream macroeconomics, focusing on its theoretical framework and emphasizing its empirical dimension. Emerging market economies is the focus of the book in terms of these aspects, emphasizing the dynamic modelling in these economies.

Theoretically, this book extends the New Consensus Macroeconomics (NCM) to better account for important economic and social features in emerging market economies; thereby filling a gap in the existing literature. In particular, the inclusion of social stratification and incorporation of household heterogeneities adds realism to the theoretical framework, which better accounts for underlying social structure in emerging economies. Moreover, financial and real estate markets that are the main components of the model, proposed by this book, have not been accounted sufficiently, if at all, in the relevant literature in terms of both advanced and emerging economies. As a result, this book provides an original contribution to this field. Empirically, this book is very relevant to the global economy, in view of the fact that emerging economies are increasingly influential globally. Consequently, improved understanding is clearly required in terms of the workings of emerging economies, particularly in relation to the socioeconomic structure and the industrialization process. In this respect, the three most important emerging market economies, namely Brazil, India and China, are considered in the book. The empirical results provide support of the theoretical framework, and in the case of these countries.

In view of the theoretical and empirical contributions of this book it is strongly recommended, especially so since the NCM macroeconomic model needs serious revisions, if not new approaches to macroeconomics, in view of the causes of the GFC.

London, UK

Prof. Philip Arestis

Preface

The Dynamic Stochastic General Equilibrium (DSGE) model, which is based on the New Consensus Macroeconomics (NCM) theoretical framework, has become the workhorse of macroeconomic analysis in academia, research institutes and monetary authorities since the 1980s. The history of macroeconomics tells us that the developments of this doctrine come from scholars' endless efforts to refine their theoretical frameworks and empirical models. Moreover, major breakthroughs in macroeconomics were typically triggered by significant economic meltdowns that expose the mismatch between theory and reality. From the birth of Keynesian economics in the great depression to the rise of Neoclassical economics in the stagflation, economists attempted to develop their model with a broader body of economic thinking and with more comprehensive structure. In such sense, scholars of this generation are privileged in that they have the opportunity to personally experience the great recession caused by the 2007/2008 subprime crisis. The faith in the NCM framework and its empirical DSGE models was severely shaken. There is a growing consensus among researchers that the mainstream macroeconomics needs to be improved, since many components, especially the financial sector, are inadequately modelled in the NCM/DSGE models.

We admit that the mainstream macroeconomics and its empirical NCM/DSGE models are seriously flawed. But we also maintain that the NCM framework inherits the spirit of major contributions in the development of economics, as it combines Keynesian and Classical elements. Moreover, such a framework is a highly flexible platform, on which new developments and improvements, both theoretical and empirical, can be feasibly incorporated. Therefore, we expect the NCM/DSGE models to be central to the future of macroeconomics. In this book, we try to make a contribution to the development of NCM/DSGE modelling, with emphasis on financial and housing markets and social stratification (asymmetric social structure).

The model we proposed in this book is Financial and Housing Sectors Asymmetric Model (FHSAM). Theoretically, it is deeply rooted in the NCM framework and draws on a broader body of economic research. Keynesian, new classical and modern financial elements are integrated into the FHSAM framework, including nominal rigidities, dynamic planning under rational expectation and financial friction. Both financial and housing sectors are explicitly modelled in this framework. The structure of the model economy in this framework is well consistent with the actual condition in emerging market economies. Technically, calibration and Bayesian estimation with the Markov Chain Monte Carlo methods and the Metropolis–Hastings algorithm are adopted in model identification. Empirically, the application of FHSAM is undertaken in three major emerging market economies, namely Brazil, India and China (BIC).

In conclusion, empirical results show good consistency of statistical features between model economy and stylized facts drawn from observed data in BIC. FHSAM exhibits strong ability to explain the inner workings of the economy in terms of both structural and dynamic qualities. Based on the FHSAM framework suggested in this book, we are looking forward to its application in economies with similar economic characteristics. Moreover, we expect certain improvements can be conducted in the future, refining it with more comprehensive model structure and advanced mathematical approaches.

Cambridge, UK
Beijing, P.R. China
December 2019

Elsa Zhang
Daniel Lukui Jia

Acknowledgements

I want to thank my loving parents, without their love and support this work could never be accomplished.

I am greatly obliged to my girlfriend and her parents, who unconditionally love and support me.

I am extremely grateful to my Ph.D. supervisor, Prof. Philip Arestis, who gives me precious supervision and valuable guidance with enormous patience and care.

Many thanks to my friends, especially Leon Deng and Prof. Xin Chang, for making my life colourful in that rainy city.

Contents

Part II Dynamic Macroeconomic Modelling

Part III The Financial and Housing Sectors Asymmetric Model for Emerging Market Economies

Acronyms

AR	Autoregression
BIC	Brazil, India and China
BoE	Bank of England
BRICS	Brazil, Russia, India, China and South Africa
CIA	Cash in Advance
CRS	Constant Return to Scale
CSV	Costly State Verification
CW	Construction Workers
DSGE	Dynamic Macroeconomic General Equilibrium
ECB	European Central Bank
EDE	Emerging & Developing Economies
FAM	Financial Accelerator Model
FED	The Federal Reserve System
FHSAM	Financial and Housing Sectors Asymmetric Model
FOC	First Order Condition
GFC	Global Financial Crisis, specifically denotes the one triggered by the 2007/2008 U.S. subprime crisis
GR	Global Recession, specifically denotes the one occurred after the 2007/2008 U.S. subprime crisis
HB	Household Borrowers
HL	Household Lenders
IID	Independent Identical Distribution
IMF	International Monetary Fund
KF	Kalman Filter
LDC	Less Developed Countries
LTI	Linear Time-Invariant

LTV	Loan to Value
MCMC	Markov Chain Monte Carlo
MIMO	Multi-Input Multi-Out
MIU	Money in the Utility
NCM	New Consensus Macroeconomics
NKE	New Keynesian Macroeconomics
NWM	Neo-Wicksellian Macroeconomics
OLG	Overlapping Generations
RBC	Real Business Cycle
RW	Migrant workers from Rural Regions
SDF	Stochastic Discount Factor

List of Figures

List of Tables

PART I

Introduction

The Dynamic Stochastic General Equilibrium (DSGE) model, which is based on the New Consensus Macroeconomics (NCM) theoretical framework, has become the workhorse of macroeconomic analysis in academia and monetary authorities since the 1980s. The dominant popularity of the DSGE type of models can be witnessed in their extensive application by central banks, such as the Bank of England (BoE), the European Central Bank (ECB), the Federal Reserve (FED) and so forth. One of the most desirable qualities of the DSGE model is its compatibility with a variety of micro- and macro-economic foundations, including short-run nominal rigidities, agent heterogeneities, monetary policy and a rich set of exogenous shocks; not that there are no problems with these aspects of the DSGE model as discussed in this book. Although a lot of efforts have been made in DSGE modelling in industrialized economies, literature of DSGE modelling in emerging market economies is rather limited, especially considering the models tailored to economic and social features of these developing economies. The models developed in this book, based essentially on the NCM/DSGE type, can be the pioneer dynamic macroeconomic models specially designed for emerging market economies.

As an introduction, this part contains two chapters. The first chapter examines the development of macroeconomics, and the second chapter summarizes the existing body of knowledge concerning modern macroeconomic models. This part also serves as a literature review, displaying the major accomplishments of and challenges to the modern mainstream macroeconomics and its empirical models.

CHAPTER 1

Introduction to Modern Macroeconomic Models

The consequences for human welfare involved in questions like these are simply staggering: Once one starts to think about them, it is hard to think about anything else.

– Lucas [1, p. 5].

1.1 Old Time Economics

The evolution of economic theory is an ongoing process of improving the understanding of economic growth and fluctuations along the growth path. A robust and convincing theory should be able to well explain and predict the economic growth and the associated variations. This is absolutely not an easy task since the economy itself is composed of enormous individuals and institutions, all of which are complicatedly connected. Historians tend to summarize the history of economics as the series of 'epochs', in which revolution and consolidation emerge. Therefore, a brief review of the story of economics in the older days helps us better understand the principal contributions of modern macroeconomics.

D. L. Jia, *Dynamic Macroeconomic Models in Emerging Market Economies*,
https://doi.org/10.1007/978-981-15-4588-7_1

Although the study of economic phenomenon can be tracked back to the ancient era,[1] economics was not a separate discipline until the eighteenth century, when Industrial Revolution started in the Western world. As this transformation from agricultural to industrial economy continued, the social and economic structures in these countries were thoroughly modified, and capitalism had gradually replaced mercantilism and feudalism in the Western world. The booming democracies and capitalistic market formed a solid basis for classical economics. As a result, many theories of value, price, supply, demand, distribution and market equilibrium were developed by a large group of famous classical thinkers,[2] 4 trying to explain capitalism's inner workings. Adam Smith's milestone contribution 'An Inquiry into the Nature and Causes of the Wealth of Nations' [6] highlights the rise of classical economics. In general, classical economists base their theories on one common belief that optimal social welfare can be achieved by free trade and market competition. Obviously, the policy implication of such theories is minimum government interference with the market that is advocated to be self-regulated. This policy implication is known as 'laissez-faire', or 'let it be'. These theories and the associated policies are well-timed in that they matched and supported the rapid growth of industrial capitalism in the eighteenth century.

The further developments of classical paradigm[3] led to the birth of neoclassical economics. Unlike traditional classical economics, neoclassical economics attempts to explain the market mechanism from the perspective of consumer's utility, rather than the cost of production. Within this framework, consumers are assumed to behave rationally, maximizing

[1] The embryonic form of economics was embedded in the earliest economic thinking in ancient China, India and Graeco-Roman world. For economic thoughts before classical economics, including medieval economists thoughts, Mercantilism and international trade theories in sixteenth to eighteenth century, see the works of Aquinas [10], who discussed 'just price', Buridan and Klima [16], who analysed the value of money, Bodin [17], who attempted to explain inflation, von Hörnigk and Wilhelm [18], who tried to analyse the principles of national economy, Locke [19], who built his social contract theory to analyse money and price, and Law [20] who studied the value of money. The contribution of Baldwin and Langholm [21] also provided a conclusive summary of medieval economics thoughts.

[2] Among them, Jean Say [2], John Mill [3], David Ricardo [4] and Eugen von Bawerk [5] are the most cited names in economics textbooks and research papers.

[3] Pioneered by the 'marginal revolution' with contributions of Menger [7], Jevons [8], Walras [9], who conducted one of the first comprehensive quantitative studies of general economic equilibrium, and many others, original classical doctrine transformed into a new stage—neoclassical economics.

their personal satisfaction. They make economic decisions based on consideration and evaluation of the utility of a good or service. This is consistent with the hypotheses of the rational behaviour theory that has profoundly influenced economists of later generations. Based on this assumption, neoclassical supporters argue that the optimal allocation of resources can be automatically realized via market competition without government interference since the forces of supply and demand can create market equilibrium.[4] Though differences and disagreements may exist among classical and neoclassical thinkers, classical school of economics, as the dominant intellectual paradigm during the early stage of capitalism in the Western world, is characterized by its emphasis on self-regulation and competition of the market, advocating a looser market strategy and a less controlling role of government in economic affairs.

But, the dominant role of a classical school in the field of economics was seriously undermined in the 1930s. The Great Depression fundamentally challenged classical economics, as major Western economies that had adopted free-market policies implied by classical economics principles encountered severe crisis with insufficient demand and underconsumption. The self-regulated market mechanism that is strongly recommended by classical economics supporters completely failed to function in this economic calamity, and the promise of efficient allocation of resource was hardly fulfilled. The Western capitalism world bitterly suffered from an extremely high level of unemployment among households, skyrocketed volume of bankruptcy in business and the collapse of the financial market. Therefore, the belief in self-regulation that supply and demand can automatically create the corresponding equilibrium through market competition and an individual's utility maximization activities were greatly shaken. In response to this failure of classical economics, scholars represented by John M. Keynes tried to provide an alternative thinking to explain the inner workings of the capitalist economy, inspiring researchers to build the theoretical framework for a new economics paradigm, which is later known as Keynesian School of economics. Based on the works of many others and the historic contribution of Keynes [11], *The General Theory of Employment Interest and Money*, announced the birth of Keynesian school of economics. In contrast to classical thinkers, Keynesian school economists systematically criticize the basis of classical economics. Firstly, they dispute the power of

[4] Early explanation of this self-adjusting market mechanism is known as the Say's Law of market, which was disputed by Keynesian economists.

market self-adjusting during recessions, arguing that due to certain market characteristics, especially the structural rigidities, underconsumption and underspending are exacerbated rather than relieved. In such sense, natural economic forces and incentives are insufficient to rebalance the market in an economic meltdown. Thus, the economic system solely based on market self-regulation is unable to restore efficiency in resource allocation, drowning the economy into, as described by Fisher [12] in the early days, later by Bernanke and Harold [13] and recently by Dalio [14], the tragedy of deflation spiral. In the second place, Keynesian economics supporters criticize the hypothesis of rational behaviour theory, illustrating that an individual's economic decision is determined not only by rational evaluation of personal utility but also by emotional factors, which Keynes noted as 'animal spirits'. As a result, Keynesian economists maintain that classical models are inaccurate to capture the real-world economic activities. Additionally, given the failure of the self-regulated market mechanism during economic crises, Keynesian economics believers, as demonstrated in the contribution of Keynesian *The End of Laissez-Faire* [15], question the policy implication of less government interference proposed by classical school, highlighting the greater importance of active government policy in preventing economic recessions and restoring economy to its equilibrium. Based on the successful applications of Keynesian economics after the 1930s, the classical school had been downplayed and Keynesianism became the orthodox intellectual paradigm widely adopted by world governments.

1.2 The New Consensus Macroeconomics

In order to conduct optimal monetary policy, central banks and monetary authorities need to adopt quantitative macroeconomic models of good precision. Before the 1970s, the so-called 'Phillips Curve', representing the inverse relationship between inflation and unemployment, along with relevant macroeconomic models, was dominant in the central banks of major Western economies. Accordingly, monetary policy was mainly focused on the trade-off between unemployment and inflation. Such framework supports the intervention conducted by the government to use both monetary policy and fiscal policy to balance unemployment and inflation, consistent with the view of the Keynesian macroeconomics. However, the stagflation in the 1970s, when major Western economies experienced both high levels of inflation and unemployment, the faith in the Phillips Curve and relevant macroeconomic models began to weaken. Stagflation in the 1970s cast severe challenges on the traditional Keynesian economics, since quantitative models based on it failed to predict and explain the stagflation. It seems that the substitution effect between unemployment and inflation described by the Phillips Curve was absent in the 1970s.

Led by Friedman [22–24] and Lucas [25], the New Classical Macroeconomics emerged in response to the failure of the Keynesian economics in stagflation. The New Classical Macroeconomics supporters try to build their framework on microeconomic foundations and the rational expectation hypothesis. The signature policy implication of the New Classical Macroeconomics is monetary targeting, which was adopted by the Fed,[5] the BoE[6] and many others[7] in the 1970s and the 1980s. However, such an approach to monetary policy seemed to be problematic.[8] As summarized by Blinder [28], monetary aggregates, due to financial deregulation and innovation, the relationship between monetary aggregate and goal variables such as GDP growth and inflation became increasingly unstable and unpredictable, making monetary aggregate no longer a good indicator for monetary policy purposes.[9] Economists had to continue their pursuit for a better theoretical framework and soon reached the consensus between

[5] In October 1979, the Fed switched its approach to monetary policy from the price of bank reserves to nonborrowed reserves, a monetary quantity variable.

[6] In 1973, BoE began to introduce an informal approach of monetary targeting, emphasizing a broad aggregate, M3. In 1976, such monetary targeting approach was adopted as BoE's formal strategy.

[7] Economies introduced monetary targeting in this period include Canada, Germany, Switzerland and so forth.

[8] For example, as demonstrated by King [26], the monetary targets set by the BoE in 1980–1981 and 1983–1984 were never achieved. What is more, Mishkin [27] concludes that targeting the nonborrowed reserves did not give rise to the decreased volatility of M1 growth as expected. Rather, the fluctuations of M1 growth in the United States increased after such a change in monetary strategy. As in the U.K., the Fed failed to match its monetary target of M1 growth in all three years of the 1979–1982 period.

[9] As a result, operating strategies of monetary targeting lost their popularity among central banks in most Western economies. In October 1982, the Fed began to change its operating strategies, moving from monetary targeting to inflation targeting. Later in February 1987, the Fed officially ceased to set any M1 targets. In July 1993, Alan Greenspan testified in the Congress that the Fed would no longer set any monetary targets for policymaking purposes. A similar story can be witnessed in the U.K., the operating procedures based on monetary targeting was abandoned by the BoE in 1985. In October 1992, the Chancellor of the Exchequer announced to adopt inflation targeting as the operating strategy of the BoE.

classical and Keynesian schools of economics. As we have discussed in the previous section, such synthesis of economic thinking seems natural in that each school focuses on one side of the market system: classical literature attempts to explain the inner workings of economy emphasizing the supply side, while Keynesian studies pay more attention to the demand side; classical doctrine advocates natural forces and incentives of market, while Keynesian paradigm highlights active government interference based on the consideration of market weakness and structural rigidities. Therefore, modern mainstream macroeconomics has been generally noted as New Consensus Macroeconomics (NCM) in the sense that it combines major characteristics of Keynesian and classical economics, not in the sense that disagreements on certain issues[10] still remain.

The NCM theoretical framework and its implications for monetary policy were initially introduced by Goodfriend and King [31], who asserted that the NCM 'inherits the spirit of the old, in that it combines Keynesian and Classical elements. Methodologically, the new synthesis involves the systematic application of intertemporal optimization and rational expectations as stressed by Robert Lucas' (p. 232). According to the work of Arestis [32], an open economy NCM framework can be summarized using the following six equations:

$$Y_t^g = \alpha_0 + \alpha_1 Y_{t-1}^g + \alpha_2 E_t(Y_{t+1}^g) + \alpha_3[R_t - E_t(P_{t+1})] + \alpha_4(rer)_t + u_1 \quad (1.1)$$

$$P_t = \beta_1 Y_t^g + \beta_2 P_{t-1} + \beta_3 E_t(P_{t+1}) + \beta_4[E_t(P_{wt+1}) - E_t(\Delta(er)_t)] + u_2 \quad (1.2)$$

$$R_t = (1-c_3)[RR^* + E_t(P_{t+1}) + c_1 Y_{t-1}^g + c_2(P_{t-1} - P^T)] + c_3 R_{t-1} + u_3 \quad (1.3)$$

[10]These issues even include the name of this theoretical framework, reflecting the diverse perspectives of scholars with different thinking of economics. A large group of macroeconomists argues that this mainstream theoretical framework is a New Keynesian Economics (NKE) contribution, since it is featured with short-term rigidities, which is the key hypothesis of Keynesian economics. In contrast, many macroeconomists refer to it as the New Neoclassical Economics or New Neoclassical Synthesis,because it is based on certain principle hypotheses of neoclassical economics, such as market competition, general equilibrium, rational expectation and long-run vertical Phillips Curve. Additionally, modern mainstream macroeconomics is often noted as Neo-Wicksellian Macroeconomics (NWM), for example the work of Woodford and Walsh [29], since it contains thinking stemming from Wicksell's original theory [30]. In this book, we denote modern mainstream macroeconomics as New Consensus Macroeconomics to reach wider acceptance among researchers.

$$(rer_t) = d_0 + d_1[[(R_t - E_t(P_{t+1})] - [(R_{wt}) - E_t(P_{wt+1})]] + d_2(CA)_t + d_3E_t(rer)_{t+1} + u_4 \tag{1.4}$$

$$(CA)_t = e_0 + e_1(rer)_t + e_2Y_t^g + e_3Y_{wt}^g + u_5 \tag{1.5}$$

$$er_t = rer_t + P_{wt} - P_t \tag{1.6}$$

In Eqs. 1.1– 1.6, Y_t^g and Y_{wt}^g represent the domestic and international aggregate output gap at time t', respectively. $(rer)_t$ stands for the real exchange rate, and $(er)_t$ for the nominal exchange rate. R is the nominal rate of interest and R_w is the world nominal interest rate. From Eq. 1.1, it is clear that the current output gap is determined not only by its previous value but also by its expected value. The current output gap is also influenced by the real interest rate and the real exchange rate. Behind this equation, the output gap is defined in such a way that it is the difference between the actual output and the potential output. The latter is a long-run variable determined by the supply side of the economy in that it represents the output level, with full price flexibility and no cyclical distortions. Equation 1.1 is based on the assumption that the assumed representative agent maximizes intertemporally her/his lifetime utility that is the reflection of optimum consumption smoothing activities subject to a budget constraint. The optimum consumption smoothing activities are achieved based on the forward-looking expectational relationship that implies the equality between the real interest rate and the marginal substitution rate between current and future consumption. Therefore, Eq. 1.1 is forward-looking, as expectations are explicitly introduced into it. Another important underlying assumption of the representative agent's intertemporal utility optimization is that all obligations are fully paid on time, meaning that there is no room for default. This assumption is known as transversality condition, in which all IOUs are safe. There is only one single interest rate for all fixed-interest financial assets in any period. Along the time path, the fluctuations of such a single rate of interest are determined by the changes of saving and borrowing propensities. In a world like this, there is no space for commercial banks, as economic agents are no longer constrained by liquidity limits. As a result, the traditional NCM framework based on transversality condition is essentially non-monetary.

Equation 1.2 is the Phillips Curve, where p is the domestic inflation and p_w is the world inflation; p^T is the target inflation rate, and RR^* is the 'equilibrium' real rate of interest. As shown in this equation, the current level of domestic inflation is determined by past and future domestic inflation, current output gap, expected changes in the nominal exchange rate and the expected world inflation. An important feature of this model lies in the fact that both short-run nominal rigidities and long-run full price flexibility are included. The typical method to introduce short-run rigidity into the model can be found in the contribution of Calvo [33]. The Phillips Curve described by Eq. 1.2 in the long'run is vertical in that $\beta_2 + \beta_3 + \beta_4 = 1$. In this equation, we can conclude that the real exchange rate is able to affect the level of demand and economic activity via influencing imports and exports. The assumption of rational expectation is prominent, as Eq. 1.2 contains forward-looking feature represented by the term $E_t(p_{t+1})$, which is the expectation of inflation. It is an important assumption, especially for central banks, in that it implies that the success of the monetary policy is determined not only by the current stance of the economy but also by the economic agents' expectations of the economic stance in the following periods in terms of inflation. Based on this assumption, it can be concluded that agents are assumed to know the dynamic mechanism of the economy and the future consequences of their current activity. Therefore, the practice of modern monetary authorities can be described as the management of private inflation expectations. In this sense, the term $E_t(p_{t+1})$ represents the credibility of the central bank. If a central bank is able to clearly send to the public its intention to achieve and maintain a lower level of inflation, the economic agents' expectations of inflation can be lowered and hence the actual inflation will be lowered as well. Consequently, it may be possible to lower the current level of inflation at a significantly lower cost in terms of output by using appropriate management of private expectations. This is the expectation channel, in which interest-rate policy operates to influence the economic activities.

Equation 1.3 is the monetary policy rule, in which the current nominal interest rate is determined by past nominal interest rate, expected inflation, past output gap, the long-run equilibrium rate of interest and the deviation of inflation from the target inflation rate. This equation is the so-called Taylor rule,[11] which has been widely used in the policymaking process of many monetary authorities. By using this equation, monetary policy can be conducted to respond to the economic fluctuations in a predictable manner, decreasing the uncertainty of monetary policy and increasing the credibility of central banks. Within this mechanism, central banks try to

[11] More details of the monetary policy based on the Taylor rule can be found in the work of Rotemberg and Woodford [34].

adopt a higher rate of interest to constrain the level of inflation, when inflation goes above the target rate. Similarly, a positive output gap in the past period also leads to a higher rate of interest rate in the current period. An equilibrium rate of interest is embedded in this equation with the notion of RR^*. It is the interest rate that can be achieved when both output gap and deviation of inflation from target are zero, meaning that the aggregate demand in Eq. 1.1 is at a level equal to trend output determined by the supply side of the economy. In this sense, it corresponds to the Wicksellian natural rate of interest, which is determined by savings and investment at the supply-side equilibrium level of income. In this equilibrium, the actual output is equal to its potential level, and inflation keeps on a constant value that is pre-set. Therefore, Eq. 1.3 indicates the case that if central banks are able to accurately estimate the value of RR^*, it is possible for them to guide the economy to this equilibrium via the monetary policy rule.

Equation 1.4 represents the exchange rate function, indicating that the exchange rate is jointly determined by the real interest rate differentials, the position of the current account and the expected exchange rate in the future. In Eq. 1.5, the position of the current account is represented as a function of the real exchange rate, domestic and world output gap. Finally, Eq. 1.6 represents the relationship between nominal and real exchange rate. In conclusion, the traditional NCM framework for an open economy can be summarized in the above six equations, corresponding to the six unknowns.

1.3 Dynamic Stochastic General Equilibrium Models

In the 1950s, Solow [35, 36] made his milestone contribution by developing a model (the Solow model) to capture the dynamics of an economy. The original Solow model is simple and straightforward: the saving ratio is exogenously determined; only two factors (labour and capital) are considered in the production function, which is Constant Return to Scale (CRS). However, this seemingly simple and intuitive model produces surprisingly good performance in explaining economic growth and provides economists with a very versatile platform to develop more sophisticated models that capture a wider range of economic features. This is indeed a quite desirable quality for economists diverse in views. The DSGE models based on the NCM theoretical framework (NCM/DSGE) originate from the Real Business Cycles (RBC) model (RBC/DSGE), which is the modern development of the Solow model. The standard stochastic RBC/DSGE models can be found in the works of Kydland and Prescott [37], and Hansen [38]. Following the inspiration of the original RBC/DSGE model, many economists try to expand it to contain more sophisticated features to better portray the economy in a more accurate way. Many other features have been added to develop more advanced DSGE models: the Cash In Advance (CIA) model developed by Cooley and Hansen [39], the model of Lucas and Stokey [40], the Money In the Utility (MIU) DSGE model inspired by the contribution of Sidrauski [41]. By introducing the short-term nominal rigidities[12] into the original RBC/DSGE model, scholars developed the first generation NCM/DSGE models. And these prototype models soon evolved to fruitful developments. Bernanke and Gertler [42] and Bernanke et al. [43] built their dynamic model (the so-called BGG model or the Financial Accelerator Model) to capture the mechanism of the economy with a financial sector of frictions, highlighting the significant role of the financial sector. Christiano et al. [44, 45] developed an important DSGE model, which is the typical DSGE model with a financial sector. Galí and Gertler [46] use the DSGE model to evaluate the impact of monetary policy. Smets and Wouters [47] developed a Bayesian Estimated DSGE model (SW model) to study the shocks and frictions in the U.S. business cycle. Iacoviello [48] and Neri [49] emphasize the important role of the real estate market in the NCM/DSGE model. The versatility of the DSGE model contributes to the prosperity and variety of its application. As we have shown above, it has been the workhorse of many academic institutes and monetary authorities. The dominant popularity of the DSGE models can be partially demonstrated by the work of Tovar [50], as shown in Table 1.1.

The European Central Bank develops its DSGE type macroeconomic model, New Area Wide Model (NAWN), which is designed for the Macroeconomic Projection Exercises regularly undertaken by ECB/Eurosystem staff. The construction of this model is demonstrated in the work of Christoffel et al. [51].[13] The Federal Reserve Board uses a DSGE type model, SIGMA,[14] to analyse the impact of a wide range of shocks such as monetary policy-related shocks, increased government spending, surge

[12] The most widely accepted method is the Calvo [33] pricing mechanism.

[13] See Fagan et al. [52] and Marcellino et al. [53] for more information.

[14] See Erceg et al. [54].

Table 1.1 The international utilization of DSGE models: some examples

Monetary authorities	*DSGE models*
European Central Bank	New Area Wide Model (NAWN)
U.S. Fed.	SIGMA
IMF	GEM, GFM, GIMF
Bank of England	BEQM
Bank of Canada	ToTEM
Central Bank of Chile	MAS
Sveriges Riksbank	RAMSES
Central Bank of Peru	MEGA-D
Norges Bank	NEMO

of housing demand, the decrease of risk premium in the capital market, long-run productivity changes and so on. The DSGE model developed and used by the Bank of England is the Bank of England Quarterly Model (BEQM).[15] It was introduced in May 1997 for the Bank of England to prepare the Monetary Policy Committee's quarterly economic projections. The original BEQM was extended during 2003 and since then it has been the major instrument and model adopted by the staff and the Monetary Policy Committee (MPC) in the construction of their projections, which is a very important part of the quarterly Inflation Report. The Bank of Canada is among the users of the DSGE models by adopting its ToTEM[16] in monetary policy operating strategies. ToTEM replaced the Quarterly Projection Model (QPM) in December 2005 and has become the bank's principal projection and policy-analysis model. The MAS model[17] is employed by the Central Bank of Chile to quantify the impact of a variety of economic shocks to the business cycle. The DSGE model developed by Sveriges Riksbank, which is the central bank of Sweden, is RAMSES.[18] The utilization of the DSGE model by the Central Bank of Peru is MEGA-D, which is demonstrated in Florian and Montoro [59] and Castillo et al. [60]. The monetary

[15] A comprehensive discussion of the BEQM is conducted by Harrison et al. [55].

[16] More information can be found in the work of Murchison and Rennison [56].

[17] For more details, see Medina and Soto [57].

[18] For more details, see Adolfson et al. [58].

authority of Norway, Norges Bnak, joins the trend of DSGE modelling by using NEMO[19] in its policy-analysis and economic projection activities.

Along with the growingly wide use of the DSGE models by academic institutes and central banks, the development of the DSGE models has become the frontier of academic research. A growing number of literature using the DSGE model as the major tool to make dynamic macroeconomic analysis have been accumulated since the 1980s. This is mainly the result of two desirable features of the DSGE models: in the first place, they provide macroeconomic models with microeconomic foundations, which are missing in the traditional structural macroeconomic models; thus, the DSGE models are robust with respect to the Lucas critique. Secondly, the DSGE models can be conveniently expanded to include more economic factors and dynamics. Quite simply, and in terms of orthodox macroeconomics, DSGE models have become the seemingly standard model to propose dynamic macroeconomic analyses.

References

1. Lucas, R. (1983). On the mechanics of economic development. *Journal of Monetary Economics*, *22*(1), 3–42.
2. Say, A. (1803). *A treatise on political economy: Or the production, distribution and consumption of wealth*. https://doi.org/10.4028/www.scientific.net/AMM.613.214.
3. Mill, J. (1901). *The principles of political economy*. London: Macmillan.
4. Ricardo, D. (1891). Principles of political economy and taxation. *The Economic Journal*, *1*(4), 769.
5. Bohm-Bawerk, E. (1894). The ultimate standard of value. *Annals of the American Academy of Political & Social Science*, *5*(5), 149–208.
6. Smith, A. (2015). An inquiry into the nature and causes of the wealth of nations. *Journal of the Early Republic*, *35*(1), 1–23.
7. Menger, C. (1871). *Principles of economics*. London: Macmillan.
8. Jevons, W. (1888). *The theory of political economy*. London: Macmillan.
9. Beach, F., Walras, L., & William, J. (1955). Elements of pure economics, or, the theory of social wealth. *Canadian Journal of Economics & Political Science*, *21*(3), 383.
10. Aquinas, T. (1702). *Summa theologica*. New York: Fordham University Press.
11. Keynes, J. (1936). *The general theory of employment interest and money*. London: Macmillan.

[19] For more details, see Brubakk et al. [61].

12. Fisher, I. (1933). The debt-deflation theory of great depressions. *Econometrica*, *1*(4), 337–357.
13. Bernanke, B., & Harold, J. (1990). *The gold standard, deflation, and financial crisis in the great depression: An international comparison* (NBER Working Papers), 8, 33–68.
14. Dalio, R. (2018). *Big debt crises.* Westport: Bridgewater.
15. Keynes, J. (2010). *The end of laissez-faire.* London: Palgrave Macmillan UK.
16. Buridan, J., & Klima, G. (2001). *Summulae de dialectica.* New Haven: Yale University Press.
17. Bodin, J. (1992). *Bodin: On sovereignty.* Cambridge: Cambridge University Press.
18. von Hörnigk., & Wilhelm, P. (1708). *Oesterreich über alles, wann es nur will.* Regensburg: Verlagsort.
19. Locke, J. (1993). *Some considerations of the consequences of the lowering of interest, and raising the value of money: In a letter to a Member of Parliament.* London: Awnsham and John Churchill.
20. Law, J. (1993). *Money and trade considered with a proposal for supplying the nation with money.* London: R. & A. Foulis.
21. Baldwin, J., & Langholm, O. (1994). Economics in the medieval schools: Wealth, exchange, value, money and usury according to the Paris theological tradition, 1200–1350. *Speculum*, *69*(1), 200.
22. Friedman, M. (1960). *A program for monetary stability.* New York: Fordham University Press.
23. Friedman, M. (1968). *Dollars and deficits.* Upper Saddle River: Prentice-Hall.
24. Friedman, M. (1981). *The roles of money and credit in macroeconomic analysis* (NBER Working Papers). https://doi.org/10.3386/w0831.
25. Lucas, R.(1976). Econometric policy evaluation: A critique. In D. V. Pritchett (Ed.), *Carnegie-Rochester Conference Series on Public Policy* (pp. 19–46). Amsterdam: Elsevier.
26. King, M. (1997). Changes in UK monetary policy: Rules and discretion in practice. *Journal of Monetary Economics*, *39*(1), 81–97.
27. Mishkin, F. (2001). *From monetary targeting to inflation targeting: Lessons from the industrialized countries* (Policy Research Working Paper Series). https://doi.org/10.1596/1813-9450-2684.
28. Blinder, S. (1999). *Central banking in theory and practice.* Cambridge: MIT Press.
29. Woodford, M., & Walsh, C. (2005). Interest and prices: Foundations of a theory of monetary policy. *Economica*, *9*(287), 550–552.
30. Wicksell, K. (1936). Interest and prices: A study of the causes regulating the value of money. *American Economic Review*, *26*(3), 493–495.

31. Goodfriend, M., & King, G. (1997). The new neoclassical synthesis and the role of monetary policy. *NBER Macroeconomics Annual, 12*, 231–296.
32. Arestis, P. (2009). New consensus macroeconomics: A critical appraisal. *SSRN Electronic Journal, 564*, 1–26.
33. Calvo, G. (1983). Staggered prices in a utility-maximizing framework. *Journal of Monetary Economics, 12*(3), 383–398.
34. Rotemberg, J., & Woodford, M. (1997). Oligopolistic pricing and the effects of aggregate demand on economic activity. *Journal of Political Economy, 100*, 1153–1207.
35. Solow, R. (1956). A contribution to the theory of economic growth. *The Quarterly Journal of Economics, 70*(1), 65–94.
36. Solow, R. (1957). Technical change and the aggregate production function. *The Review of Economics and Statistics, 39*(3), 312–320.
37. Kydland, F., & Prescott, E. (1982). Time to build and aggregate fluctuations. *Econometrica, 50*(6), 1345–1370.
38. Hansen, G. (1985). Indivisible labor and the business cycle. *Journal of Monetary Economics, 16*(3), 309–327.
39. Cooley, T., & Hansen, G. (1989). The inflation tax in a real business cycle model. *The American Economic Review, 79*(4), 733–748.
40. Lucas, R., & Stokey, N. (1987). Money and interest in a cash-in-advance economy. *Econometrica, 55*(3), 491–513.
41. Sidrauski, M. (1967). Rational choice and patterns of growth in a monetary economy. *The American Economic Review, 57*(2), 534–544.
42. Bernanke, B., & Gertler, M. (1989). Agency costs, net worth, and business fluctuations. *The American Economic Review, 79*(1), 14–31.
43. Bernanke, B., Gertler, M., & Gilchrist, S. (1999). The financial accelerator in a quantitative business cycle framework. *Handbook of Macroeconomics, 1*, 1341–1393.
44. Christiano, L., Eichenbaum, M., & Evans, C. (2005). Nominal rigidities and the dynamic effects of a shock to monetary policy. *Journal of Political Economy, 113*(1), 1–45.
45. Christiano, L., Motto, R., & Rostagno, M. (2010). *Financial factors in economic fluctuations* (European Central Bank Working Papers), 1192.
46. Galí, J., & Gertler, M. (2007). Macroeconomic modelling for monetary policy evaluation. *The Journal of Economic Perspectives, 21*(4), 25–45.
47. Smets, F., & Wouters, R. (2007). Shocks and frictions in US business cycles: A Bayesian DSGE approach. *The American Economic Review, 97*(3), 586–606.
48. Iacoviello, M. (2005). House prices, borrowing constraints, and monetary policy in the business cycle. *The American Economic Review, 95*(3), 739–764.
49. Iacoviello, M., & Neri, S. (2010). Housing market spillovers: Evidence from an estimated DSGE model. *American Economic Journal: Macroeconomics, 2*(2), 125–164.

50. Tovar, C. (2009). DSGE models and central banks. *Economics: The Open-Access, Open-Assessment E-Journal, 3*(16), 2178–2178.
51. Christoffel, K., Coenen, G., & Warne, A. (2008). The new area-wide model of the Euro area: A micro-founded open-economy model for forecasting and policy analysis. *Social Science Electronic Publishing, 119*(35), 171–192.
52. Fagan, G., Henry, J., & Mestre, R. (2005). An area-wide model for the Euro area. *Economic Modelling, 22*(1), 39–59.
53. Marcellino, M., Stock, J., & Watson, M. (2003). Macroeconomic forecasting in the Euro area: Country specific versus area-wide information. *European Economic Review, 47*(1), 1–18.
54. Erceg, C., Guerrieri, L., & Gust, C. (2006). *SIGMA: A new open economy model for policy analysis* (International Finance and Economics Discussion Papers), 835.
55. Harrison, R., Nikolov, K., Quinn, M., Ramsay, G., Scott, A., & Thomas, R. (2005). *The Bank of England quarterly model.* London: Bank of England.
56. Murchison, S., & Rennison, A. (2006). ToTEM: The Bank of Canada's new quarterly projection model. *The Bank of Canada Technical Reports, 1994*, 23–38.
57. Medina, J., & Soto, C. (2007). *The Chilean business cycles through the lens of a stochastic general equilibrium model* (Central Bank of Chile Working Papers), 457.
58. Adolfson, M., Laséen, S., Lindé, J., & Villani, M. (2007). RAMSES—-A new general equilibrium model for monetary policy analysis. *Sveriges Riksbank Economic Review, 2*, 5–41.
59. Florian, D., & Montoro, C. (2009). *Development of mega-D: A DSGE model for policy analysis.* Lima: Central Reserve Bank of Peru.
60. Castillo, P., Montoro, C., & Tuesta, V. (2006). An estimated stochastic general equilibrium model with partial dollarization: A Bayesian approach. *Documentos de Trabajo (Banco Central de Chile), 381*, 1–72.
61. Brubakk, L., Husebø, T., Maih, J., Olsen, K., & Østnor, M. (2006). Finding NEMO: Documentation of the Norwegian economy model. *Norges Bank Staff Memo, 6*, 1–87.

CHAPTER 2

Time to Improve the Existing Models

Do DSGE Models Have a Future? I see the current DSGE models as seriously flawed, but they are eminently improvable and central to the future of macroeconomics. To improve, however, they have to become less insular, by drawing on a much broader body of economic research.

– Blanchard [1, p. 1].

2.1 Criticism on Existing DSGE Models

Just as Goodfriend and King [2] suggest in their work, the history of macroeconomics can be best portrayed as a field, in which intellectual disarray, with continuous and vital disagreements concerning the theoretic assumptions, methodologies and models among competing schools of thought evolves. The NCM framework and its macroeconomic policy implications are inevitably placed in the centre of the heated debate among macroeconomists. Although the NCM framework and its macroeconomic model—DSGE model, and according to the proponents[1] of them, have contributed to the low rate of inflation and high economic growth in

[1] The success of inflation management after the 1980s in the Western world is generally credited to the monetary policy of inflation targeting widely adopted by central banks in their DSGE models. Evidence and discussion can be found in the contributions of Svensson [3], who concludes that inflation targeting is superior to money growth or exchange rate targeting in that it decreases inflation variability, Christopher et al. [4], who argue that optimal policy

D. L. Jia, *Dynamic Macroeconomic Models in Emerging Market Economies*,
https://doi.org/10.1007/978-981-15-4588-7_2

major Western economies during the 1980s to 2007; they have been seriously questioned after the Global Financial Crisis (GFC) in 2007/2008 and the subsequent Global Recession (GR). In fact, the mainstream macroeconomics was so thoroughly challenged that many scholars refer to such phenomenon as the 'intellectual collapse' of the Chicago School in the 'dark age of macroeconomics'. As Krugman [7] and Blanchard [1] summarize, the failure to predict the GFC only reflects a small portion of the flaws of modern macroeconomics framework and its NCM/DSGE models. Economists have to face up to certain fundamental weaknesses of modern-day macroeconomic models. As a synthesis, the NCM framework inherits the advancements of classical and Keynesian economics over the last decades. But it has to bear with the criticism on both schools as well.

The heaviest criticism of modern macroeconomics lies in the issue of aggregation based on the assumption of representative agents, namely the fallacy of composition. In NCM/DSGE models, economic aggregates are derived from the representative agent's optimization behaviour. This is the microfoundation of the NCM framework, indicating its classical/neoclassical component. The early debate of whether we can build macroeconomic models from the microeconomic functions at the firm or household level took place in the 1930s, and this question has constantly been in dispute thereafter. As noted by Hartley [8], 'the aggregate demand curve must be exactly the same as the rigorously derived individual curve' (p. 4). Additionally, Kirman [9] maintains that the assumption of representative agent fails to depict the coordination and interaction among economic agents. The single representative agent assumption implies that all economic agents in each sector are identical. But this assumption is highly vulnerable. Just as King [10] suggests: 'There is thus no reason for them to trade with each other, no reason why their decision should be coordinated, and therefore no role for the markets' (p. 293). Therefore, the assumption of microeconomic rationality seems to have no simple equivalent macroeconomic implications. We believe that human behaviour can only be understood in the context of social and economic interactions.

rule responds not only to price inflation but also to aggregate output gap or wage inflation due to staggered nominal contracts and monopolistic competition, and Kim and Mehrotra [5], who find the complementary effects among inflation targeting and macroprudential policies in Asia-Pacific economies. Bernanke et al. [6] provide an international survey of the economic performance of inflation targeting policies in nine countries, showing that such a policy scheme improves the climate for economic growth.

Therefore, in our model, we try to improve the existing framework by introducing more types of households, according to their intrinsic heterogeneities, with strong social and economic connections.

Another important issue is the lack of a financial sector in NCM/DSGE models. Dou et al. [11] point out, the crucial role of the financial system in monetary policy and macroeconomic analysis has been largely overlooked in the formal macroeconomic models used by major central banks. As explained by Arestis [12], 'the NCM model is characterized by an interest rate rule, where the money market and financial institutions are typically not mentioned let alone modelled' (p. 10). The traditional NCM framework fails to account for the interaction between interest rate fluctuations, financial asset prices and the credit. But in the real world, financial intermediaries, especially commercial banks that absorb savings and grant credit, are crucial to business cycles. The financial sector and the corresponding services it provides are key factors in the modern market system. This conclusion has been reconfirmed by the GFC and the following GR. Therefore, without properly modelling the financial sector in the NCM framework, the failure of this framework and its DSGE model to anticipate such crisis seems to be rather 'reasonable'.[2]

After the painful experience of the GFC and GR, scholars generally accept the view that price stability alone is insufficient to achieve macroeconomic and financial stability. Asset prices, especially the property prices, are key determinants of economic fluctuations, meaning that a robust macroeconomic model is required to contain housing market components. Some economists further advocate that monetary authorities should consider asset price changes in their policy rules, and make appropriate adjustments of monetary policy in response to significant asset price fluctuations. For example, Cecchetti [14] argues that monetary policy should not focus solely on the inflation rate. Asset price fluctuations must be considered within the monetary policy framework as well. Goodhart [15] supports this point of view by suggesting that it is unguaranteed for central banks to narrow their focus on inflation rate only, asset prices such as real estate prices and stock market prices need to be included in a general inflation rate target framework. Ahearne et al. [16], after analysing international cases of housing markets, assert that pre-emptive adjustments of monetary policy to asset price fluctuations would be a better choice than a passive one,

[2] Colander et al. [13] further claim that the widely acceptance of such incomprehensive NCM/DSGE models is one of the causes of the GFC.

considering the balance of possible costs and potential benefits. In one word, based on current knowledge, it may not be plausible to add asset price as one of the determinants of monetary policy. But, the door should remain open as our knowledge and circumstances change.

In conclusion, lessons we learn over the last decades have shown the urgent necessity to modify traditional NCM/DSGE modelling, by expanding and refining economic features included in the DSGE model. A robust dynamic macroeconomic model should be grounded more solidly in the realities of modern economy, in which financial and the housing markets play the key role. And the dynamics of such a model need to be consistent with real-world structures. In the following section, we discuss each of these improvements in greater detail, with emphasis on emerging market economies.

2.2 New Dynamic Macroeconomic Models for Emerging Market Economies

When we review the evolution of economic development, certain conclusions can be drawn. Among them is that many previous patterns and phenomenon in developed markets, both social and economic, will occur in emerging market economies in the future. This catching-up process of poorer countries is also known as their economic 'convergence' with developed countries. Post-WWII history has witnessed such trends in countries including Japan, South Korea, Singapore and so forth, all of which have successfully joined the club of developed economies. Many others, such as China, India, Brazil and the countries in East Europe, are still in their process of catching up. The outcomes of such economic convergence include certain major economic and social changes, such as the improved role of market in resource allocation, enhanced integrity to the global market, general adoption of market principle and financial deepening, all of which have substantially contributed to higher economic growth in the corresponding economies. Emerging market economies began to share more similarities with their developed counterparts. As summarized by Verspagen [17], Van Elkan [18], Kolodko [19], Wei [20], Lee and Lim [21] and Gill and Kharas [22], the success of catching up involves capital accumulation, technology spillovers (to emerging market economies, it means technological capability building), integration of the global markets and marketization in domestic economic systems. In other words, as emerging market economies' market share in world trade began to rise at a fast pace, the similarities of market dynamics in these economies and advanced economies quickly increased as well. Therefore, learning the evolution of macroeconomic theoretic frameworks and models developed for advanced economies may provide us with valuable guidance and suggestions to deal with the problems in emerging markets now, since similar counterparts of these problems may be easily found in the history of developed markets. This is also an important reason for us to carefully study the above relevant literature of models developed for advanced economies.

On the other hand, emerging market economies, compared to the advanced ones, are more challenged, in the sense that not only do they need to encounter the issues challenging both developing and developed economies, but also the issues concerning the unique characteristics relating to their own social and economic condition. Such challenges lead to the economic phenomenon of 'middle-income trap', as many catching-up economies suffered from growth slowdowns after they reached middle-income threshold, being trapped in this stage for a considerably long time.[3] As Kharas and Kohli [24] point out, how to avoid falling into the middle-income trap has become the major challenge and concern of developing countries. This has been more severe especially after the GR, when the economic growth in developing countries slowed down and the economic gap between several emerging market economies and advanced economies even widened. Therefore, we believe that the monetary policy decision-making system and its theoretical framework and models should be adjusted to cater to the problems faced by emerging market economies. This is so since the latter need to deal not only with current issues, which all economies are faced with, but also the ones that are unique to emerging market economies themselves. As a result, dynamic macroeconomic modelling in emerging market economies requires modification of and extension to existing theoretical framework and models. Doing so could be very meaningful and valuable for both emerging markets and advanced economies.

[3] The definition of middle-income trap may vary as different economies exhibit different performance during this period. According to Felipe et al. [23], there are two types of middle-income trap: the lower-middle-income trap and the higher-middle-income trap. The first occurs when economies climb up from lower-middle-income to higher-middle-income, and the latter from higher-middle-income to high-income.

2.2.1 Financial Sector

Inadequate modelling of the financial sector meant they (the DSGE models) were ill-suited for predicting or responding to a financial crisis.

– Stiglitz [25, p. 1].

Analysing the dynamics between financial markets and the overall economic performance has been among the most popular research topics over the last decades. The great importance of financial intermediates, particularly the banking sector, in the macroeconomic system has been emphasized in the works of Tooke and Newmarch [26], Bagehot [27] and Schumpeter [28], all of whom made early efforts to understand the economic role of the financial sector. They believe that the services, such as bridging potential lenders and borrowers, risk management, liquidity enhancement and project analysis, provided by the financial intermediates, are all essential for the growth of productivity. A heated debate on the function of the banking system and its relationship with economic fluctuations, emerged from a very early age. Some economists argue that developments in the financial markets and their impact on the overall economic growth is unimportant[4] and 'over-stated' (Lucas [30]). Even within the group of scholars who admit the importance of financial intermediation to economic growth, different opinions on the dynamic mechanism exist. For example, although both Hayek [31] and Schumpeter [28] are Wicksellian economists and their theories of bank credit are deeply rooted in the endogeneity of credit introduced by Wicksell [32] in his analysis of 'cumulative process', they hold very different explanations of how the changes of bank credit contribute to business cycles.[5] In general, two branches of theoretical thinking emerged. Scholars in the first branch attempt to develop economic theories from the static real state of a barter economy, without the functioning of financial intermediates, and then enrich this basic model with the dynamics of monetary and financial activities. On the other hand, economists in the second branch try to build theoretical frameworks on the endogenous nature of credit money. In this theoretical regime, one can hardly introduce financial intermediaries without radically modifying

[4] Representative literature is the work conducted by Robinson [29], who maintains that development of the financial market is merely a passive result of general economic growth.

[5] For more detailed discussion on this issue, see the contribution conducted by Festré [33].

the economic system developed in the case of a barter economy; this is so since, credit is assumed to substitute real savings. Such theoretical issue is still in today's debate among economists.

Though theoretical arguments remain, a growing amount of empirical evidence indicates that the financial market is vital to economic growth. The level of development in financial markets is significantly connected with the overall economic growth. In the works of Goldsmith [34] and Revell and Goldsmith [35],[6] the positive relationship between the level of banking credit and overall economic growth is theoretically hypothesized and empirically confirmed. A similar conclusion can be witnessed in the work of McKinnon [36]. His research expands the reach of the financial sectors analysis by introducing Less Developed Countries (LDCs)[7] into his study. By analysing statistics collected in these LDCs from the end of World War II to the 1970s, he finds that the economic growth in LDCs exhibits greater reliance on the financial sector than developed economies. According to his study, the development of financial intermediates determines the economic performance of LDCs. Thus, it is now safe to maintain that development of the financial sector is not just the natural result of economic growth but a decisive factor to the success of economic development.[8]

The functions of financial intermediaries in the economy have been greatly widened and changed as the result of advancements in information technology, financial deregulation and globalization. Modern economic history has further emphasized the key role played by financial intermediates as they actively connect borrowers and lenders. According to the work of King and Levine [38], who analysed cross-country data from 1960 to 1989, the dynamic interactions between the level of development in financial intermediates and real economic growth, the rate of physical capital accumulation and the overall economic and social performance are significantly positive. Statistics indicate a strong connection between financial fluctuations and business cycles. As mentioned by Bernanke et

[6] They analysed the long-run time series of the U.S. economic data and conclude that development of financial sectors is closely linked to the overall economic growth.

[7] These LDCs include Japan, Korea, India, Mexico, Colombia, Brazil and so on.

[8] Just as Levine and Zervos [37, p. 1] concluded, 'Do well-functioning stock markets and banks promote long-run economic growth? …show that stock market liquidity and banking development both positively predict growth, capital accumulation, and productivity improvements…'.

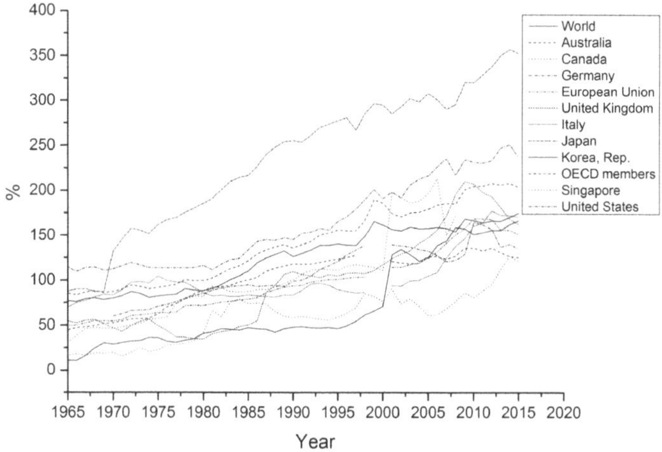

Fig. 2.1 Financial depth in advanced economies (*Source* International monetary fund)

al. [39], changes in the financial markets are not just a passive reflection of economic fluctuations but one of the driving forces and amplifying factors of business cyclic movements. This is even more so in emerging market economies as they are still in the process of industrialization and capital accumulation. Financial intermediaries like banks make decisive contributions to capital resource allocation and thus the overall output in these economies.To quantify the link between developments in the financial market and economic growth (or the level of capital accumulation), certain economists such as Revell and Goldsmith [35] and McKinnon [36] use indicators to measure financial sector development or the so-called 'financial depth'. According to their work, the ratio of the size of the financial sector to the overall economic outcome (in most cases, GDP is preferred) can be used to quantify the financial depth of an economy. By using ratios of this type,[9] we can clearly observe the difference of financial development among different economies. As demonstrated in Fig. 2.1, advanced economies

[9] King and Levine [38] use four kinds of indicators to define the level of financial developments. For simplicity, we only use one indicator—the ratio of domestic credit created by financial sector to GDP. The same conclusions can be obtained by using other indicators as well, such as M2 to GDP ratio.

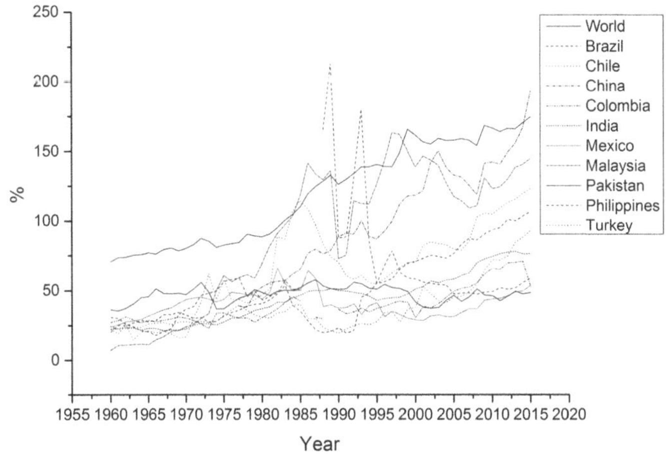

Fig. 2.2 Financial depth in less developed economies (*Source* International monetary fund)

including the United States, the United Kingdom, Germany and Japan tend to have heavier dependence on financial market developments. The average financial depth in OECD countries is significantly higher than the world average. On the other hand, less developed economies are typically identified with less developed financial markets. As shown in Fig. 2.2, almost all emerging market economies have lower financial depth than the world average. Figure 2.3 indicates that similar conclusions can be drawn if we group economies according to their income level.

Another fact displayed in Figs. 2.1, 2.2, and 2.3 is the trend of growing reliance on financial development in all economies regardless of their income level. Such a growing trend tends to accelerate after 2007 as economies adopted an easy monetary policy to stimulate economic growth. Although financial depth in less developed economies is lower than that in advanced economies, certain emerging market economies benefit from the developments in their financial sectors, stimulating the rate of physical capital accumulation and improving the utilization efficiency of that capital. This finding is consistent with the work of McKinnon [36] and many others, who attribute the diverse economic performance of LDCs to the difference in financial developments among these economies. Given this stylized fact that the level of financial development is significantly

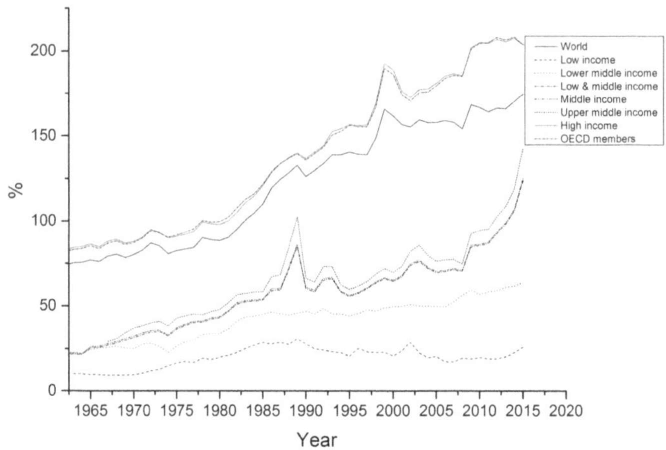

Fig. 2.3 Financial depth in different groups of economies (*Source* International monetary fund)

important to the success of LDCs' catching up, the dynamic macroeconomic models designed for emerging market economies should give sufficient attention to the financial sector. Therefore, we build our model with consideration of the financial sector in each examined country.

2.2.2 Real Estate Market

> *The experience of the U.S. housing market at the beginning of the 21st century has led many to raise the spectre that the developments in the housing market are not just a passive reflection of macroeconomic activity but might themselves be one of the driving forces of business cycles.*
>
> – Iacoviello and Neri [40, p. 2].

The subprime crisis in 2007 is not the first housing crisis, but it demonstrates the massive effects the housing market is able to create to the overall economy. As the volume of the housing market grows and its links with the financial markets tightened, real estate has become one of the major investment assets. The amplification effect and dynamic connections of the housing market to business fluctuations have greatly intensified. There is a growing concern that dynamic macroeconomic models should not ignore the role of the housing market when evaluating economic performance and business cycles. For example, Kiyotaki and Moore [41] have built a model, in which durable assets (including real estate assets) are used as collateral to loans. In this model, the positive interaction between credit limits and asset prices can be a significant transmission and amplification mechanism, through which asset prices change, credit cycles and business fluctuations are firmly connected. Therefore a small shock of asset prices can give rise to greatly amplified economic changes. This finding is consistent with Higgins and Osler [42], whose finding supports the view that real estate prices can substantially affect real and financial activities. Empirical evidence in industrialized countries can be found in the International Monetary Fund's World Economic Outlook.[10] Based on these findings, Iacoviello [43] and Iacoviello and Neri [40] use DSGE modelling with an explicit housing market component to explain the economic performance in the United States. Their works empirically quantify the economic dynamics contributed by the housing market, highlighting the active role of real estate in busines cycles.

Household wealth in emerging market economies exhibits higher level of concentration in real estate assets as households in these economies tend to be more reliant on real estate investment. This is supported by much empirical evidence. According to the report by China Household Finance Survey (CHFS) in the Southwestern University of Finance and Economics,[11] in 2014, real estate assets accounted for more than 83% of household wealth on average in Beijing and 66% in China. Other emerging market economies share this feature. As shown in Table 2.1, according to the reports of World Bank in 2019 and Credit Suisse [44] in 2018, the non-financial asset (primarily housing and land) accounts for more than 60% of total wealth per adult in all the listed emerging market economies, except the Philippines (56%) and Malaysia (59%). In certain countries, this ratio is extremely high: India (91%), Indonesia (88%) and Russian Republic (82%). Unfortunately, despite the growing literature of DSGE modelling with the housing market component in advanced economies, we can hardly find literature using the DSGE models that include the housing

[10] Full report is available online at https://www.imf.org/media/Websites/IMF/imported-flagshipissues/external/pubs/ft/weo/2000/01/pdf/chapter3pdf.ashx.

[11] Available at http://chfs.swufe.edu.cn/ListPage/ListPageIndex?categoryid=20.

Table 2.1 Household wealth breakdown in emerging market economies[a]

Economies	*Wealth per adult (USD)*	*Non-financial asset per adult (USD)*	*Non-financial asset ratio*
Brazil	23,278	17,114	74%
Czech Republic	44,975	29,550	66%
India	4,706	4,302	91%
Indonesia	11,839	10,444	88%
Malaysia	27,007	15,846	59%
Philippines	8,799	4,956	56%
Poland	26,056	17,919	68%
Russian Federal	10,976	9,043	82%

[a] *Source* World bank

market component to analyse the economic performance in emerging market economies.

After carefully considering the empirical evidence found in advanced economies and the high level of concentration of household wealth in property investment, we decided to explicitly introduce the housing market into our model.

2.2.3 Social Structure and Household Stratification

Another feature of these emerging market economies, we need to take into account, is the severe uneven distribution of income, wealth and public resources. This feature, we believe, is sadly missing in most of the DSGE models of emerging market economies. Clear separation of different social classes can be easily witnessed in these countries. Inspired by the Financial Accelerator Model, which introduces the heterogeneities of firms into the baseline NCM model, we develop our model to further account for the heterogeneities and stratification in the household sector. Quite intuitively, rural and urban regions in some emerging market economies naturally separate the households into two distinct social groups with different economic characteristics. Table 2.2 summarizes the urbanization rate in some major emerging market economies.[12] It is evident that some of these economies such as China, India, Indonesia, Poland and the Philippines have large

[12] The original data can be accessed at http://data.worldbank.org/indicator/SP.URB.TOTL.IN.ZS.

Table 2.2 Urbanization ratio in emerging market economies 2018

Countries	*Urbanization ratio%*
Brazil	87
China P.R.	59
Czech Republic	74
India	34
Indonesia	55
Malaysia	76
Philippines	47
Poland	60
Russian Federal	74

portions of their population living in the rural area. In emerging market economies, statistics show that people from different social layers, such as rural and urban parts, can have huge differences in income, wealth and access to public and financial services. Therefore, we need to account for such social stratification in these economies, and this is where the basic idea of asymmetrical characterization in different social groups comes from.

Besides the separation of rural and urban parts, households in emerging market economies fall into distinct social layers by income and wealth as well. Without a dominating mid-class social group as it is in developed economies, several distinguished social groups exist in emerging market economies. Figure 2.4 demonstrates three evident social classes in India.[13] The same phenomenon can be seen in China and Brazil as well.[14] These social groups have distinct economic behaviour patterns, and therefore it is necessary to use more than one single representative agent in the household sector to model the aggregate economics. As a result, even though not all

[13] According to McKinsey Global Institute, these social layers are categorized according to the annual income: globals $\geq$ 1,000,000 rupees; strivers = 500,000–1,000,000 rupees; seekers = 200,000–499,999 rupees; aspirers = 90,000–199,999 rupees; deprived $\leq$ 90,000 rupees. Strivers and seekers are defined as middle class in India.

[14] There are several important studies on this issue: Riskin et al. [45], Yang [46], Chen and Fleisher [47], Zhou [48, 49]. These contributions provide empirical evidence of income inequality in China over the last decades. For the income inequality in Brazil, see Deininger and Squire [50] (this study contains data sets and analysis of a variety of economies including Brazil), Azzoni [51], Szwarcwald et al. [52], Barros et al. [53] and Messias [54]. The income inequality in India is well studied in Piketty and Qian [55], Salaimartin [56], Subramanian et al. [57] and Dreze and Sen [58].

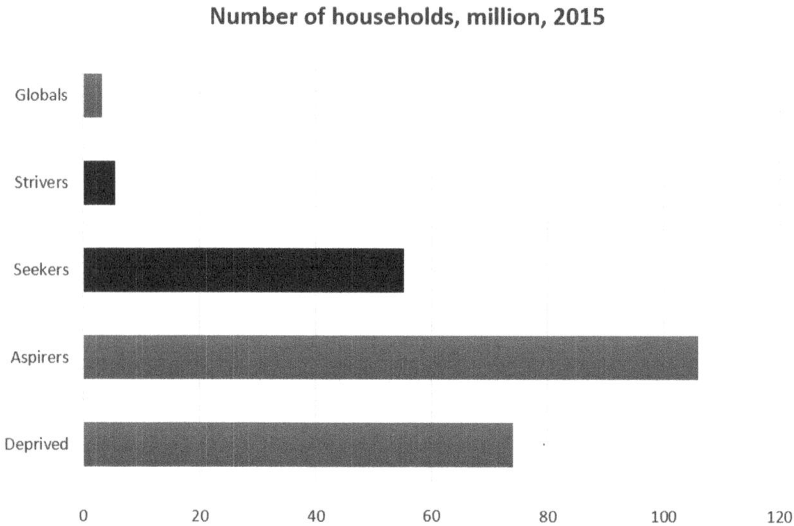

Fig. 2.4 Distinct social classes in India (*Source* World bank and McKinsey global institute)

emerging market economies are divided by large rural and urban parts, they still need to be analysed with different social groups.

2.2.4 *Why Emerging Market Economies and Why Brazil, India and China*

According to the definition made by MSCI, an economy is considered as emerging market when it shares certain characteristics of developed market economies but fails to meet the full standard to be a developed market. World Bank classifies developing countries that are neither part of the least developed countries, nor of the newly industrialized countries as emerging market economies. These countries are considered to be at their transition phase to become developed from developing. Although the definition of emerging market economies may be different, there is a wide agreement that examples of these economies include many countries in Africa, most countries in Eastern Europe, some countries in Latin America, some countries in the Middle East, some countries in the Southeast Asia and finally Russia. In this book, a general definition by Bremmer [59] is adopted. He

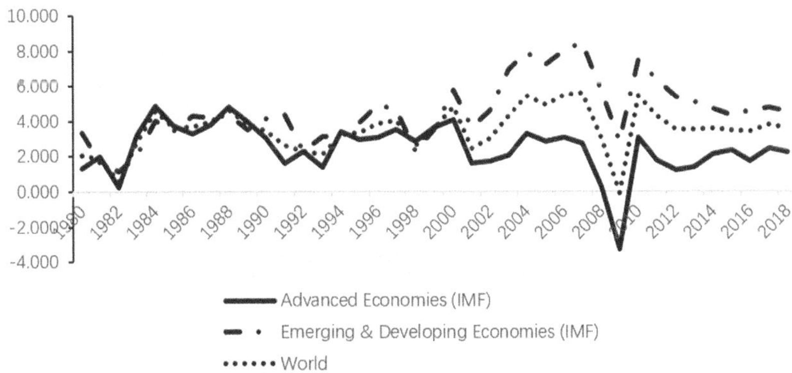

Fig. 2.5 The GDP growth rates in advanced and emerging market economies

defines an emerging market as 'a country where politics matters at least as much as economics to the markets' (p. 3) (Fig. 2.5).

In spite of these conceptual disagreements, scholars are deeply impressed that emerging market economies have gained great success over the past decades. They are contributing a growingly large share of the global economy. As globalization, financial deregulation and international collaboration strongly intensified after the 1980s, the performance of these economies has become more and more critical to the world economy. This growing importance of emerging market economies can be witnessed in the statistics in terms of their GDP, net export, capital inflow and their contribution to global economic growth. As shown in Fig. 2.6, emerging market and developing economies, and by the end of 2018, accounted for roughly 40% of the global GDP, more than doubled the ratio in 1999. And such a trend is even more evident in terms of purchasing power parity GDP, accounting for over 58% of global output, as shown in Fig. 2.7. Figure 2.5 illustrates that emerging market economies materially exceed their advanced counterparts and the world average in economic growth after 2000, and Fig. 2.8 tells us that emerging and developing economies have become the major accelerator of global economy. By the end of 2018, EDE accounted for 67.54% of the global economic growth, compared to 32.46% contributed by advanced economies.

Among these economies, Brazil, Russia, India, China and South Africa, the so-called 'BRICS' are the five largest countries among all the emerging

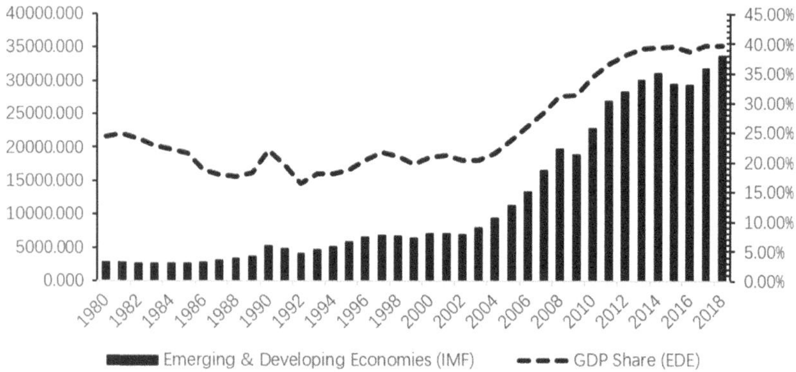

Fig. 2.6 The share of EDE's GDP to the overall global output

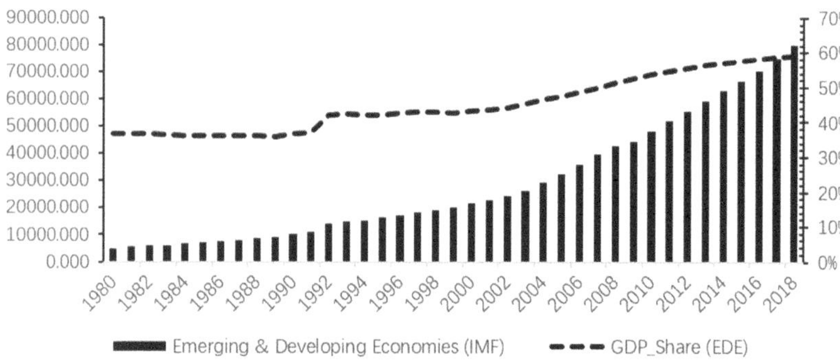

Fig. 2.7 The share of EDE's GDP to the overall global output (Purchasing power parity)

market economies, in terms of not only population and GDP, as summarized in Table 2.3, but also geographic coverage and international influence. In this book, we focus on three largest emerging market economies: China, India and Brazil.

As the economic volume and importance of emerging market economies increase, literature studying the dynamics of these economies began to grow. The application of the DSGE model in emerging market economies is currently at the frontier of DSGE modelling. Among them, the literature of DSGE modelling in analysing Brazilian economy can be seen in the

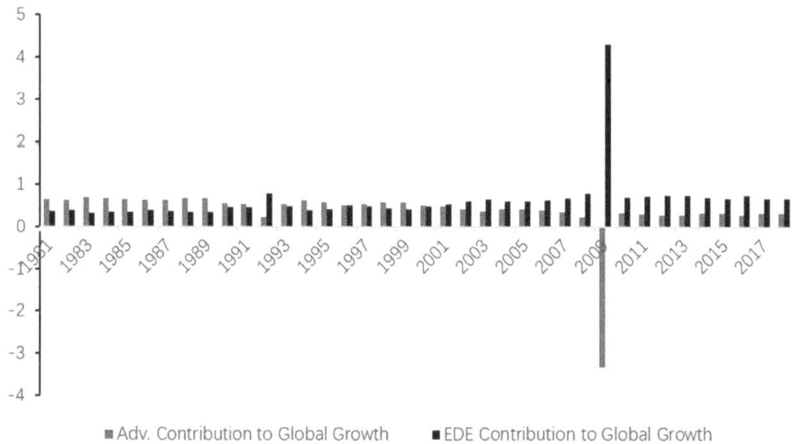

Fig. 2.8 The contribution ratio of EMDE to the global economic growth

Table 2.3 Population and GDP ranking 2019 (top 10)[a]

Ranking	*Economies*	*Population (k)*	*Ranking*	*Economies*	*GDP (billions USD)*
1	China	1,392,730	1	U.S.	21,439
2	India	1,352,617	2	China	14,140
3	U.S.	327,167	3	Japan	5,154
4	Indonesia	267,663	4	Germany	3,863
5	Pakistan	212,215	5	India	2,935
6	Brazil	209,469	6	U.K.	2,743
7	Nigeria	195,875	7	France	2,707
8	Bangladesh	161,356	8	Italy	1,988
9	Russia	144,478	9	Brazil	1,847
10	Japan	126,529	10	Canada	1,730

[a] *Source* World bank

works of Silveira [60] and Cabezon [61]. Peiris et al. [62] and Gabriel et al. [63] develop DSGE models for the Indian economy. Bin [64] and Chen et al. [65] adopt DSGE models to study the Chinese economy. These contributions are theoretically inspiring and empirically encouraging, as they provide certain plausible results, but none of them give full consideration of the financial and the housing markets in their DSGE models. Additionally, the social stratification and household heterogeneities are missing. Therefore, we try to expand the existing body of knowledge in terms of the DSGE modelling for emerging market economies by developing the new dynamic framework with fuller consideration of these issues.

References

1. Blanchard, O. (2016). Do DSGE models have a future? *Policy Briefs*, *8*(11), 1–12.
2. Goodfriend, M., & King, G. (1997). The new neoclassical synthesis and the role of monetary policy. *NBER Macroeconomics Annual*, *12*, 231–296.
3. Svensson, L. (1997). Inflation forecast targeting: Implementing and monitoring inflation targets. *European Economic Review*, *41*(6), 1111–1146.
4. Christopher, E., Henderson, D., & Levin, A. (1997). Inflation forecast targeting: Implementing and monitoring inflation targets. *Journal of Monetary Economics*, *46*(2), 281–313.
5. Kim, S., & Mehrotra, A. (2018). Effects of monetary and macroprudential policies-evidence from four inflation targeting economies. *Journal of Money Credit & Banking*, *50*(5), 967–992.
6. Bernanke, B., Laubach, T., Mishkin, F., & Posen, A. (1999). Inflation targeting: Lessons from the international experience. *The Canadian Journal of Economics*, *32*(5), 1334–1338.
7. Krugman, P. (2009). How did economists get it so wrong? *The New York Times*, *9*(10), 1–13.
8. Hartley, J. (2002). *The representative agent in macroeconomics*. London: George Routledge and Sons.
9. Kirman, A. (1992). Whom or what does the representative individual represent? *The Journal of Economic Perspectives*, *6*(2), 117–136.
10. King, J. (2012). *The Elgar companion to post Keynesian economics*. Cheltenham: Edward Elgar Publishing.
11. Dou, W., Lo, A., Muley, A., & Uhlig, H. (2017). Macroeconomic models for monetary policy: A critical review from a finance perspective. *Social Science Electronic Publishing*, *1*(14), 1–174.
12. Arestis, P. (2009). New Consensus macroeconomics and Keynesian critique. In E. Hein, T. Niechoj, & E. Stockhammer (Eds.), *Macroeconomic policies on shaky foundations whither mainstream economics* (pp. 629–653). Marburg: Metropolis.
13. Colander, D., Goldberg, M., Haas, A., Juselius, K., Kirman, A., Lux, T., et al. (2009). The financial crisis and the systemic failure of the economics profession. *Social Science Electronic Publishing*, *1*(14), 1–174.
14. Cecchetti, S. (2000). *Asset prices and central bank policy*. London: Centre for Economic Policy Research.
15. Goodhart, C. (2001). Monetary transmission lags and the formulation of the policy decision on interest rates. *Federal Reserve Bank of St. Louis Review*, *83*(124), 1654–1674.
16. Ahearne, G., Ammer, J., Doyle, M., Kole, S., & Martin, R. (2005). House prices and monetary policy: A cross-country study. *Social Science Electronic Publishing*, *1*(49), 65–78.

17. Verspagen, B. (1991). A new empirical approach to catching up or falling behind. *Structural Change and Economic Dynamics, 2*(2), 359–380.
18. Van Elkan, R. (1996). Catching up and slowing down: Learning and growth patterns in an open economy. *Journal of International Economics, 41*(1–2), 95–111.
19. Kolodko, G. (2001). Globalization and catching-up: From recession to growth in transition economies. *Communist and Post-Communist Studies, 34*(3), 279–322.
20. Wei, Y. (2001). Decentralization, marketization, and globalization: The triple processes underlying regional development in China. *Asian Geographer, 20*(1–2), 7–23.
21. Lee, K., & Lim, C. (2001). Technological regimes, catching-up and leapfrogging: Findings from the Korean industries. *Research Policy, 30*(3), 459–483.
22. Gill, I., & Kharas, H. (2007). *An East Asian renaissance: Ideas for economic growth*. Washington, DC: World Bank Publications.
23. Felipe, J., Abdon, A., & Kumar, U. (2012). *Tracking the middle-income trap: What is it, who is in it, and why?* (Economics Working Papers), 715.
24. Kharas, H., & Kohli, H. (2011). What is the middle income trap, why do countries fall into it, and how can it be avoided? *Global Journal of Emerging Market Economies, 3*(3), 281–289.
25. Stiglitz, J. (2017). Where modern macroeconomics went wrong? *Oxford Review of Economic Policy, 34*(1–2), 70–106.
26. Tooke, T., & Newmarch, W. (2002). *A history of prices, and of the state of the circulation, during the nine years 1848–56*. London: Routledge Thoemmes Press.
27. Bagehot, W. (1873). *Lombard street: A description of the money market*. London: Scribner, Armstrong and Company.
28. Schumpeter, J. (1912). *Theorie der wirtschaftlichen Entwicklung*. New York: Springer.
29. Robinson, J. (1952). *The generalization of the general theory*. London: Macmillan.
30. Lucas, R. (1988). On the mechanics of economic development. *Journal of Monetary Economics, 22*(1), 3–42.
31. Hayek, F. (1939). *Profits, interest, and investment, and other essays on the theory of industrial fluctuations*. London: George Routledge and Sons.
32. Wicksell, K. (1988). The influence of the rate of interest on prices. *Economic Journal, 17*(66), 213–220.
33. Festré, A. (1988). Money, banking and dynamics: Two Wicksellian routes from Mises to Hayek and Schumpeter. *American Journal of Economics and Sociology, 61*(2), 439–480.
34. Goldsmith, R. (1988). *Financial intermediaries in the American economy since 1900* (NBER Working Paper), 581.

35. Revell, J., & Goldsmith, R. (1970). Financial structure and development. *Studies in Comparative Economics, 80*(318), 31–45.
36. McKinnon, R. (2010). *Money and capital in economic development.* Washington, DC: Brookings Institution Press.
37. Levine, R., & Zervos, S. (1998). Stock markets, banks, and economic growth. *The American Economic Review, 88*(3), 537–558.
38. King, R., & Levine, R. (1993). Finance and growth: Schumpeter might be right. *The Quarterly Journal of Economics, 108*(3), 717–737.
39. Bernanke, B., Gertler, M., & Gilchrist, S. (1999). The financial accelerator in a quantitative business cycle framework. *Handbook of Macroeconomics, 1*, 1341–1393.
40. Iacoviello, M., & Neri, S. (2010). Housing market spillovers: Evidence from an estimated DSGE model. *American Economic Journal: Macroeconomics, 2*(2), 125–164.
41. Kiyotaki, N., & Moore, J. (1997). Credit cycles. *Journal of Political Economy, 105*(2), 211–248.
42. Higgins, M., & Osler, C. (1997). Asset market hangovers and economic growth: The OECD during 1984–93. *Oxford Review of Economic Policy, 13*(3), 110–134.
43. Iacoviello, M. (2005). House prices, borrowing constraints, and monetary policy in the business cycle. *American Economic Journal: Macroeconomics, 2*(2), 125–164.
44. Suisse, C. (2018). *Global wealth report 2018.* Credit Suisse Research Institute Reports. Available via DIALOG. https://www.credit-suisse.com/about-us-news/en/articles/news-and-expertise/global-wealth-report-2018-us-and-china-in-the-lead-201810.html Cited 15 June 2019.
45. McKinnon, R. (2010). *China's retreat from equality: Income distribution and economic transition.* New York: M. E. Sharpe.
46. Yang, D. (1999). Urban-biased policies and rising income inequality in China. *The American Economic Review, 89*(2), 306–310.
47. Chen, J., & Fleisher, B. (1996). Regional income inequality and economic growth in China. *Journal of Comparative Economics, 22*(2), 141–164.
48. Zhou, X. (2000). Economic transformation and income inequality in urban China: Evidence from panel data. *American Journal of Sociology, 105*(4), 1135–1174.
49. Zhou, X. (2000). Accounting for income inequality in rural China: A regression-based approach. *Journal of Comparative Economics, 32*(2), 348–363.
50. Deininger, K., & Squire, L. (1996). A new data set measuring income inequality. *The World Bank Economic Review, 10*(3), 565–591.
51. Azzoni, C. (2001). Economic growth and regional income inequality in Brazil. *The World Bank Economic Review, 10*(3), 565–591.

52. Szwarcwald, C., Bastos, F., Viacava, F., & De Andrade, C. (1999). Income inequality and homicide rates in Rio de Janeiro. *Brazil. American Journal of Public Health, 89*(6), 845–850.
53. Barros, R., De Carvalho, M., Franco, S., & Mendonca, R. (2010). Income inequality and homicide rates in Rio de Janeiro, Brazil. In L. López-Calva & N. Lustig (Eds.), *Declining inequality in Latin America: A decade of progress* (pp. 137–174). Washington, DC: Brookings Institution Press.
54. Messias, E. (2003). Income inequality, illiteracy rate, and life expectancy in Brazil. *American Journal of Public Health, 93*(8), 1294–1296.
55. Piketty, T., & Qian, N. (2009). Income inequality and progressive income taxation in China and India, 1986–2015. *American Economic Journal: Applied Economics, 1*(2), 53–63.
56. Salaimartin, X. (2002). *The disturbing "rise" of global income inequality* (NBER Working Papers), 8904.
57. Subramanian, S., Kawachi, I., & Smith, G. (2007). Income inequality and the double burden of under- and over-nutrition in India. *Journal of Epidemiology and Community Health, 34*(1–2), 70–106.
58. Dreze, J., & Sen, A. (1995). *India: Economic development and social opportunity.* Oxford: Oxford University Press.
59. Bremmer, I. (2005). Managing risk in an unstable world. *Harvard Business Review, 83*(6), 51–60.
60. Silveira, M. (2008). Using a Bayesian approach to estimate and compare new Keynesian DSGE models for the Brazilian economy: The role for endogenous persistence. *Revista Brasileira de Economia, 62*(3), 333–357.
61. Cabezon, E. (2014). *Working capital, financial frictions and monetary policy in Brazil* (University of North Carolina Working Papers), 11.
62. Peiris, S., Saxegaard, M., & Anand, R. (2010). *An estimated model with macro-financial linkages for India* (IMF Working Papers), 1021.
63. Gabriel, V., Levine, P., Pearlman, J., & Yang, B. (2010). *An estimated DSGE model of the Indian economy* (Universidade do Minho Working Papers), 29.
64. Bin, L. (2008). Development and application of the DSGE model for monetary policy analysis in China. *Journal of Financial Research, 10*, 4–24.
65. Chen, Q., Funke, M., & Paetz, M. (2012). *Market and non-market monetary policy tools in a calibrated DSGE model for mainland China* (Bank of Finland Quantitative Macroeconomics Working Papers), 16.

PART II

Dynamic Macroeconomic Modelling

Part II aims to examine the dynamic macroeconomic modelling in greater detail. We attempt to derive the fundamentals of the dynamic macroeconomic models. This part contains two chapters. Chapter 3 focuses on the traditional dynamic macroeconomic models, namely the Solow model and the RBC/DSGE models. Chapter 4 examines modern dynamic modelling, with emphasis on the NCM/DSGE models. Based on these two chapters, we demonstrate and summarize the most important features of modern DSGE modelling exercises. These desirable qualities help us develop new dynamic models in the following part.

CHAPTER 3

Traditional Dynamic Macroeconomic Models

3.1 It All Starts from Solow

The structur of Solow growth model (or, the Solow model for short) [1, 2] is simple and straightforward. It contains three basic assumptions:

1. The production function is CRS (Constant-Return-to-Scale);
2. Physical capital used to produce goods can be accumulated;
3. Saving ratio is exogenously determined.

Based on these assumptions, we can write the production function as:

$$Y_t = A_t F(K_t, H_t) \tag{3.1}$$

In this equation, the aggregate output Y_t is produced using the combination of capital K_t and labour H_t under certain technological conditions A_t. Equation 3.1 can be written in the per capita form:

$$y_t = \frac{Y_t}{H_t} = A_t f(k_t, 1) \equiv A_t f(k_t) \tag{3.2}$$

If we denote n as the constant population growth rate and δ the capital depreciation rate, the growth path of this model can be summarized as:

$$k_{t+1} = g(k_t) = \frac{(1-\delta)k_t + \delta A_0 f(\bar{k})}{1+n} \tag{3.3}$$

D. L. Jia, *Dynamic Macroeconomic Models in Emerging Market Economies*,
https://doi.org/10.1007/978-981-15-4588-7_3

A major weak point of the above model is the assumption of the exogenously determined saving ratio. In order to endogenously include saving ratio in the model, Samuelson [3] and Diamond [4] developed an Overlapping generations model (OLG model), within which the life of each individual consists of two parts: young and senior. All the individuals leave the system at the end of their senior period, with nothing left for the next generation. The sense of overlapping generation is in that within each time period t, two generations coexist: the young ones born in this period and the senior ones born in the previous period, $t-1$. Each agent tries to maximize the sum of his/her consumption in two periods. Therefore, the determination of the saving ratio becomes a dynamic planning scheme of intertemporal utility maximization.

If we move further assuming no transaction between generations in the capital market, the capital stock in time t, K_t, is inherited from the previous time period $t-1$, and will be fully depreciated in the time period t. Therefore, the constraint in time period t is

$$Y(t) = F(K(t), H(t)) \geq \sum_{h=1}^{N(t)} c_t^h(t) + \sum_{h=1}^{N(t-1)} c_{t-1}^h(t) + K(t+1) \tag{3.4}$$

In an economy where perfect competition holds in all the markets, no arbitrage exists and thus:

$$rental(t) = F_K(K(t), H(t)) = F_H(K(t), H(t)) = r_t \tag{3.5}$$

Therefore, we can combine the constraints for an individual in his/her whole life of two periods:

$$c_t^h(t) + \frac{c_t^h(t+1)}{r_t} = w_t h_t^h(t) + \frac{w_{t+1} h_t^h(t+1)}{r_t} \tag{3.6}$$

$$= F_H(K(t), H(t)) h_t^h(t) + \frac{F_H(K(t+1), H(t+1)) h_t^h(t+1)}{r_t} \tag{3.7}$$

The meaning of this equation is quite intuitive: the present value of total consumption should be equal to the present value of total wage income.

By assuming that the life of each agent contains two consecutive parts, OLG models endogenously determine the saving ratio via the agent's intertemporal optimization behaviour. Another way to achieving the endogeneity of the saving ratio in macroeconomic modelling is to treat individuals as families who live for infinite time periods. Under such assumption, each individual (family) tries to maximize his/her utility for infinite time periods:

$$\sum_{i=0}^{\infty} \beta^i u(c_{t+i}) \tag{3.8}$$

In this equation, $u()$ is the sub-utility function and $0 < \beta < 1$ is the discount factor. The single period constraints of each individual are:

$$k_{t+1} = (1 - \delta)k_t + i_t \tag{3.9}$$

$$y_t = f(k_t) \geq c_t + i_t \tag{3.10}$$

Under these constraints, Eq. 3.8 can be rewritten as:

$$\sum_{i=0}^{\infty} \beta^i u(f(k_{t+i}) - k_{t+i-1} + (1 - \delta)k_{t+i}) \tag{3.11}$$

The corresponding Euler equation is

$$f'(k_t) + (1 - \delta) = \frac{u'(f(k_{t-1} - k_t + (1 - \delta)k_{t-1})}{\beta u'(f(k_t - k_{t+1} + (1 - \delta)k_t)} \tag{3.12}$$

In the steady state, $k_{t-1} = k_t = k_{t+1} = \bar{k}$, therefore

$$f'(\bar{k}) = \frac{1}{\beta} + \delta - 1 \tag{3.13}$$

This indicates that in the steady state, the marginal output of capital is equal to the sum of real interest rate $\frac{1}{\beta} - 1$ and the depreciation rate, δ.

3.2 The Stochastic Models

Although Solow model and its variants achieved promising results in explaining economic growth, they are based on basic assumptions that are highly ideal. The models of such kind do not incorporate key aspects of economic behaviour in a world full of uncertainties. In order to close this gap between theory and reality, scholars introduce rational expectation hypothesis and its applications into the original model. Dynamic models contain stochastic terms that capture the potential innovations of the economic system. Economic agents are assumed to be rational in the sense that their economic decision is based on rational expectation of future realization of uncertainties. Therefore, the dynamic property of the RBC/DSGE model is summarized as the intertemporal maximization of utility. In this section, we demonstrate the fundamentals of the stochastic RBC/DSGE model. A standard stochastic RBC/DSGE models can be found in the works of Kydland and Prescott [5], and Hansen [6].

An agent's aim is to maximize his/her discounted utility function:

$$max \sum_{t=0}^{\infty} \beta^t u(c_t, l_t) \tag{3.14}$$

where l_t denotes the leisure the agent chooses to take in time period t (therefore, $h_t = 1 - l_t$).

We further define the utility function as:

$$u(c_t, l_t) = u(c_t, 1 - h_t) = \ln c_t + A \ln(1 - h_t), A > 0 \tag{3.15}$$

The corresponding budget constraint for the household is

$$c_t + k_{t+1} = w_t l_t + (1 - \delta)k_t + r_t k_t \tag{3.16}$$

The production function is Cobb–Douglas function with random term:

$$f(\lambda_t, k_t, h_t) = \lambda_t k_t^{\theta} h_t^{1-\theta} \tag{3.17}$$

$$\lambda_{t+1} = \gamma \lambda_t + \epsilon_{t+1} \tag{3.18}$$

in which $0 < \gamma < 1$, and random shock $\epsilon_t > 0$ obeys I.I.D. (Independent Identical Distribution) with average value $1 - \gamma$. Under such assumption, the average of λ_t is 1 and the production cannot be negative.

Under the budget constraints, as shown in 3.9 and 3.10, the Bellman function[1] can be written as:

$$V(\lambda_t, k_t) = max[\ln c_t + A \ln(1 - h_t) + \beta E_t[V(\lambda_{t+1}, k_{t+1})]] \tag{3.19}$$

[1] The full definition and deduction of the Bellman function is provided in the work of Bellman [7].

Therefore the first order conditions (FOCs) are:

$$\frac{\partial V(\lambda_t, k_t)}{\partial k_{t+1}} = 0 \tag{3.20}$$

$$\frac{\partial V(\lambda_t, k_t)}{\partial h_t} = 0 \tag{3.21}$$

Using the Benveniste–Scheinkman Envelop Theorem,[2] we get

$$\frac{\partial V(\lambda_t, k_t)}{\partial k_t} = \frac{\theta \lambda_t k_t^{\theta-1} h_t^{1-\theta} + (1-\delta)}{\lambda_t k_t^{\theta} h_t^{1-\theta} + (1-\delta)k_t - k_{t-1}} \tag{3.22}$$

Under perfect competition condition, $w_t = (1-\theta)\lambda_t k_t^{\theta} h_t^{-\theta}$ and $r_t = \theta \lambda_t k_t^{\theta-1} h_t^{1-\theta}$ Together with the FOCs, we have

$$\frac{1}{c_t} = \beta E_t[\frac{r_{t+1} + (1-\delta)}{c_{t+1}} \mid \lambda_t] \tag{3.23}$$

$$(1-h_t)w_t = Ac_t \tag{3.24}$$

In equilibrium, $k_t = k_{t+1} = k_{t+2} = \overline{k}$. Thus, we can solve for the value of each control variable in the steady state:

$$\overline{h} = \frac{1}{1 + \frac{A}{1-\theta}[1 - \frac{\beta\delta\theta}{1-\beta(1-\delta)}]} \tag{3.25}$$

$$\overline{k} = \overline{h}[\frac{\theta\overline{\lambda}}{\frac{1}{\beta} - (1-\delta)}]^{\frac{1}{1-\theta}} \tag{3.26}$$

3.3 Money and Finance in RBC/DSGE Models

Until now, money and financial intermediaries play no role in RBC/DSGE macroeconomic models. In order to portrait the better image of the macroeconomic mechanism, many economists take efforts to expand original DSGE models to include money in the basic structure of the model economy. To do so, economists developed two types of models: the money

[2] The details of Envelop Theorem are provided in the work conducted by Benveniste and Scheinkman [8].

in utility (MIU) model and the cash in advance (CIA) model, both of which are derived in the following subsections.

3.3.1 *Money in the Utility*

As shown in its name, MIU/DSGE models explicitly introduce the real money balance into the utility function of households. In his work, Sidrauski [9] maintains that money provides additive utility to households, in that it serves as

1. Unit of account
    a. It is used to measure the value of everything else in the economy.
2. Medium of exchange
    a. It solves the problem of double coincidence of wants in a barter economy, and thus facilitates transactions and other economic activities.
3. Store of value
    a. It is a special asset that is an important component of wealth.

Therefore, the household's flow budget constraint captured in Eq. 3.27 becomes

$$c_t + k_{t+1} + B_t + \frac{M_t}{p_t} = w_t h_t + (1-\delta)k_t + r_t k_t + (1+i_{t-1})B_{t-1} + \frac{M_{t-1}}{p_t} \quad (3.27)$$

p_t is the price level at time period t, and $m_t \equiv \frac{M_t}{p_t}$ is the real money balance. Moreover, the household utility function described in Eq. 3.15 is modified as

$$u(c_t, l_t, m_t) = u(c_t, 1-h_t, m_t) = \ln c_t + A\ln(1-h_t) + \phi\frac{(\frac{M_t}{p_t})^{1-\nu} - 1}{1-\nu} \quad (3.28)$$

This equation indicates that holding money brings direct utility to households.

In an economy where the central bank is exclusively responsible for monetary policy that follows the fashion shown below

$$\ln(M_t)-\ln(M_{t-1}) = (1-\rho_M)\pi^* + \rho_M(\ln(M_{t-1})-\ln(M_{t-2})) + \epsilon_{M,t} \quad (3.29)$$

If we define the growth rate of money supply as $\Delta M_t = \ln(M_t) - \ln(M_{t-1})$, then Eq. 3.29 turns into

$$\Delta M_t = (1-\rho_M)\pi^* + \rho_M \Delta M_{t-1} + \epsilon_{M,t} \quad (3.30)$$

where ρ_M is the parameter of persistence, π^* is the target inflation rate set by the central bank, and $\epsilon_{M,t}$ is the unexpected money supply shock, which is assumed to be white noise.

Combining Eqs. 3.27 and 3.28 produces the Lagrangian function

$$L = max E \sum_{t=0}^{\infty} \beta^t \Big(\ln c_t + A \ln(1-h_t) + \phi \frac{(\frac{M_t}{p_t})^{1-\nu} - 1}{1-\nu} - \lambda_t (c_t + k_{t+1} + B_t + \frac{M_t}{p_t} - w_t h_t - (1-\delta)k_t - r_t k_t - \Big(1 + i_{t-1})B_{t-1} - \frac{M_{t-1}}{p_t}\Big)\Big) \quad (3.31)$$

λ_t is the Lagrangian multiplier.

Differentiating Eq. 3.31 with respect to consumption, c_t, yields the corresponding first order condition

$$\lambda_t = \frac{1}{c_t} \quad (3.32)$$

Similarly, the first order conditions for labour, h_t, and capital, k_t, can be written as

$$\frac{1}{1-h_t} = \frac{1}{c_t} w_t \quad (3.33)$$

$$\lambda_t = \beta E_t(\lambda_{t+1}(r_{t+1} + 1 - \delta)) \quad (3.34)$$

Differentiating Eq. 3.31 with respect to bond investment, b_t, and real money balance, m_t, produces the first order conditions

$$\lambda_t = \beta E_t(\lambda_{t+1}(\frac{1+i_t}{1+\pi_{t+1}})), \pi_t \equiv \frac{p_t}{p_{t-1}} \quad (3.35)$$

$$\phi(m_t)^{-\nu} = \frac{1}{c_t}\frac{i_t}{i_{t+1}} \quad (3.36)$$

This is the money demand curve. Based on these first order conditions and the identification of parameters, the MIU/DSGE models can be solved. The solution to dynamic macroeconomic system will be discussed in Chapter 9.

3.3.2 *Cash in Advance*

Cash in advance (CIA) models developed by Cooley and Hansen [10], and Lucas and Stokey [11] are based on the assumption that households hold money for trading purposes. Before households purchase final goods and services, they need to possess sufficient amount of money to complete the corresponding transactions. This implies an additional constraint for households. Thus, the constraint for household is (g_t represents the nominal money growth rate at time t):

$$P_t c_t^i \leq m_{t-1}^i + (g_t - 1)M_{t-1} \tag{3.37}$$

The ith household budget constraint under CIA model is

$$c_t^i + k_{t+1}^i + \frac{m_t^i}{P_t} = w_t h_t^i + r_t k_t^i + (1-\delta)k_t^i + \frac{m_{t-1}^i + (g_t - 1)M_{t-1}}{P_t} \tag{3.38}$$

Equation 3.38 implies that in CIA model money is directly distributed to households, without the channel of financial intermediaries. Cooley and Quadrini [12] and Fuerst [13] expand the original CIA model to contain the financial intermediaries, which connect households and firms through deposits and in-period loans. Under such condition, the CIA constraint for household indexed by i is

$$P_t c_t^i \leq m_{t-1}^i - N_t^i \tag{3.39}$$

$$\frac{m_t^i}{P_t} + k_{t+1}^i = w_t h_t^i + r_t k_t^i + (1-\delta)k_t^i + \frac{r_t^n N_t^i}{P_t} \tag{3.40}$$

in which N_t^i represents the household's nominal deposit in financial intermediary, which pays nominal interest rate r_t^n to the household. This implies that money can be used not only to purchase consumption but also to generate deposits at financial intermediaries.

For financial intermediaries, the constraint can be written as

$$r_t^f(N_t + (g_t - 1)M_{t-1}) = \int_0^1 r_t^n N_t^i di = r_t^n N_t \tag{3.41}$$

The interest payment to financial intermediaries by firm borrowing to pay wages is r_t^f.

The equilibrium condition of financial market is

$$r_t^f(N_t + (g_t - 1)M_{t-1}) = r_t^n N_t = P_t w_t H_t \tag{3.42}$$

Similar to 3.13, on the production side, the steady state is accomplished at the same condition:

$$\overline{r} = \frac{1}{\beta} - 1 + \delta \tag{3.43}$$

$$\overline{r^n} = \frac{\overline{g}}{\beta} = \overline{r}^f \tag{3.44}$$

So far, we have discussed the principal components of the RBC/DSGE model with detailed mathematical deduction. It successfully incorporates the contributions of the Solow model and the rational expectation hypothesis. As its name suggests, the economic fluctuations in this model are purely determined by real shocks to the economy, which is captured by the random term ϵ_t in Eq. 3.18. The highly ideal assumptions of the RBC/DSGE models limit their robustness and accuracy. But models of this kind provide a considerably flexible platform, to which economists can easily add on economic features. By introducing nominal rigidities to the RBC model, scholars soon developed the NCM/DSGE model, which is carefully discussed in the following chapters.

References

1. Solow, R. (1956). A contribution to the theory of economic growth. *The Quarterly Journal of Economics*, *70*(1), 65–94.
2. Solow, R. (1957). Technical change and the aggregate production function. *The Review of Economics and Statistics*, *39*(3), 312–320.
3. Samuelson, P. (1958). An exact consumption-loan model of interest with or without the social contrivance of money. *The Journal of Political Economy*, *66*(6), 467–482.
4. Diamond, P. (1965). National debt in a neoclassical growth model. *The American Economic Review*, *55*(5), 1126–1150.

5. Kydland, F., & Prescott, E. (1982). Time to build and aggregate fluctuations. *Econometrica, 50*(6), 1345–1370.
6. Hansen, G. (1985). Indivisible labor and the business cycle. *Journal of Monetary Economics, 16*(3), 309–327.
7. Bellman, R. (1956). Dynamic programming and Lagrange multipliers. *Proceedings of the National Academy of Sciences of the United States of America, 42*(10), 767–769.
8. Benveniste, L. M., & Scheinkman, J. A. (1982). Duality theory for dynamic optimization models of economics: The continuous time case. *Journal of Economic Theory, 27*(1), 1–19.
9. Sidrauski, M. (1967). Rational choice and patterns of growth in a monetary economy. *The American Economic Review, 57*(2), 534–544.
10. Cooley, T., & Hansen, G. (1989). The inflation tax in a real business cycle model. *The American Economic Review, 79*(4), 733–748.
11. Lucas, R., & Stokey, N. (1987). Money and interest in a cash-in-advance economy. *Econometrica, 55*(3), 491–513.
12. Cooley, T., & Quadrini, V. (1999). A neoclassical model of the Phillips curve relation. *Journal of Monetary Economics, 44*(2), 165–193.
13. Fuerst, T. (1992). Liquidity, loanable funds, and real activity. *Journal of Monetary Economics, 29*(1), 3–24.

CHAPTER 4

Modern Mainstream Macroeconomic Models

4.1 Manufacturer Firms

In this section, we demonstrate the application of Calvo [1] pricing mechanism in a DSGE model by following the procedure introduced by Bernanke et al. [2]. In our model, we use a similar mechanism to instal short-term nominal rigidity. Under such mechanism, firms fall into two categories: ones that produce intermediate goods, and another that bundles these intermediate goods into the final goods. Intermediate goods firms possess pricing power as the market of intermediate goods is not perfectly competitive. Producers can price their intermediate goods over the marginal cost to maximize their profits, because these intermediate goods are heterogeneous. The market of final goods is assumed to be frictionless. We assume that the intermediate producers indexed by j are evenly distributed in the continuum $[0, 1]$, $j \in [0,\ 1]$. Then, at time t, producer j's products are bundled into final goods by the final goods producer subject to the constant elasticity of substitution (CES) assumption.

4.1.1 *Intermediate Manufacturer*

Each intermediate manufacturer j follows the standard Cobb–Douglas production function as

$$Y_t(j) = A_t \overline{k}_t(j)^{\alpha} N_t(j)^{1-\alpha} \tag{4.1}$$

D. L. Jia, *Dynamic Macroeconomic Models in Emerging Market Economies*,
https://doi.org/10.1007/978-981-15-4588-7_4

in which the capital used by the firm is denoted by $\overline{k}_t(j)$ and

$$\overline{k}_t(j) = u_t k_t(j) \tag{4.2}$$

where u_t refers to the utilization rate of capital.

The aim of these intermediate goods producers is to minimize the factor costs of capital ($\overline{k}_t(j)$) and labour ($N_t(j)$) at given level of production, meaning that

$$\min_{\overline{k}_t(j), N_t(j)} \quad W_t^p N_t(j) + R_t^p \overline{k}_t(j) \tag{4.3}$$

subject to

$$Y_t(j) = A_t \overline{k}_t(j)^\alpha N_t(j)^{1-\alpha} \leq (\frac{p_t(j)}{p_t})^{-\epsilon_p} Y_t \tag{4.4}$$

Equations 4.3 and 4.4 produce the Lagrangian function of the intermediate goods producer, $L = -W_t^p N_t(j) - R_t^p(j)\overline{k}_t(j) + (A_t \overline{k}_t(j)^\alpha N_t(j)^{1-\alpha} - \phi_t(\frac{p_t(j)}{p_t})^{-\epsilon_p} Y_t)$. Thus, the first order conditions of capital and labour are

$$R_t^p = \phi_t(j)\alpha A_t \overline{k}_t(j)^{\alpha-1} N_t(j)^{1-\alpha} \tag{4.5}$$

and

$$W_t^p = \phi_t(j)(1-\alpha) A_t \overline{k}_t(j)^\alpha N_t(j)^{-\alpha} \tag{4.6}$$

respectively.

By nature, Eqs. 4.5 and 4.6 are the demand curves of intermediate producer j for capital and labour. Therefore, the aggregate demand of intermediate manufacturers for capital and labour can be written as

$$\overline{k}_t = \int_0^1 k_t(j)dj \tag{4.7}$$

and

$$N_t = \int_0^1 N_t(j)dj \tag{4.8}$$

respectively.

Combining equations from 4.5 to 4.8, we can conclude that all intermediate manufacturers that are minimizing their costs according to Eq. 4.3 exhibit same capital/labour ratio:

$$\frac{W_t}{R_t} = \frac{1-\alpha}{\alpha}\frac{\overline{k}_t}{N_t} \tag{4.9}$$

If the marginal cost of firm j, $mc_t(j)$, is defined as the total factor cost of producing an additional product, then we get $mc_t(j) = R_t\overline{k}_t(j) + W_tN_t(j)$. Together with the production function

$$A_t\overline{k}_t(j)^{\alpha}N_t(j)^{1-\alpha} = 1 \tag{4.10}$$

and Eqs. 4.5, 4.6, and 4.9, the marginal cost can be rewritten as

$$mc_t = mc_t(j) = \frac{1}{1-\alpha}W_t\frac{(\frac{\alpha}{1-\alpha}\frac{W_t}{R_t})^{\alpha}}{A_t} \tag{4.11}$$

By rearranging it, we get the final expression of the marginal cost for intermediate manufacturers who minimizea their factor costs as shown in Eq. 4.3

$$mc_t = \left(\frac{1}{1-\alpha}\right)^{1-\alpha}\left(\frac{1}{\alpha}\right)^{\alpha}\frac{W_t^{1-\alpha}R_t^{\alpha}}{A_t} \tag{4.12}$$

This equation holds for all intermediate goods producers, regardless of their heterogeneities.

4.1.2 *Final Goods Producer*

Unlike intermediate manufacturers, whose heterogeneities are reflected by their differentiated products, final goods producer is assumed to pack intermediate goods into undifferentiated goods in a costless manner. Thus, the final manufacturer is often cited as the final goods packer. Because the final goods are identical and the packing process is costless, the final goods market is perfectly competitive, leading to the zero profit condition for final goods firm. This implies that the final goods producer is purely a price-taker, who considers the price level as given. Therefore, the demand curve of final manufacturer for intermediate goods is downward sloping.

By adopting Dixit–Stiglitz aggregation function, we can derive the output of final goods producer

$$Y_t = \Big(\int_0^1 Y_t(j)^{\frac{\epsilon_p - 1}{\epsilon_p}} dj\Big)^{\frac{\epsilon_p}{\epsilon_p - 1}} \tag{4.13}$$

in which ϵ_p is a parameter describing the elasticity of price substitution between intermediate goods. By definition, the larger ϵ_p is, the stronger the price substitution effect.[1] The economic decision-making for final goods producer is thus equivalent to determine the quantity of $Y_t(j)$ with given level of price $p_t(j)$

$$\max_{Y_t(j)} p_t Y_t - \int_0^1 p_t(j) Y_t(j) dj \tag{4.14}$$

According to the zero profit condition for final goods packer, Eq. 4.14 implies

$$p_t Y_t = \int_0^1 p_t(j) Y_t(j) dj \tag{4.15}$$

The zero profit condition also implies that final goods producer keeps on increasing their demand, $Y_t(j)$, until the marginal cost and benefit are equal. Therefore, differentiating Eq. 4.15 with respect to $Y_t(j)$ produces

$$p_t(j) = p_t \frac{\epsilon_p - 1}{\epsilon_p} (\int_0^1 Y_t(j)^{\frac{\epsilon_p - 1}{\epsilon_p}} dj)^{\frac{\epsilon_p}{\epsilon_p - 1} - 1} \frac{\epsilon_p}{\epsilon_p - 1} Y_t(j)^{\frac{\epsilon_p - 1}{\epsilon_p} - 1} \tag{4.16}$$

This derives the downward sloping demand curve of final manufacturer

$$Y_t(j) = Y_t \Big(\frac{p_t(j)}{p_t}\Big)^{-\epsilon_p} \tag{4.17}$$

Equation 4.17 indicates the inverse relationship between the relative price level of *jth* intermediate good, $\frac{p_t(j)}{p_t}$, and the demand of final manufacturer for it, $Y_t(j)$. Substituting Eq. 4.17 in Eq. 4.15, we can write the

[1] In fact, goods are completely substitutable with each other when $\epsilon_p \to \infty$.

price level of final goods, p_t, in terms of the intermediate goods price, $p_t(j)$,

$$p_t = \left(\int_0^1 p_t(j)^{1-\epsilon_p} dj \right)^{\frac{1}{1-\epsilon_p}} \tag{4.18}$$

4.1.3 *Price Rigidity*

The most widely accepted method to incorporate short-term nominal rigidity into the dynamic model is developed by Calvo. In this pricing mechanism, not all intermediate goods producers can adjust their prices. Rather, in each time period, a fractional of intermediate manufacturers, denoted by $1-\theta_p$, are randomly selected as price adjuster. The rest of the intermediate goods producers, θ_p, keep their price same as the previous value. Based on such pricing mechanism, the degree of price rigidity in the NCM/DSGE model can be modified to meet the reality by assigning corresponding value to parameter θ_p.[2]

For an intermediate goods firm j, the profit generated by price adjusting can be expressed as

$$\frac{p_t(j)}{p_t} - mc_t Y_t(j) \tag{4.19}$$

Because each intermediate goods producer only knows the probability of being able to adjust its price in the next time period, it uses stochastic discount factor (SDF) to make economic decisions. More specifically, the dynamic operating function of firm j is

$$\max_{p_t(j)} E_t \sum_{s=0}^{\infty} \left(\theta_p \beta\right)^s \frac{u'(C_{t+s})}{u'(C_t)} \left(\frac{p_t(j)}{p_{t+s}} \left(\frac{p_t(j)}{p_{t+s}} \right)^{-\epsilon_p} Y_{t+s} - mc_{t+s} \left(\frac{p_t(j)}{p_{t+s}} \right)^{-\epsilon} Y_{t+s} \right) \tag{4.20}$$

As a result, the optimal price, p_t^*, satisfies

$$p_t^* = \frac{\epsilon_p}{\epsilon_p - 1} \frac{X_{1t}}{X_{2t}} \tag{4.21}$$

[2] It is easy to observe that the degree of price rigidity grows as the value of parameter, θ_p increases. In fact, the market is perfectly elastic (inelastic) if $\theta_p = 0$ (θ_p=1).

in which X_{1t} and X_{2t} can be written in their recursive expressions

$$X_{1t} = \lambda_t mc_t p_t^{\epsilon_p} Y_t + \theta_p \beta E_t X_{1t+1} \tag{4.22}$$

and

$$X_{2t} = \lambda_t p_t^{\epsilon_p - 1} Y_t + \theta_p \beta E_t X_{2t+1} \tag{4.23}$$

respectively.

4.2 Household Sector

In the NCM/DSGE model, households are labour suppliers and final goods consumers. They are ultimate owners of the manufacturer firms and thus enjoy the profits generated by these firms. Therefore, their economic decisions on working, consuming and investing directly affect labour supply, consumption and capital accumulation. This section explains the economic behaviours of the households. In the labour market, we introduce nominal wage rigidity into the DSGE model by using a similar mechanism as explained in the goods market. This section is composed of two subsections: the first describes the determination of labour supply, and the second discusses the dynamic behaviours of households and their connection with the rest of the economy.

4.2.1 Labour Market

The nominal wage rigidity can be introduced into the DSGE model as well. To do so, scholars adopt Calvo pricing mechanism in the labour market. A similar structure is assumed in the labour market as in the goods market. Households provide differentiated labour in the labour market, equivalent to the intermediate goods producers in the goods market. There is a labour packer who packs these labour of heterogeneities into undifferentiated final labour (N_t in Eq. 4.8). Similar to the final goods producer described in 4.1.2, the final labour packer works costlessly.

Suppose there is a continuum households in the economy indexed by i, the corresponding labour provided by the ith household is $N_t(i)$. The Dixit–Stiglitz aggregation of household labour produces

$$N_t = \left(\int_0^1 N_t(i)^{\frac{\epsilon_W - 1}{\epsilon_W}} dj \right)^{\frac{\epsilon_W}{\epsilon_W - 1}} \tag{4.24}$$

in which parameter ϵ_w represents the elasticity of wage substitution, just as ϵ_p does in Eq. 4.13.

Therefore, the final labour packer's aim is to maximize its profit by adjusting the demand for labour $N_t(i)$

$$\max_{N_t(i)} W_t N_t - \int_0^1 W_t(i) N_t(i) di \tag{4.25}$$

The first order partial differentiation of this equation with respect to $N_t(i)$ produces the downward sloping demand curve for labour

$$N_t(i) = N_t \left(\frac{W_t(i)}{W_t} \right)^{-\epsilon_w} \tag{4.26}$$

This is equivalent to Eq. 4.17 in Sect. 4.1.2. The corresponding wage of final labour, W_t, can be calculated in terms of the idiosyncratic wages, $W_t(i)$, as

$$W_t = \left(\int_0^1 W_t(i)^{1-\epsilon_w} \right)^{\frac{1}{1-\epsilon_w}} \tag{4.27}$$

The Calvo pricing mechanism in the labour market implies that a subset of the households, in each time period, are randomly selected to adjust their wage request, while the wage for the remaining households remains its previous value. Thus, households need to adopt SDF to make optimal economic decisions on wage $W_t(i)$. This yields the optimal wage of final labour W_t^*

$$(W_t^*)^{1+\eta\epsilon_w} = \frac{\epsilon_w}{\epsilon_w - 1} \frac{H_{1t}}{H_{2t}} \tag{4.28}$$

in which H_{1t} and H_{2t} can be written in recursive forms

$$H_{1t} = \Phi W_t^{\epsilon_w(1+\eta)} N_t^{1+\eta} + \theta_w \beta E_t (\pi_{t+1})^{\epsilon_w(1+\eta)} H_{1t+1} \tag{4.29}$$

and

$$H_{2t} = \lambda_t W_t^{\epsilon_w} N_t + \theta_w \beta E_t (\pi_{t+1})^{\epsilon_w - 1} H_{2t+1} \tag{4.30}$$

By nature, households are consumers, labour suppliers and ultimate owners of capital. Their utility is a function of consumption, C_t, labour,

N_t, and the real money balance, $m_t \equiv \frac{M_t}{p_t}$.

$$u(C_t, N_t, M_t) = ln(C_t - bC_{t-1}) - \theta \frac{N_t^{1+\eta}}{1+\eta} + \phi \frac{m_t^{1-\nu} - 1}{1-\nu} \tag{4.31}$$

The first term on the right side of this equation summarizes the positive utility of consumption, with b as the habit formation parameter. The second term represents the negative utility of work, and the third term the positive utility of real money balance. The corresponding budget constraint for households is

$$\begin{aligned} C_t + Inv_t + b_{t+1} + m_{t+1} = {} & W_t N_t + R_t u_t k_t \\ & + \frac{\pi_t}{p_t} - T_t - RC_t + (1 + i_{t-1}) b_t + m_t \end{aligned} \tag{4.32}$$

The use of economic resources by households is summarized in the terms on the left side of Eq. 4.32, and the economic resources on the right side. Inv_t is the capital investment, $\frac{\pi_t}{p_t}$ is the real profits generated by intermediate goods manufacturers, T_t is the tax paid to the government, and b_t is the bond investment that yields interest income, i_{t-1}, at the end of each time period. The rental income of capital is captured by $R_t u_t k_t$, and the wage income by $W_t N_t$. RC_t is the cost of adjusting capital utilization rate. One thing worth mentioning is that all entries in Eq. 4.32 are in real terms.

According to Christiano et al. [3], the investment costs consist of two components. The first component is the cost of capital utilization adjustment, RC_t, in the household budget constraint Eq. 4.32

$$RC_t = \frac{k_t}{z_t}(\chi_1(u_t - 1) + \chi_2(u_t - 1)^2) \tag{4.33}$$

The second component is the cost of investment adjustment

$$k_{t+1} = z_t\left(1 - \frac{\tau}{2}\left(\frac{Inv_t}{Inv_{t-1}} - 1\right)^2\right)Inv_t + (1 - \delta)k_t \tag{4.34}$$

It shows that this cost increases as investment deviates further from its previous value.

4.3 The General Equilibrium

The demand function of final goods packer for the intermediate goods, Eq. 4.17, and the production function of intermediate manufacturers, Eq. 4.1, jointly determine the equilibrium in the goods market on the supply side

$$Y_t = \frac{A_t \bar{k}_t(j)^{\alpha} N_t(j)^{1-\alpha}}{\int_0^1 (\frac{p_t(j)}{p_t})^{-\epsilon_p} dj} \tag{4.35}$$

Government collects tax, T_t, paid by the households, to purchase final goods, G_t.

$$G_t = w_t^G Y_t \tag{4.36}$$

in which the ratio of government expenditure to the aggregate output, w_t^G, follows

$$w_t^G = (1 - \rho_G) w^G + \rho_G w_{t-1}^G + \epsilon_t^G \tag{4.37}$$

Parameter w^G is the ratio of government expenditure to the aggregate output in the steady state, and ϵ_t^G is the government expenditure shock. Under balanced budget assumption, the government expenditure equals the tax it collects

$$G_t = T_t \tag{4.38}$$

Central bank in the NCM/DSGE model independently conducts monetary policy following the Taylor rule

$$i_t = (1 - \rho_i) i^* + \rho_i i_{t-1} + (1 - \rho_i)(\theta_\pi(\pi_t - \pi^*) + \theta_Y(log Y_t - log Y_{t-1})) + \epsilon_t^i \tag{4.39}$$

This is corresponding to the discussion of monetary policy, Eq. 1.3, in Sect. 1.2. In Eq. 4.39, i^* is the equilibrium interest rate, and π^* is the target inflation rate set by the central bank. $(log Y_t - log Y_{t-1})$ represents the output gap in period t. ϵ_t^i is the unexpected monetary policy shock, which is assumed to be white noise. ρ_i, θ_π, and θ_Y are parameters, whose values can be either calibrated or estimated.[3]

[3] The details of model identification will be discussed in Chapter 10, along with the empirical analysis using our model.

The general equilibrium of the economy is achieved when all markets contained in the model, including the goods market and labour market, clear out

$$Y_t = C_t + G_t + Inv_t + \frac{RC_t k_{t-1}}{z_t} \tag{4.40}$$

This accounting identity fully explains the composition of aggregate output of the economy at aggregate level. Conclusively, we derive the fundamentals of the NCM/DSGE model that contains many significant qualities such as nominal rigidities, intertemporal optimization, rational expectations and dynamic planning. This chapter summarizes the principles of the existing NCM/DSGE models and concludes this part. In the following part, we try to demonstrate our contribution to develop new models for selected emerging market economies.

References

1. Calvo, G. (1983). Staggered prices in a utility-maximizing framework. *Journal of Monetary Economics, 12*(3), 383–398.
2. Bernanke, B., Gertler, M., & Gilchrist, S. (1999). The financial accelerator in a quantitative business cycle framework. *Handbook of Macroeconomics, 1*, 1341–1393.
3. Christiano, L., Eichenbaum, M., & Evans, C. (2005). Nominal rigidities and the dynamic effects of a shock to monetary policy. *Journal of Political Economy, 113*(1), 1–45.

PART III

The Financial and Housing Sectors Asymmetric Model for Emerging Market Economies

In this part, we propose the new dynamic macroeconomic framework designed for the emerging market economies, namely the financial and housing sectors asymmetric model (FHSAM). Essentially, the financial market and the housing market are explicitly modelled in this framework. Moreover, the basic structure of the model economy draws on a broader body of economic and social features in emerging market economies. It is composed of four chapters. The first chapter provides an overview and summarizes the general assumptions underlying the FHSAM. The rest three chapters examine the modelling exercise, from the basic model to the full model.

CHAPTER 5

Overview and General Assumptions

5.1 The Incentives to Build New Dynamic Macroeconomic Models for Emerging Market Economies

Based on the literature review and the study of existing DSGE modelling, we find that although a significant volume of literature and research has been conducted and that a growing number of researchers are making progress in the DSGE modelling in emerging market economies, models with emphasis on housing and financial markets are still rare. Additionally, emerging market economies are facing certain economic and social features that can hardly be described by the traditional DSGE models with insufficient consideration of heterogeneities in the household sector. Several distinct household groups with materially different economic and social features simultaneously exist within one economy. This household structure needs to be carefully considered in the DSGE models with housing and financial markets, as these household groups, although share some basic economic features such as consumption and willingness to take leisure, enjoy distinct access to these markets and thereby have different economic activity patterns. As we have shown in Chapter 2, the most simple and straightforward household grouping in the BIC countries is the urban–rural structure.[1] Thirdly, there is lack of research that employs the DSGE

[1] One may argue that the urbanization ratio in Brazil is 85%, as high as the level in developed economies, but we can still treat the Brazilian economy in terms of two social classes with a

D. L. Jia, *Dynamic Macroeconomic Models in Emerging Market Economies*,
https://doi.org/10.1007/978-981-15-4588-7_5

models to compare and explain the distinct economic performance in these emerging market economies.

Therefore, the principle incentive to build new DSGE models for emerging market economies, such as the BIC countries, is to modify the original NCM/DSGE models to capture the social household structure in these economies. Another contribution of our new DSGE models is the explicit introduction of the housing market in emerging market economies. As we have discussed in Chapter 2, because of certain issues, such as immature financial market, insufficient infrastructure in the rural areas, natural, governmental and social barriers between urban and rural areas, and so on, real estate accounts for a crucial share in household wealth. The average share of housing to total household wealth is much higher than that in developed economies, where the household may possess alternative investments, such as stocks, bonds and funds. Therefore, DSGE models for the emerging market economies should pay attention to the role played by the housing market. We can also study the welfare effect of changes in the social household structure and provide quantified policy implication for public policy analysis. This is an important issue since social and economic inequality may lead to instability or even political and governmental failure. Models proposed in this part may help policymakers to quantify the impacts of their policies, thus making their policy more accurate and effective. As these three economies are under the intensive process of internalization and modernization, all of them are trying to build strong middle class and decrease the number of households living in poverty. New models in this book may provide helpful quantified information of how to achieve this goal in a more stable and effective way, with minimum adverse by-products to other household groups and to the aggregate output.

In order to accommodate all these important issues, we are trying to build new DGSE models with multiple household groups to capture the heterogeneities of households in these economies. Additionally, housing and financial markets are explicitly included in the new dynamic system, producing a broader and deeper insight of the economic mechanism in these economies. In general, this is the first DSGE framework designed for

small modification of the original urban–rural structure. The basic two groups of Brazilian households can be categorized as developed household group with full access to the financial market and possessing marketable real estate properties and underdeveloped household group who have very limited access to the financial market, from where they can get loans, and have no or little marketable real estate assets.

emerging market economies with special emphasis on household heterogeneities and with major concern of housing and financial markets.

The basic procedure to develop the FHSAM consists of three steps, and in each step model is improved by incorporating a broader body of economic details[2]: a basic two-layer DSGE model is developed to depict the simplest social stratification structure; the advanced models with more sophisticated social structure and economic agents are then proposed, based on the basic two-layer model; finally, the fully fledged model is developed via adding comprehensive economic and social features into the basic and the advanced models. For each model, we calculate the steady-state value of each variable as the initial value for Dynare to make further stochastic analysis.

5.2 General Assumptions

As its name, the model we propose in this part, the Financial and Housing Sectors Asymmetric Model (FHSAM), has the major concern of the financial and housing markets, both of which have been proved to be major sources of economic fluctuations. We discussed the importance of financial and housing markets in an economy theoretically in Chapter 2. Empirical evidence and the stylized facts are summarized as well.

Firstly, along with the growing volume of empirical evidence showing the great importance of the financial markets and the services they provide, more and more scholars agree with the view that financial sector plays a key role in the modern economy, in which both households and entrepreneurs heavily rely on financial services. Therefore, changes in the financial markets can give rise to fluctuations in real terms. In the second place, housing market has regained public attention, especially after the subprime crisis. It again convinces that those changes in the housing market may give rise to large scale international economic fluctuations. To quantify the effects of the housing market to other parts of the economy, we need a DSGE model with an explicit housing market. This necessity seems more urgent in emerging market economies, since households in these economies exhibit much higher concentration of wealth on real estate assets. Thirdly, the existing DSGE models have traditionally focused on the heterogeneities in production, by introducing heterogeneities in the household sector, the

[2] This is consistent with the standard procedure to develop comprehensive DSGE models with large volume of variables.

framework suggested by this book is able to capture the social stratification in emerging market economies; or put it in another way, the lack of representative middle-class households. Several social groups (or classes) exist, each contains a large amount of people. Households in different social groups have very different access to financial assets, properties and physical capital. As a result, they are diverse in economic behaviour patterns. These heterogeneities in the household sector constraint the application of mainstream DSGE models, most of which did not pay much attention to these issues, in emerging market economies.

The basic idea of household heterogeneities is intuitive. It assumes that the overall population can be categorized into several exclusive groups. At the micro level, if the magnitude of the *i*th individual is denoted as φ_i, then the aggregate magnitude (denoted as *Agg* below) can be calculated as:

$$Agg = \Sigma_{i=1}^{N} \varphi_i \tag{5.1}$$

If we divide the whole population into P groups, with M_j as the population in group *j*, then we can get:

$$Agg = \Sigma_{j=1}^{P} (\Sigma_{k=1}^{N} \varphi_{k,j}) \tag{5.2}$$

Here $\varphi_{k,j}$ is the magnitude of the *k*th individual in group j, and $\Sigma_{j=1}^{P} M_j = N$. Within one group, if we denote g_j as the aggregate magnitude of all the individuals in group *j*, then:

$$Agg = \Sigma_{j=1}^{P} g_j \tag{5.3}$$

In this equation, $g_j = \Sigma_{k=1}^{M_j} \varphi_{k,j}$. As P increases, M_j decreases. That is to say, the more groups we divide the whole population into, the smaller the size we get in each group. At the extreme condition, if $P \to N$, then $M_j \to 1$, and $g_j \to \varphi_j$. In a continuum, we can further denote the g_j as:

$$g_j = \Sigma_{i=1}^{N} \varphi_i = \int_{t_{t-j}}^{t} \varphi_t \, dt, 0 \leq t_{t-j} < t \leq 1, t_0 = 0, t_P = 1 \tag{5.4}$$

Therefore, the *Agg* can be written as:

$$Agg = \Sigma_{j=1}^{P} \int_{t-j}^{t} \varphi_t \, dt \tag{5.5}$$

The application of this aggregation method in our model is straightforward. We use the simple double-group social structure as an example. If an economy has two exclusive social groups—the urban A_u and the rural A_r, we can model these two groups of households and their dynamic connections in the economy. The final aggregates A can be solved by

$$A_u = \int_0^1 \varphi_{u,t} dt \tag{5.6}$$

$$A_r = \int_0^1 \varphi_{r,t} dt \tag{5.7}$$

$$Agg = \omega_1 A_u + \omega_2 A_2, \omega_1 + \omega_2 = 1 \tag{5.8}$$

It is evident that the more groups we divide the overall population into, the more accurate the model is. In an extreme case, if we exactly divide the entire population, N, into N groups and model all the dynamics of these N individuals, we can get the full picture of the economy. As the population within an economy is usually very large, it is almost impossible to model each individual separately. More importantly, macroeconomic models need to account for the complicated connection between each pair of economic agents. Therefore, as the number of economic agents, N, increases, the volume of the relationships that need to be modelled surges. As a result, economists need to find the subtle balance between improving accuracy and reducing the overwhelming complicity. Here in this part of the book, we begin from a basic model, and then move to the advanced and the full models with four exclusive social groups in the household sector. This is to address the features of social structure in the emerging market economies.

The major qualities and assumptions of the FHSAM are:

- The short-term nominal price rigidity implied by staggered pricing mechanism proposed by Calvo [1] is one of the basic features of the FHSAM. The mechanism of staggered pricing in our model is consistent with that in the models developed by Bernanke et al. [2], Christiano et al. [3], and Iacoviello and Neri [4].
- We introduce short-term nominal rigidity in the consumption goods market but keep the housing market with flexible prices. This is because the majority of real estate transactions are made in a case-by-case manner. Each side of the deal has plenty of time to adjust their economic decision. The same assumption can be seen in Iacoviello [5] and Iacoviello and Neri [4].

- Inspired by the contributions made by Iacoviello [5], Davis and Heathcote [6], and Iacoviello and Neri [4], the FHSAM explicitly contains the housing market, reflecting the heterogeneities in housing and non-housing sectors. We also realize the principles of the model in Iacoviello and Neri [4] by allowing a fraction of households to get credit, using real estate wealth as collateral. Their contribution models two groups of households: household borrowers and household lenders. But in our model, we go one step further by considering the heterogeneities in households in terms of income, access to the financial and housing markets, capital ownership and the economic patterns.
- The asymmetry between households in the less-developed regions (or from the lower class of the society) and those in the urban areas (or from the middle and high classes of the society) are independently modelled in our research. In emerging market economies, a large portion of the population suffers from highly restricted (or limited) access to financial services and investments. Therefore, in our FHSAM system, this part of households is studied as an independent sector compared to the original household sector in previous studies. This is to capture the evident social stratification in emerging market economies.
- Within the FHSAM framework, an important hypothesis is that amplification effects, in both financial and housing sectors, heavily influence the real-term aggregate outcomes. The financial acceleration effect and the housing market effect can explain the higher level of economic volatility in emerging market economies.
- A rich set of shocks are included in the FHSAM. This feature gives us the freedom to depict more details of the emerging market economies as they are facing uncertainties, not just from purely economic factors but also from certain strong government interventions and social changes. Our model can better evaluate the outcomes of these activities and thus provide decent policy suggestions.
- By modelling social stratification in the model economy, FHSAM helps us better understand the economic impacts of the social structure. Thus, this framework is a good platform to analyse the economic dynamics in economies with multiple social classes.
- Since financial and housing markets are accommodated in the FHSAM framework, monetary policy based on the FHSAM is more effective in predicting potential threats caused by the fluctuations in these two markets, leading to smoother growth path of the overall outcomes.

- The FHSAM framework can be converted to different versions for different economies with unique characteristics such as fixed exchange rate, direct credit control, dependent central bank, etc., all of which are not rare in emerging market economies.

References

1. Calvo, G. (1983). Staggered prices in a utility-maximizing framework. *Journal of Monetary Economics, 12*(3), 383–398.
2. Bernanke, B., Gertler, M., & Gilchrist, S. (1999). The financial accelerator in a quantitative business cycle framework. *Handbook of Macroeconomics, 1*, 1341–1393.
3. Christiano, L., Eichenbaum, M., & Evans, C. (2005). Nominal rigidities and the dynamic effects of a shock to monetary policy. *Journal of Political Economy, 113*(1), 1–45.
4. Iacoviello, M., & Neri, S. (2010). Housing market spillovers: Evidence from an estimated DSGE model. *American Economic Journal: Macroeconomics, 2*(2), 125–164.
5. Iacoviello, M. (2005). House prices, borrowing constraints, and monetary policy in the business cycle. *American Economic Journal: Macroeconomics, 95*(3), 739–764.
6. Davis, M. A., & Heathcote, J. (2007). The price and quantity of residential land in the United States. *Journal of Monetary Economics, 54*(8), 2595–2620.

CHAPTER 6

The Basic Model

6.1 Theoretical Framework

6.1.1 Household Sector

As we have discussed previously, in the basic two-layer FHSAM, there are two exclusive groups of households: urban households, who own the capital; and rural households who work and consume but do not possess any physical capital. Households in each group have different utility functions and constraints according to their economic characteristics.

As for the urban households, they try to maximize the lifetime utility by:

$$maxE_t\beta_u^t\sum_t^{\infty}(\frac{c_{u,t}^{1-\sigma_u}}{1-\sigma_u}+\gamma_u\frac{m_{u,t}^{1-\xi_u}}{1-\xi_u}-\psi_u\frac{n_{u,t}^{1+\nu_u}}{1+\nu_u}) \tag{6.1}$$

Here, we introduce the real money, m_t, into the model using the MIU method, which is proposed by Sidrauski [1]. The real money balance enters directly into the household's utility function.

Likewise, the rural households try to maximize their lifetime utility by:

$$maxE_t\beta_r^t\sum_t^{\infty}(\frac{c_{r,t}^{1-\sigma_r}}{1-\sigma_r}+\gamma_r\frac{m_{r,t}^{1-\xi_r}}{1-\xi_r}-\psi_r\frac{n_{r,t}^{1+\nu_r}}{1+\nu_r}) \tag{6.2}$$

The economic meaning of these two utility functions is straightforward. Households get utility from consumption, $c_{u,t}$ for urban household and $c_{r,t}$ for rural households, and real balance of money, $m_{u,t}$ for urban households

D. L. Jia, *Dynamic Macroeconomic Models in Emerging Market Economies*,
https://doi.org/10.1007/978-981-15-4588-7_6

and $m_{r,t}$ for rural households. Working, or providing labour, brings negative utility for households as it decreases the leisure time. Therefore, we can see the term $-\psi_u \frac{n_{u,t}^{1+\nu_u}}{1+\nu_u}$ in urban households' utility function and $-\psi_r \frac{n_{r,t}^{1+\nu_r}}{1+\nu_r}$ in rural households' utility function.

Another feature that needs to be emphasized is the discount factors for urban and rural households. Different from other DSGE models with only one household class, this basic model contains two different classes of households with diverse economic characteristics. As a result, these two classes of households value the utility in the future using different discount factors (here, we use β_u for urban households and β_r for rural households). As we demonstrate in the following equations, urban and rural households have different compositions of wealth: physical capital is assumed to be possessed exclusively by urban households. The only resource of wealth for rural households is their wage income and real money balance. This wealth status gives rise to the fact that urban and rural households discount the future utility using different rates. Because urban households hold all the physical capital, they have the claim on the capital rent income in the future, giving them more freedom to balance their optimal utility between current and future period of time. Therefore, urban households value utility in the future with higher value than rural households do, since the latter focus more on utility in the current period of time. Thus, we conclude that $\beta_u > \beta_r$. This assumption is consistent with the one in Iacoviello and Neri [2], which assumes that the discount factor for patient households, β, is higher than that for impatient households, β'.

The budget constraints for urban and rural households are:

$$c_{u,t} + k_t + m_{u,t} = w_{u,t}n_{u,t} + R_t k_{t-1} + (1-\delta)k_{t-1} + \frac{g_{t-1}m_{u,t-1}}{\pi_t} \tag{6.3}$$

$$c_{r,t} + m_{r,t} = w_{r,t}n_{r,t} + \frac{g_{t-1}m_{r,t-1}}{\pi_t} \tag{6.4}$$

respectively. From the differences between Eqs. 6.3 and 6.4, we can clearly see the diverse wealth status of these two groups of households. Urban households own the capital, k_t, and thus enjoy the rental income of capital, R_t. The only income of rural households is the real wage, w_t, gained by providing labour, $n_{r,t}$. The different parameters indicate the different economic behaviour patterns of these two different social groups. Because urban households hold capital, they discount future income less than do the rural households, who rely on wage as their sole income source, that is

$\beta_u \geq \beta_r$. Thus, rural households are less working averse than urban ones: $\psi_u \geq \psi_r$.

The rational decision making process implies that households maximizes their lifetime utility, subject to the corresponding constraints. Mathematically, this is equivalent to solving the first order conditions of the Lagrangians given by Eqs. 6.1, 6.2, 6.3, and 6.4. These FOCs of urban and rural households are shown in equations from 6.5 to 6.9.

$$c_{u,t}^{-\sigma_u} = c_{u,t+1}^{-\sigma_u}\beta_u(R_{t+1} + 1 - \delta) \tag{6.5}$$

If we put the budget constraint of urban households and the corresponding utility maximization function 6.3 together. By partially differentiating it with respect to capital k_t, we get Eq. 6.5. On the left side, term $c_{u,t}^{-\sigma_u}$ is the marginal utility of one unit consumption. On the right side, term $\beta_u(R_{t+1} + 1 - \delta)$ is the present value of the postponed one unit of consumption, which has been invested and yields return, $(R_{t+1} + 1 - \delta)$, in the next time period. Therefore, Eq. 6.5 describes the equality of utilities for urban households in two cases: they may directly spend one unit of consumption in current period or postpone this one unit of consumption and invest it to get $\beta_u(R_{t+1} + 1 - \delta)$ amount of real consumption in the next period. In fact, Eq. 6.5 is the supply curve of physical capital in this model.

$$\psi_u = w_{u,t}c_{u,t}^{-\sigma_u} \tag{6.6}$$

$$\psi_r = w_{r,t}c_{r,t}^{-\sigma_r} \tag{6.7}$$

The above two equations are the first order conditions of labour for urban and rural households, respectively, showing that the marginal disutility (ψ_u and ψ_r) of working should be fully compensated by the utility of consumption using the wages, $w_{u,t}$ and $w_{r,t}$, earned by working that much. In fact, Eqs. 6.6 and 6.7 are the supply curves of labour.

$$c_{u,t}^{-\sigma_u} = \gamma_u m_{u,t}^{-\xi_u} + \beta_u \frac{g_t c_{u,t+1}^{-\sigma_u}}{\pi_{t+1}} \tag{6.8}$$

$$c_{r,t}^{-\sigma_r} = \gamma_r m_{r,t}^{-\xi_r} + \beta_r \frac{g_t c_{r,t+1}^{-\sigma_r}}{\pi_{t+1}} \tag{6.9}$$

By using households' budget constraints shown in Eqs. 6.3 and 6.4, together with the utility maximization functions, we solve for the first order conditions of real money balance for urban and rural households. Similar to the explanation of Eq. 6.5, left side of the equations represents the marginal utility of one unit of consumption and the right side is the utility of postponing that amount of consumption, holding it as real balance of money ($\gamma_u m_{u,t}^{-\xi_u}$ and $\gamma_r m_{r,t}^{-\xi_r}$) and spending it in the next period ($\beta_u \frac{g_t c_{u,t+1}^{-\sigma_u}}{\pi_{t+1}}$ and $\beta_r \frac{g_t c_{r,t+1}^{-\sigma_r}}{\pi_{t+1}}$). In conclusion, 6.8 and 6.9 are the demand curves of real money.

6.1.2 Production Sector

Now, it is the time for us to move on to the production sector in the model economy. We use the Cobb–Douglas production function in this sector

$$y_t = z_t k_t^{\alpha} (n_{u,t}^{f} n_{r,t}^{1-f})^{1-\alpha} \tag{6.10}$$

in which z_t is the technology shock at time t, and α is the contribution share of the physical capital in goods production, which is assumed to be a positive constant. In view of our introduction of two household groups into this model, we need to decide the shares of contribution in production for each group of households. In Eq. 6.10, it is captured by parameter f. More specifically, parameter f represents the share of contribution in production for urban households (thus $1 - f$ is the share for rural households). A larger value of f indicates the higher labour contribution of urban households in production and thus the lower labour contribution of rural households in production.

In the fully competitive capital and labour markets, the real wages, $w_{u,t}$ and $w_{c,t}$, are equal to the marginal product of labour; and the capital rental rate, R_t, to the marginal product of capital. Therefore, the first order conditions of labour for production can be drawn as Eqs. 6.11 and 6.12, and the first order condition of capital as Eq. 6.13.

$$w_{u,t} = z_t k_t^{\alpha} (1-\alpha)(n_{u,t}^{f} n_{r,t}^{1-f})^{-\alpha} f n_{u,t}^{f-1} n_{r,t}^{1-f} \tag{6.11}$$

$$w_{r,t} = z_t k_t^{\alpha} (1-\alpha)(n_{u,t}^{f} n_{r,t}^{1-f})^{-\alpha} (1-f) n_{u,t}^{f} n_{r,t}^{-f} \tag{6.12}$$

In fact, 6.11 and 6.12 are the labour demand curves in this model.

$$R_t = z_t \alpha k_t^{\alpha-1} (n_{u,t}^{f} n_{r,t}^{1-f})^{1-\alpha} \tag{6.13}$$

This is the capital demand curve, in which the real aggregate outputs are either consumed or invested. Therefore, the capital accumulation function is (the left side of this equation represents the real investment: $inv_t = y_t - c_{u,t} - c_{r,t}$):

$$y_t - c_{u,t} - c_{r,t} = k_t - (1-\delta)k_{t-1} \tag{6.14}$$

In this model, the supply of money follows the AR(1) process. The nominal growth rate of money, g_t, and the output technological condition, z_t, follow the patterns of:

$$\log g_t = (1-d)\log \overline{g} + d \log g_{t-1} + \epsilon_1 \tag{6.15}$$

$$\log z_t = \rho_z \log z_{t-1} + \epsilon_2 \tag{6.16}$$

6.1.3 The Steady State

In this basic model, there are 14 unknowns and 14 equations (from 6.3 to 6.16). Thus, the solution to the basic model can be solved.[1] To find the solution, we need to linearize this DSGE model to get its state-space representation. We have also discussed several mathematical techniques to fulfil linearization. Here we adopt the technique advocated by Uhlig [4] to linearize this basic model.[2] The mathematics behind this method is not too complex and the procedure to use it is straightforward: we use $\overline{x}e^{\widetilde{x}_t}$ to substitute x_t for all the variables in this model, with $\overline{x}$ represents the steady-state value of variable x_t. After this substitution, we can transfer the original non-linear equations into linear equations using approximations of $\lim_{\widetilde{x}_t\to 0} e^{\widetilde{x}_t} \approx 1+\widetilde{x}_t$, $\lim_{\widetilde{x}_t\to 0} e^{\widetilde{x}_t^a} \approx 1+a\widetilde{x}_t$, and $\lim_{\widetilde{x}_t\to 0,\widetilde{y}_t\to 0} 1+\widetilde{x}_t\widetilde{y}_t \approx 1$. For example, Eq. 6.13 can be rewritten as

$$\overline{R}e^{\widetilde{R}_t} = \overline{z}e^{\widetilde{z}_t}\alpha\overline{k}^{\alpha-1}e^{(\alpha-1)\widetilde{k}_t}\overline{n}_u^{f(1-\alpha)}e^{f(1-\alpha)\widetilde{n}_{u,t}}\overline{n}_r^{(1-f)(1-\alpha)}e^{(1-f)(1-\alpha)\widetilde{n}_{r,t}} \tag{6.17}$$

[1] We use Dynare 4.4.3 to undertake the empirical analysis of this model. For the details of the Dynare package, see Chapter 10 and the contribution made by Adjemian et al. [3].

[2] Same results can be achieved using other linearization methods. To save space, we only demonstrate the method as in the text.

In equilibrium, $\overline{R} = \overline{z}\alpha\overline{k}^{\alpha-1}\overline{n}_u^{f(1-\alpha)}\overline{n}_r^{(1-f)(1-\alpha)}$. Therefore, by eliminating steady-state values and higher order terms, Eq. 6.17 changes into:

$$\widetilde{R}_t = \widetilde{z}_t + (\alpha - 1)\widetilde{k}_t + f(1-\alpha)\widetilde{n}_{u,t} + (1-f)(1-\alpha)\widetilde{n}_{r,t} \tag{6.18}$$

which is the linearized expression of Eq. 6.13. By using the same technique on all the rest 13 equations, we can fully transfer the original non-linear model into the following linear equations.

The budget constraint of urban household (6.3) is linearized as

$$\begin{aligned}\overline{c}_u\widetilde{c}_{u,t} + \overline{k}\widetilde{k}_t + \overline{m}_u\widetilde{m}_{u,t} = \overline{w}_u\overline{n}_u(\widetilde{n}_{u,t} + \widetilde{n}_{r,t}) + \overline{R}\overline{k}(\widetilde{R}_t + \widetilde{k}_{t-1})\\ + (1-\delta)\overline{k}\widetilde{k}_{t-1} + \overline{g}\overline{m}_u\overline{\pi}^{-1}(\widetilde{g}_t + \widetilde{m}_{u,t} + \widetilde{n}_{u,t})\end{aligned} \tag{6.19}$$

Correspondingly, the linearized rural household's budget constraint is

$$\overline{c}_r\widetilde{c}_{r,t} + \overline{m}_r\widetilde{m}_{r,t} = \overline{w}_r\overline{n}_r(\widetilde{w}_{r,t} + \widetilde{n}_{r,t}) + \overline{g}\overline{m}_r\overline{\pi}^{-1}(\widetilde{g}_t + \widetilde{m}_{r,t} + \widetilde{n}_{r,t}) \tag{6.20}$$

Eq. 6.5, which is the capital supply curve, can be linearized as

$$1 - \sigma_u\widetilde{c}_{u,t} = \beta_u(1 - \delta + \overline{R} + \overline{R}\widetilde{R}_t - \sigma_u\overline{R}\widetilde{c}_{u,t+1} - \sigma_u\widetilde{c}_{u,t+1} + \delta\sigma_u\widetilde{c}_{u,t+1}) \tag{6.21}$$

The labour supply curves described in Eqs. 6.6 and 6.6 are linearized as

$$\widetilde{w}_{u,t} = \sigma_u\widetilde{c}_{u,t} \tag{6.22}$$

$$\widetilde{w}_{r,t} = \sigma_r\widetilde{c}_{r,t} \tag{6.23}$$

The linearized expressions of Eqs. 6.8 and 6.9 are

$$1 - \sigma_u\widetilde{c}_{u,t} = -\overline{m}_u^{\xi_u} + \beta_u\overline{c}_u^{-\sigma_u}\overline{\pi}(1 + \widetilde{g}_t - \sigma_u\widetilde{c}_{u,t} - \widetilde{\pi}_{t+1}) \tag{6.24}$$

$$1 - \sigma_r\widetilde{c}_{r,t} = -\overline{m}_r^{\xi_r} + \beta_r\overline{c}_r^{-\sigma_r}\overline{\pi}(1 + \widetilde{g}_t - \sigma_r\widetilde{c}_{r,t} - \widetilde{\pi}_{t+1}) \tag{6.25}$$

The production function's linear expression is

$$\widetilde{y}_t = \widetilde{z}_t + \alpha\widetilde{k}_t + f(1-\alpha)\widetilde{n}_{u,t} + (1-f)(1-\alpha)\widetilde{n}_{r,t} \tag{6.26}$$

The linear labour demand curves are demonstrated in Eqs. 6.27 and 6.28

$$\widetilde{w}_{u,t} = \widetilde{z}_t + \alpha\widetilde{k}_t - \alpha f\widetilde{n}_{u,t} + (1-f)(1-\alpha)\widetilde{n}_{r,t} + (f-1)\widetilde{n}_{u,t} + (1-f)\widetilde{n}_{r,t} \tag{6.27}$$

$$\widetilde{w}_{u,t} = \widetilde{z}_t + \alpha\widetilde{k}_t - \alpha f\widetilde{n}_{u,t} + (1-f)(1-\alpha)\widetilde{n}_{r,t} + f\widetilde{n}_{u,t} - f\widetilde{n}_{r,t} \tag{6.28}$$

The capital accumulation Eq. 6.14 can be linearized as

$$\widetilde{y\bar{y}}_t - \tilde{c}_u\bar{c}_{u,t} - \tilde{c}_r\bar{c}_{r,t} - \widetilde{k\bar{k}}_t - (1-\delta)\widetilde{k\bar{k}}_{t-1} \tag{6.29}$$

Thus, we find all corresponding linearized equations for the basic DSGE model, which has been represented in a non-linear manner through equations from 6.3 to 6.16. Note that all the variables with overline, $\overline{x}$, appeared in linear equations above, are the steady-state values[3] and therefore they can be treated as constant like all the other parameters.

We should emphasize that, prior to the dynamic analysis, the steady-state solution of the DSGE model should be calculated. Without an accurate solution to the steady-state values, Dynare can not solve the model. In this basic model, the steady-state solution is calculated manually. The basic principle to solve for the steady-state values is often referred to as the 'great ratio' method.[4] To simplify the computation we further assume that the inflation rate is constant and equal to the growth rate of money supply ($g^{ss} = \pi^{ss} = 1$), consistent with the MIU assumption of this basic model.

$$\pi^{ss} = g^{ss} = 1 \tag{6.30}$$

Secondly, Eq. 6.4 (or 6.20 in the linear expression) leads to Eq. 6.31 when $g^{ss} = \pi^{ss} = 1$. Thus, we get Eq. 6.30. In this equation, we can clearly see that the steady-state value of rural households' working hour is solely determined by parameter Ψ_r, which denotes the degree of disutility of work to rural households. The higher the value of Ψ_r the lower the number of hours rural households tend to work. This is consistent with the theoretical assumption of our model. Because rural households do not hold physical capital, their consumption is exclusively supported by their working wage. Therefore, the steady-state working hours are completely determined by rural households' willingness to work, which is parameter Ψ_r.

$$n_r^{ss} = \frac{1}{\Psi_r} \tag{6.31}$$

[3] In this thesis, we use $\overline{x}$ and x^{ss} interchangeably, meaning that equality $\overline{x} = x^{ss}$ holds for all the variables in this model.

[4] For greater details of the 'great ratio' method, one may refer to the works of Del Negro and Schorfheide [5] and Fagiolo and Roventini [6]. An alternative way to find the steady-state solution is to linearize the model at the steady state and then to solve the resulting equations either by band or using software.

If we cancel out the equal part ($c_{u,t}^{ss}$) in capital supply Eq. 6.5 (or in the linear version 6.21) at the steady state, we get Eq. 6.32, by which we can compute the steady-state capital rental rate R^{ss}. This equation indicates that in equilibrium, the rent of physical capital should compensate the discount effect, $\frac{1}{\beta_u} - 1$, and depreciation of such capital, δ. Higher depreciation rate requires higher level of capital rental rate. Additionally, the steady-state capital rental rate is negatively correlated with the discount factor of the capital owner, β_u,

$$R^{ss} = \frac{1}{\beta_u} + \delta - 1 \tag{6.32}$$

Unlike computing steady-state working hours of rural households, things get more complex when we compute the steady-state value of urban households' working hour, n_u^{ss}, as they own physical capital that can yield capital rental income, R^{ss}. However, with the value of R^{ss}, n_r^{ss}, and physical capital demand curve of Eq. 6.13, we can compute the value of n_u^{ss}, according to Eq. 6.33. The economic meaning of this equation matches our economic intuition: because urban households have capital rental income, R^{ss}, their willingness to work, n_u^{ss}, is negatively correlated with the value of R^{ss}—the higher capital income the lower the willingness for urban households to work as the additional capital income can be used as the source of consumption.

$$n_u^{ss} = \frac{\frac{1}{\Psi_u} R^{ss}(1-\alpha) f}{R^{ss} - R^{ss}(1-\alpha)(1-f) - \alpha\delta} \tag{6.33}$$

Therefore, by using the budget constraint of urban households, Eq. 6.8, and eliminating the equal terms of real money balance on both sides of it, we can compute the steady-state value of physical capital, k^{ss}, as shown in Eq. 6.34. In general, the steady-state value of capital is positively correlated with capital return rate, R^{ss}. This is consistent with our economic intuition that higher capital return leads to greater amount of capital stock.

$$k^{ss} = \left(\frac{\frac{R^{ss}}{\alpha} - \delta}{\frac{1}{\Psi_u}\left(n_u^{ss\,f} n_r^{ss\,1-f}\right)^{1-\alpha}(1-\alpha) f \frac{1}{n_u^{ss}} + \frac{1}{\Psi_r}\left(n_u^{ss\,f} n_r^{ss\,1-f}\right)^{1-\alpha}(1-\alpha)(1-f)\frac{1}{n_r^{ss}}} \right)^{\frac{1}{\alpha-1}} \tag{6.34}$$

Using the value of n_u^{ss}, n_r^{ss}, and k^{ss} in the production function 6.10, we calculate the steady-state output, y^{ss} as in Eq. 6.35.

$$y^{ss} = k^{ss^{\alpha}} (n_u^{ss^f} n_r^{ss^{1-f}})^{1-\alpha} \tag{6.35}$$

Therefore, labour demand curve, Eqs. 6.11 and 6.12, produce the steady-state value of real wage for urban, w_u^{ss}, and rural households, w_r^{ss}, as shown in Eqs. 6.36 and 6.37, showing that the real wage is positively correlated with overall output, y^{ss}, the share of labour contribution in production, $1 - \alpha$, and the corresponding shares of labour of urban, f, and rural households, $1 - f$.

$$w_u^{ss} = \frac{y^{ss}}{n_u^{ss}}(1 - \alpha)f \tag{6.36}$$

$$w_r^{ss} = \frac{y^{ss}}{n_r^{ss}}(1 - \alpha)(1 - f) \tag{6.37}$$

The labour supply curves, Eqs. 6.6 and 6.7, yield the steady-state values of consumption for urban, c_u^{ss}, and rural households, c_r^{ss}, as shown in Eqs. 6.38 and 6.39. These equations indicate that the steady-state value of consumption is positively determined by the real wages, w_u^{ss} and w_r^{ss} and negatively by their willingness to take leisure, Ψ_u and Ψ_r. Such implication is well consistent with our economic logic: when households get more real wages, their consumption expenditure tends to increase accordingly; if households show higher desire to enjoy leisure, Ψ_u and Ψ_r increase, (or, put it in another way, less willingness to work), and their steady-state consumption decreases.

$$c_u^{ss} = \frac{1}{\Psi_u} w_u^{ss} \tag{6.38}$$

$$c_r^{ss} = \frac{1}{\Psi_r} w_r^{ss} \tag{6.39}$$

Finally, real money demand curve, Eqs. 6.8 and 6.9, tell us the steady-state values of real money balance for urban, m_u^{ss}, and rural households, m_r^{ss}, as shown in the following two equations

$$m_u^{ss} = \frac{\nu_u c_u^{ss} p^{ss}}{\pi^{ss} - \beta} \tag{6.40}$$

$$m_r^{ss} = \frac{\nu_r c_r^{ss} p^{ss}}{\pi^{ss} - \beta} \tag{6.41}$$

In conclusion, all the steady-state conditions of our basic two-layer model can be summarized in the above equations from 6.30 to 6.41 (the variable ending with 'ss' denote the steady-state value of that variable). Based on these values, Dynare can solve the dynamic model.

6.2 Theoretical Summary and Testable Hypotheses

We have now put together the components of our basic model including how to linearize it and how to compute the steady-state values. The main purpose of this model is to make preliminary analysis of how heterogeneities in households affect the overall economic performance.

The economic structure of the basic model is illustrated in Fig. 6.1. The major difference between rural and urban households lies in the fact that only urban households own physical capital assets and thus their rental return. Therefore, they value future income with a higher discount rate ($\beta_u > \beta_r$). Both of these two groups of households work in production sector to earn wages. Their contribution shares in the production sector are f and $(1 - f)$, respectively. Let us consider one extreme situation, if $f \rightarrow 1$, this basic model is exactly the same as the standard RBC/DSGE model with only one group of households. As f decreases, the labour share of urban households in production drops accordingly. If $f \rightarrow 0$, we arrive at another extreme case where only rural households are working while urban households completely rely on capital rental income. Different values of f may lead to diverse economic outcomes including consumption, investment and aggregate output. Thus, parameter f is a very important factor determining the structure (or social classification) of an economy. In general, we expect that as f increases, the real wage for urban households, w_u, becomes higher as well (that is to say, when $(1 - f)$ increases, the real wage for rural households, w_r, becomes higher.) This is so because if production becomes more dependent on one particular group of households, the real wage for such households surely rises. What is more, because consumption is positively correlated with real wages, the real consumption of that group of households increases to a certain degree. Based on the theoretical features of this basic model, we also expect that when $(1 - f)$ gets larger, both the physical capital stock, k, and capital investment, inv, increase (equivalently, there is a negative correlation between f and k and inv.). The theoretical logic behind this hypothesis is that as $(1 - f)$ increases, the share of urban households'

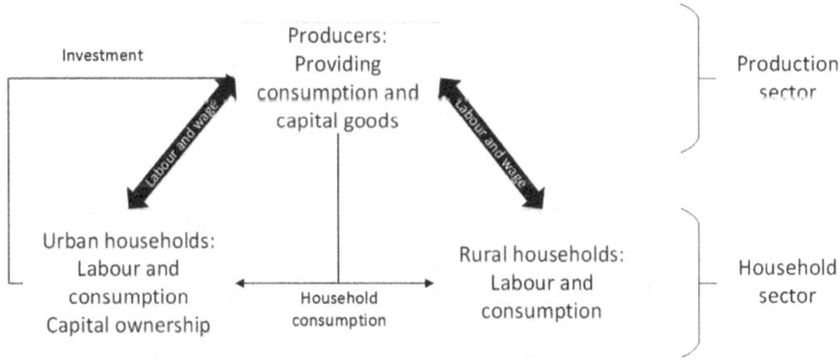

Fig. 6.1 Structure of the basic model

contribution to production is lower; they, thus, get less real wages, and rely more on capital rental income. As a result, the demand for capital increases. Additionally, this basic model also implies that aggregate output, y_t, is positively correlated with consumption, $c_{u,t}$ and $c_{r,t}$, physical capital stock, k_t, and investment, inv_t, which means that consumption and investment are procyclical variables. Similarly, higher aggregate output leads to increasing real wages for both urban and rural households and higher level of capital rental rate. Therefore, we expect that the basic model implies that real wages and capital return are also procyclical variables. As we have discussed previously, this basic model implies several important theoretical hypotheses that need to be reviewed and evaluated in the empirical analysis. To better demonstrate these hypotheses, we summarize them in Table 6.1.

Economists want to accurately quantify how certain economic variables, such as aggregate output, GDP_t, investment, Inv_t,and household consumption, $c_{u,t}$ and $c_{r,t}$, react against exogenous economic or technological innovations and shocks such as unexpected interest-rate shocks, productivity shocks and housing preference shocks. Generally, this type of analysis is called impulse response analysis, as it captures the response of certain variables to an exogenous shock. DSGE models provide a very feasible way to conduct such a dynamic analysis. In our basic model, we introduce a productivity shock, z_t, to quantify the dynamic relationships between such shock and economic variables. A positive productivity shock will push up aggregate output and thus the real wage for households. This increase in wage income leads to higher household consumption. Another effect of the positive productivity shock is that it pushes up the demand for physical capital assets. Therefore, this will be followed by the increase of real

Table 6.1 Theoretical hypotheses of the basic two-layered model: correlations

Economic factors	*Hypothesized correlations*
Urban household's labour share in production, f, and labour provided by urban household, n_u	Positive
Rural household's labour share in production, $1-f$, and labour provided by rural household, n_r	Positive
Rural household's labour share in production, $1-f$, and real wage for rural household, w_r	Positive
Urban household's labour share in production, f, and stock of physical capital, k	Negative
Urban household's labour share in production, f, and investment in physical capital, inv	Negative
Aggregate output, y_t, and investment in physical capital, inv_t	Positive
Aggregate output, y_t, and household consumption, $c_{u,t}$ and $c_{r,t}$	Positive
Household consumption, $c_{u,t}$ and $c_{r,t}$, and investment in physical capital, inv_t	Positive
Household consumption, $c_{u,t}$ and $c_{r,t}$, and households' real wage, $w_{u,t}$ and $w_{r,t}$	Positive
Real capital rental rate, R_t, and aggregate output, y_t	Positive
Real capital rental rate, R_t, and investment in physical capital, inv_t	Positive
Real capital rental rate, R_t, and urban household consumption, $c_{u,t}$	Positive

Table 6.2 Theoretical hypotheses of the basic two-layered model: impulse responses

Economic variables	*Exogenous shock (positive)*	*Hypothesized responses*
Urban household's consumption, $c_{u,t}$	Productivity shock	Gradually rise to a new level
Rural household's consumption, $c_{r,t}$	Productivity shock	Gradually rise to a new level
Urban household's real wage, $w_{u,t}$	Productivity shock	Gradually rise to a new level
Rural household's real wage, $w_{r,t}$	Productivity shock	Gradually rise to a new level
Aggregate output, y_t	Productivity shock	Instantly increase and gradually return to a new level
Investment, inv_t	Productivity shock	Instantly increase and gradually return to a new level
Real capital rent, r_t	Productivity shock	Instantly increase and gradually return to the original level
Inflation	Productivity shock	Instantly decrease and gradually return to the original level

capital rent. Since the aggregate output instantly increases after the positive productivity shock, while the households' wages and consumption go up in a gradual way, the initial reaction of inflation to such productivity shock is negative. As households' wages and consumption gradually increase, the level of inflation gradually returns to its original level in the following periods. The summarized hypotheses of theses dynamics are shown in Table 6.2.

References

1. Sidrauski, M. (1967). Rational choice and patterns of growth in a monetary economy. *The American Economic Review*, *57*(2), 534–544.
2. Iacoviello, M., & Neri, S. (2010). Housing market spillovers: Evidence from an estimated DSGE model. *American Economic Journal: Macroeconomics*, *2*(2), 125–164.
3. Adjemian, S., Bastani, H., Karame, F., Juillard, M., Maih, J., Mihoubi, F., et al. (2017). *Dynare: Reference manual* (Dynare Working Papers No. 1).
4. Uhlig, H. (1999). *A toolkit for analyzing nonlinear dynamic stochastic models easily* (Federal Reserve Bank of Minneapolis Working Papers No. 101).
5. Del Negro, M., & Schorfheide, F. (2008). Forming priors for DSGE models and how it affects the assessment of nominal rigidities. *Journal of Monetary Economics*, *55*(7), 1191–1208.
6. Fagiolo, G., & Roventini, A. (2012). *Macroeconomic policy in DSGE and agent-based models* (Observatoire Français des Conjonctures Economiques Working Papers No. 124).

CHAPTER 7

The Advanced Model

7.1 Theoretical Framework

Similar to the basic model, the advanced model assumes that rural households do not possess any capital, all of which are exclusively owned by the household lenders. Within the rural household group, it is further divided into two sub-groups: rural migrant[1] workers, who work in the non-housing sector and rural migrant construction workers, who work only in the real estate industry. This is consistent with the real social structure in most emerging market economies.[2] Additionally, the advanced model considers production as a more sophisticated process that produces both housing and non-housing products. Thus, this model captures the effects of different technology conditions and structures in these two sectors. Finally, we introduce a rich set of shocks into the advanced model, making it possible to analyse the detailed dynamic information of the model to a variety of shocks.

[1] The word 'migrant' reflects the fact that these agents are from rural parts of the economy but live and work in the urban areas. According to China's National Bureau of Statistics, the number of migrant workers rose to 280 million in 2019.

[2] Compared to goods production, the production of real estate assets, or put it in another way, building construction, is of a lower level of technology and skill, especially concerning the property development in emerging market economies. Therefore, the majority of the working force in the building construction industry are workers from rural areas.

D. L. Jia, *Dynamic Macroeconomic Models in Emerging Market Economies*,
https://doi.org/10.1007/978-981-15-4588-7_7

7.1.1 *Household Sector*

In the basic model, we try to introduce heterogeneities of households by categorizing households into urban and rural ones, according to their economic and social characteristics. As we have mentioned previously, the definition of urban and rural is not limited by their geographic meaning. They can be feasibly expanded to two social classes of households, with one more developed and the other less developed, or one with ownership of capital and the other with no capital ownership. In general, household heterogeneities in emerging market economies can be better depicted by considering more details of the economic properties and characteristics of these households. In the countries we focus on, several different household classes exist, each with their unique economic features in terms of industries they work in, access to the financial market and capital ownership. Moreover, each of these social classes includes a large number of households. After considering the study of social layers and classification in emerging market economies in Chapter 2, urban and rural households are further classified into 4 groups in the economy of this advanced model. More specifically, they are household borrowers, household lenders, rural workers and rural migrant construction workers. Their economic behavioural patterns and budget constraints are discussed as per below.

As we have discussed in the basic model, one of the most distinguished features of emerging market economies is that they typically have a larger portion of working force or potential working force coming from the rural or less developed parts of these economies. As the process of industrialization and urbanization proceeds in these economies, they flush into the urban or more developed areas. In relevant literature, scholars use the term 'rural migrant workers' to identify them. Because they are of less education and working skills, they mainly participate in labour-intensive industries, such as housing construction and low-end manufacturing sectors. These workers share many common economic characteristics, such as the limited access to capital and financial market, negligible holding of housing assets and higher willingness to work. Therefore, it becomes natural to analyse the heterogeneities of these rural migrant workers according to the industries they work in. What is more, one of the most important developments of this advanced model is that it contains a housing market, as housing assets are explicitly included in household's utility functions and housing production is introduced to the supply side of this model. In the production of housing services (i.e. real estate development process), developers need to hire labour to build up new housing products. In emerging market economies, such work is mainly provided by rural migrant workers (therefore, we denote them as rural migrant construction workers), as this industry is more labour-concentrated and requires less techniques and skills. It is, thus, one of the most common choices for rural migrant workers to work in. The rural migrant construction workers solve the maximization problem

$$maxE_t \sum_{t=0}^{\infty}(\beta_{cw}^t(\ln(c_{cw,t} - b_{cw}c_{cw,t-1}) - \psi_{cw}\frac{n_{cw,t}^{(1+\eta_{cw})}}{1+\eta_{cw}}) \tag{7.1}$$

Here, $\ln(c_{cw,t} - b_{cw}c_{cw,t-1})$ captures the habit formation feature[3] in household's utility function, in which the parameter b_{cw} is the habit formation parameter for rural construction worker households. The utility of rural migrant construction workers is simple and straightforward. They work in the construction industry to produce real estate, which they do not possess. The only source of their wealth is their wage income, $w_{cw,t}$ (by providing labour, $n_{cw,t}$). Therefore, their budget constraint is

$$c_{cw,t} = w_{cw,t}n_{cw,t} \tag{7.2}$$

As discussed previously, the rural workers are essentially similar to rural migrant construction workers but work in other industries like low-end manufacturing or service industries. They do not own any housing or capital either. They work (providing labour $n_{rw,t}$) to get a real wage, $w_{rw,t}$. The only difference between rural workers and rural migrant construction workers is that they work in different sectors: the former work in the non-housing sector while the latter in the housing sector. As a result, the maximization of utility and budget constraint of rural workers can be written as:

$$maxE_t \sum_{t=0}^{\infty}(\beta_{rw})^t\left(\ln(c_{rw,t} - b_{rw}c_{rw,t-1}) - \psi_{rw}\frac{n_{rw,t}^{1+\eta_{rw}}}{1+\eta_{rw}}\right) \tag{7.3}$$

$$c_{rw,t} = w_{rw,t}n_{rw,t} \tag{7.4}$$

[3] For more details on habit formation in household consumption function, one may refer to Bouakez et al. [1].

Based on budget constraints and utility functions of rural construction workers (cw) and rural workers (rw), we have the corresponding F.O.Cs:

F.O.C wrt $n_{cw,t}$:

$$\psi_{cw} n_{cw,t}^{eta_{cw}} = u_{c,t}^{cw} w_{cw,t} \tag{7.5}$$

F.O.C wrt $n_{rw,t}$:

$$\psi_{rw} n_{rw,t}^{eta_{rw}} = u_{c,t}^{rw} w_{rw,t} \tag{7.6}$$

Equations 7.5 and 7.6 are labour supply curves for construction workers ($n_{cw,t}$) and rural immigrant workers ($n_{rw,t}$). The economic meaning of these two equations is clear: the negative utility of working (or sacrifice leisure time) should be equally compensated by the positive utility of consumption using money earned by working. To put it simply, the higher the wage the more the labour supply.

Unlike rural households, household borrowers and lenders own marketable housing property (household lenders have $h_{lh,t}$ and borrowers $h_{bh,t}$), which directly goes into their utility functions. This assumption is consistent with the reality in that real estate does provide utility and is one of the most important investments for households.[4] Therefore, the household lenders try to maximize their utility by:

$$maxE_t \sum_{t=0}^{\infty} (\beta_{lh})^t (\ln(c_{lh,t} - b_{lh} c_{lh,t-1}) - \psi_{lh} \frac{n_{lh,t}^{1+\eta_{lh}}}{1+\eta_{lh}} + j_t \ln h_{lh,t} \tag{7.7}$$

Likewise, the household borrowers solve

$$maxE_t \sum_{t=0}^{\infty} (\beta_{bh})^t (\ln(c_{bh,t} - b_{bh} c_{bh,t-1}) - \psi_{bh} \frac{n_{bh,t}^{1+\eta_{bh}}}{1+\eta_{bh}} + j_t \ln h_{bh,t} \tag{7.8}$$

Loans are made only between household borrowers and lenders. This is to fit the situation where rural workers and rural migrant construction workers do not have marketable housing property, upon which they can claim to get loans. This is also because those rural households are refrained from the financial market in which loans are made. Like the assumptions in the FAM [2] and the model proposed by Iacoviello and Neri [3], loans are made against real estate as collateral. The amount of borrowing cannot exceed a certain ratio, m, of the underlying collateral.

[4] The importance of real estate in overall household wealth has been discussed at length in the literature review and further demonstrated in the data analysis chapter.

Based on the above assumptions, we can summarize the economic activities of the household lenders: besides the similarities with construction workers and migrant workers in that they all work to earn wages and purchase consumption goods, they own all the physical capitals including capital used in non-housing and housing sector ($k_{c,t}$ and $k_{h,t}$, respectively), make loans to household borrowers, collect interest repayments from the borrowers, hold land and finally, enjoy the dividends from retailers who are working in a monopolistic competitive market. The budget constraint of household lender is:

$$\begin{aligned} & c_{lh,t} + k_{c,t} + k_{h,t} + k_{b,t} + p_{h,t}h_{lh,t} + p_{l,t}l_t + L_{lh,t} \\ & \quad = w_{lh,t}n_{lh,t} + p_{h,t}(1-\delta_h)h_{lh,t-1} \\ & \quad + (1-\delta_{kc})k_{c,t-1} + (1-\delta_{kh})k_{h,t-1} \\ & \quad + R_{c,t}k_{c,t-1} + R_{h,t}k_{h,t-1} + p_{b,t}k_{b,t} \\ & \quad + \frac{r_{t-1}L_{lh,t-1}}{\pi_t} + (p_{l,t} + r_{l,t})l_{t-1} + div_t \end{aligned} \tag{7.9}$$

This equation shows that the income of household lenders consists of a variety of components. As we explained above, household lenders own capital and land. They rent capital (both $k_{c,t}$ in the goods market and $k_{h,t}$ in the housing market) to firms on the production side to get rental income ($r_{c,t}$ and $r_{h,t}$, respectively). The price of housing is $p_{h,t}$, and housing depreciation rate is δ_h. There are two kinds of capital, $k_{c,t}$ and $k_{h,t}$, which are used in the production of consumption goods and housing accordingly. Capital depreciates at the rate of δ_{kc} and δ_{kh}, respectively. Land, l_t, the price of which is $p_{l,t}$, is totally owned by the household lenders. The rental return rate of land is $r_{l,t}$. We also assume that firms are owned by household lenders as well. Therefore, the dividends of these firms, div_t, are accumulated by household lenders, which can be calculated as:

$$div_t = y_t \frac{x_t - 1}{x_t} \tag{7.10}$$

The household borrowers maximize their lifetime utility under the budget constraint:

$$c_{bh,t} + p_{ht}h_{bh,t} + \frac{r_{t-1}b_{bh,t-1}}{\pi_t} = w_{bh,t}n_{bh,t} + p_{h,t}(1-\delta_h)h_{bh,t-1} + L_{bh,t} \tag{7.11}$$

Their borrowing constraint is:

$$L_{bh,t} \leq m E_t(\frac{p_{h,t+1} h_{bh,t} \pi_{t+1}}{r_t}) \tag{7.12}$$

The household borrowers get loans ($L_{bh,t}$) from household leaders using their property ($h_{bh,t}$) as collateral. The amount of loans that can be granted is determined by the expected value of this property in the next period ($E_t p_{h,t+1} h_{bh,t}$) divided by the expected rate of inflation (π_{t+1}), the Loan-to-Value (LTV) ratio (m) and current interest rate (r_t). Using budget constraints and utility functions of urban households (household lenders and household borrowers), we can derive the FOCs in the following equations:

F.O.C wrt $n_{bh,t}$:

$$\psi_{bh} n_{bh,t}^{eta_{bh}} = u_{c,t}^{bh} w_{bh,t} \tag{7.13}$$

F.O.C wrt $n_{lh,t}$:

$$\psi_{lh} n_{lh,t}^{eta_{lh}} = u_{c,t}^{lh} w_{lh,t} \tag{7.14}$$

Equations 7.13 and 7.13 bear the same economic meaning as 7.5 and 7.6. They are labour supply functions of $n_{bh,t}$ and $n_{lh,t}$, depicting the upward sloping labour supply curve to the real wage.

F.O.C wrt $h_{bh,t}$:

$$\frac{j_t}{h_{bh,t}} + u_{c,t}^{bh} m p_{h,t} \frac{\pi_{t+1}}{r_t} + \beta_{bh} u_{c,t+1}^{bh} p_{h,t+1}(1-\delta_h) = u_{c,t}^{bh} p_{h,t} + \beta_{bh} u_{c,t}^{bh} m p_{h,t+1} \frac{r_{t+1}}{r_t} \tag{7.15}$$

F.O.C wrt $h_{lh,t}$:

$$\frac{j_t}{h_{lh,t}} + \beta_{lh} u_{c,t+1}^{lh} p_{h,t+1}(1 - \delta_h) = u_{c,t}^{lh} p_{h,t} \tag{7.16}$$

Equations 7.15 and 7.16 are the housing demand equations for household borrowers and household lenders, respectively. These two equations work together with the housing supply curve described below to determine the equilibrium in the housing market. The supply of capital ($k_{c,t-1}$ and $k_{h,t-1}$), intermediate goods ($k_{b,t}$), land (l_{t-1}) and loans ($L_{lh,t}$) can be derived from the first order conditions of household lenders as they are the ultimate owners of capital, intermediate goods and land. The following equations describe these F.O.C.s.

F.O.C wrt l_{t-1}:

$$u_{c,t}^{lh} p_{l,t} = \beta_{lh} u_{c,t+1}^{lh} (p_{l,t+1} + r_{l,t+1}) \tag{7.17}$$

F.O.C wrt $k_{b,t}$:

$$u^{lh}_{c,t}(p_{b,t} - 1) = 0 \tag{7.18}$$

F.O.C wrt $k_{c,t-1}$:

$$u^{lh}_{c,t} = \beta_{lh} u^{lh}_{c,t+1}(r_{c,t} + (1 - \delta_{kc})) \tag{7.19}$$

F.O.C wrt $k_{h,t-1}$:

$$u^{lh}_{c,t} = \beta_{lh} u^{lh}_{c,t+1}(r_{h,t} + (1 - \delta_{kh})) \tag{7.20}$$

The economic meanings of these first order conditions are: Eq. 7.17 represents the land supply of household lenders, and Eq. 7.18 is the supply curve of intermediate goods ($k_{b,t}$). Equations 7.19 and 7.20 depict the household lenders' optimal choice of capital in goods production and housing production, respectively. Therefore, they are supply curves of physical capital, $k_{c,t}$ and $k_{h,t}$. Finally, the utility-maximization strategy of household lenders leads to the loan supply function:

$$u^{lh}_{c,t} = \beta_{lh} u^{lh}_{c,t+1} r_t / \pi_{t+1} \tag{7.21}$$

From the perspective of household lenders, loans lent to household borrowers are their assets, bearing interest income, $r_t L_{lh,t}$. Therefore, household lenders' choice of loan amount granted to borrowers is to balance between the utility of consuming in the current period and the utility of saving such amount of consumption as loans to borrowers, getting interest income and consuming it in the next period. Accordingly, the left side of Eq. 7.21 represents the marginal utility of current consumption, $u^{lh}_{c,t}$, and its right side the marginal utility of making loans, getting interest income, and spending that amount in the next period (after discounting and considering inflation), $\beta_{lh} u^{lh}_{c,t+1} r_t / \pi_{t+1}$.

7.1.2 *Production and Technology*

As we have discussed previously, the pricing mechanism is similar to that in the model suggested by Bernanke et al. [2], as in the works conducted by Iacoviello and Neri [3], and Christiano et al. [4], which is the Calvo's staggered pricing mechanism [5]. One important feature of the pricing mechanism in our model is that it only contains price rigidity in the consumption sector, as in the model of Iacoviello [6] and Iacoviello and Neri [3]. We do not introduce wage rigidity in the labour market because of the weaker bargaining power of workers in emerging market economies. Labour unions in these countries are of so little influence that they rarely manage to achieve significant benefits for their workers. We do not instal price rigidity in housing market either. This is based on the fact that the real estate transactions are normally conducted case by case. Both sides of the deal may have plenty of time to negotiate and reconsider. Thus, the price of each deal can be quickly adjusted to reflect the changes in circumstances. This assumption is consistent with the empirical analysis and is similar to the consumption in Iacoviello [6], Iacoviello and Neri [3], Barsky et al. [7]

In general, there are two types of producers on the supply side: the wholesale firms and the retailers (final good producers). The wholesale firms operate in a fully competitive consumption market and housing market (flexible prices of consumption and housing). They hire labour, $n_{rw,t}, n_{lh,t} and n_{bh,t}$, and capital services, $k_{y,t}$, to produce wholesale goods y_t. They also hire labour and capital services together with intermediate goods of non-housing (consumption) sector, $k_{b,t}$, capital and land to provide new houses IH_t. While the final good producers differentiate all the wholesale goods (including consumption and housing) into retail goods and sell them to all the consumers in both consumption and housing markets. The production of y_t and IH_t by wholesale firms can be expressed as:

$$\begin{aligned} Y_t &= A_{c,t}((n_{lh,t}^{\beta_1} n_{bh,t}^{\beta_2} n_{rw,t}^{\beta_3}))^{1-\alpha} k_{c,t-1}^{\alpha}, \\ \beta_i &\geq 0 \; for \; all \; i = 1, 2, 3, \; and \; \beta_1 + \beta_2 + \beta_3 = 1 \end{aligned} \tag{7.22}$$

$$\begin{aligned} IH_t &= A_{h,t} n_{rw,t}^{\mu_1} k_{b,t}^{\mu_2} l_{t-1}^{\mu_3} k_{h,t-1}^{\mu_4}, \\ \mu_i &\geq 0 \; for \; all \; i = 1, 2, 3, 4 \; and \; \mu_1 + \mu_2 + \mu_3 + \mu_4 = 1 \end{aligned} \tag{7.23}$$

These wholesale firms are assumed to maximize their profits by solving:

$$\begin{aligned} & max \frac{Y_t}{x_t} + p_{h,t} IH_t \\ & - (w_{rw,t} n_{rw,t} + w_{lh,t} n_{lh,t} + w_{bh,t} n_{bh,t} + w_{cw,t} n_{cw,t} \\ & + r_{c,t} k_{c,t} + r_{l,t} l_{t-1} + r_{h,t} k_{h,t-1} + r_{b,t} k_{b,t}) \end{aligned} \tag{7.24}$$

Equation 7.22 shows that urban households (both household lenders and household borrowers) and rural workers provide labour to wholesale producers ($n_{lh,t}$, $n_{bh,t}$, and $n_{rw,t}$, respectively). In Eq. 7.23, only rural migrant construction workers provide labour ($n_{cw,t}$) input in the production of new properties. This is consistent with our theoretical assumption of the household classification. The factors $A_{c,t}$ and $A_{h,t}$ represent the total factor productivity level in non-housing and housing sectors, respectively.

If we put the production process described in Eqs. 7.22 and 7.23 together with the profit-maximizing process shown in Eq. 7.24 together, we can find the optimum conditions for wholesale firms by solving the first order conditions to the input variables. The following equations summarize the corresponding F.O.Cs.

F.O.C. wrt $k_{c,t-1}$ (this equation describes the capital demand in non-housing [goods] production)

$$\alpha Y_t = r_{c,t} k_{c,t-1} x_t \tag{7.25}$$

F.O.C. wrt $k_{h,t-1}$, this equation describes the wholesale firms' demand for capital in housing production.

$$\mu_4 p_{h,t} I H_t = r_{h,t} k_{h,t-1} \tag{7.26}$$

F.O.C. wrt $n_{cw,t}$, this is the equation where the wholesale firms' demand for labour $n_{cw,t}$ in the housing market is determined.

$$\mu_1 p_{h,t} I H_t = w_{cw,t} n_{cw,t} \tag{7.27}$$

F.O.C. wrt $n_{rw,t}$, the demand function of wholesale firms for labour of rural workers $n_{rw,t}$ in the goods market.

$$(1-\alpha)\beta_3 Y_t = n_{rw,t} w_{rw,t} x_t \tag{7.28}$$

F.O.C. wrt $n_{lh,t}$, the demand function of wholesale firms for labour of household lenders $n_{lh,t}$ in the goods market.

$$(1-\alpha)\beta_1 Y_t = n_{lh,t} w_{lh,t} x_t \tag{7.29}$$

F.O.C. wrt $n_{bh,t}$, the demand function of wholesale firms for labour of household borrowers $n_{bh,t}$ in the goods market.

$$(1-\alpha)\beta_2 Y_t = n_{bh,t} w_{bh,t} x_t \tag{7.30}$$

F.O.C. wrt $k_{b,t}$, this is the demand function of wholesale firms for intermediate goods $k_{b,t}$.

$$\mu_2 p_{h,t} I H_t = p_{b,t} k_{b,t} \tag{7.31}$$

F.O.C. wrt l_{t-1}, this is the demand function of wholesale firms for land l_{t-1}.

$$\mu_3 p_{h,t} I H_t = r_{l,t} l_{t-1} \tag{7.32}$$

From these F.O.C. equations, we can clearly see that the demand for labour ($n_{rw,t}$, $n_{cw,t}$, $n_{bh,t}$, and $n_{lh,t}$) is negatively correlated with wages ($w_{rw,t}$, $w_{cw,t}$, $w_{bh,t}$, and $w_{lh,t}$, respectively) and positively correlated with its contribution share in the production process (captured by $(1-\alpha)\beta_3$, μ_1, $(1-\alpha)\beta_2$, and $(1-\alpha)\beta_1$, respectively), consistent with the basic economic intuition. Similarly, the demand for capital in goods production ($k_{c,t-1}$), capital in the housing market ($k_{h,t-1}$), land (l_{t-1} and intermediate goods ($k_{b,t}$) increases as their shares of contribution in the production process (α, μ_4, μ_3,, and μ_2, respectively) grow, and decreases as their price ($p_{b,t}$ for intermediate goods $K_{b,t}$) or rent rates ($r_{c,t}$, $r_{h,t}$ and $r_{l,t}$ for $k_{c,t-1}$, $k_{h,t}$, and l_t, respectively) become larger. In conclusion, these demand equations together with the supply equations derived in the F.O.C.s in the private sector jointly determine the market-clearing condition of labour ($n_{rw,t}$, $n_{cw,t}$, $n_{bh,t}$, and $n_{lh,t}$), capital ($k_{c,t}$ and $k_{h,t}$), intermediate goods ($k_{b,t}$) and land (l_t).

7.1.3 Nominal Rigidity

As in the standard Calvo pricing mechanism in modern NCM/DSGE models such as models of Bernanke et al. [2], Iacoviello [6], Christiano et al. [4] and so forth, price rigidity in the non-housing (consumption) sector is introduced by retailers, who work in a monopolistic market. Thus, these retailers have the ability to adjust their price to maximize their profit, following the Calvo pricing mechanism. They buy wholesale goods, y_t, produced by the wholesale producers at the price of $p_t^{wholesale}$, since the wholesale market is a perfectly competitive market. After that, they differentiate these purchased wholesale products, with no costs, and then sell them at the price of $p_{y,t} = X_{y,t} p_{y,t}^{wholesale}$, in which $X_{y,t}$ represents the markup of retailer price above the wholesale price. This repacking process undertaken by retailers follows the Constant Elasticity Substitution (CES) aggregation (using the Dixit–Stiglitz aggregator[5]):

[5] The details of CES aggregation and Dixit–Stiglitz aggregator can be found in Dixit and Stiglitz's contribution [8].

$$Y_t = (\int_0^1 Y_t(i)^{\frac{\epsilon_p - 1}{\epsilon_p}} di)^{(\frac{\epsilon_p}{\epsilon_p - 1})} \tag{7.33}$$

In this equation, $Y_t(i)$ represents the production of goods produced by the ith wholesale producer and ϵ_p is the elasticity of substitution among different final goods.[6] Retailers convert the CES aggregates of the wholesale goods into homogenous consumption and investment goods. Under the Calvo-style pricing mechanism, only a fraction $(1 - \theta_\pi)$ of retailers are randomly selected to have the ability to adjust their price to maximize their profit. While the other fraction (θ_π) retailers can only index their price to the inflation in the previous period. For those retailers who can adjust their price, they solve for

$$\max_{Y_t(i)} \int_0^1 p_t(i) Y_t(i) di - p_{y,t}^{wholesale} Y_t \tag{7.34}$$

Together with Eq. 7.33, we have

$$\max_{Y_t(i)} \int_0^1 p_t(i) Y_t(i) di - p_{y,t}^{wholesale} (\int_0^1 Y_t(i)^{\frac{\epsilon_p - 1}{\epsilon_p}} di)^{(\frac{\epsilon_p}{\epsilon_p - 1})} \tag{7.35}$$

Therefore, under optimum condition, the following equation can be derived (F.O.C wrt $Y_t(i)$):

$$p_{y,t}^{wholesale} \frac{\epsilon_p - 1}{\epsilon_p} (\int_0^1 Y_t(i)^{\frac{\epsilon_p - 1}{\epsilon_p}} di)^{\frac{\epsilon_p}{\epsilon_p - 1} - 1} \frac{\epsilon_p}{\epsilon_p - 1} Y_t(i)^{\frac{\epsilon_p - 1}{\epsilon_p} - 1} = p_t(i) \tag{7.36}$$

The left side of Eq. 7.36 is the marginal cost to the retailers and the right-hand side represents the marginal benefit. Therefore, this equation produces the retailer's downward sloping demand curve of item i produced by the ith wholesale producer.

[6] $\epsilon_p > 1$ and the elasticity of substitution among different final goods increase as ϵ_p becomes larger. In the extreme case $\epsilon_p \to \infty$, which means perfect substitution.

At the aggregate level, the final goods price is

$$p_t = (\int_0^1 p_t(i)^{1-\epsilon_p} di)^{\frac{1}{1-\epsilon_p}} \tag{7.37}$$

Therefore, retailer's profit $((x_t - 1) * Y_t)$ can be written as

$$(x_t - 1)Y_t = \int_0^1 p_t(i)Y_t(i)di - p_{y,t}^{wholesale} Y_t \tag{7.38}$$

Under the standard Calvo-style pricing mechanism, in each period of time, not all retailers are able to adjust their price. Only a fraction $(1 - \theta_\pi)$, of retailers are randomly selected to adjust their prices, maximizing their profits shown in Eq. 7.38. While the remaining fraction (θ_π) of retailers can only index their price to the inflation in the previous period. In this mechanism, the average life of the final goods price is $\frac{1}{1-\theta_\pi}$, completely determined by θ_π.[7] As a result, the inflation in non-housing market follows the Philips curve as shown in Eq. 7.39.

$$\begin{aligned} \ln \pi_t - \rho_\pi \ln \pi_{t-1} &= \beta_{lh}(E_t(\ln \pi_{t+1}) - \rho_\pi \ln \pi_t) \\ &\quad - \frac{(1-\theta_\pi)(1-\beta_{lh}\theta_\pi)}{\theta_\pi} \ln \frac{x_t}{x_{ss}} + \varepsilon_{\pi,t} \end{aligned} \tag{7.39}$$

7.1.4 *Monetary Policy*

This advanced model assumes that the central bank adopts the Taylor rule to set the interest rate r_t as shown in Eq. 7.40, where r^{ss} and π^{ss} are the rates of interest and inflation in the steady state, respectively.

$$\begin{aligned} r_t &= (1 - \rho_r)r^{ss} + \rho_r r_{t-1} + (1 - \rho_r)(\rho_{\pi,r}(\pi_t - \pi^{ss})) \\ &\quad + \rho_{GDP}(\ln GDP_t - \ln GDP_{t-1}) + \varepsilon_{r,t} \end{aligned} \tag{7.40}$$

Central bank adjusts the interest rate (r_t) to its value in the previous period (r_{t-1}) with an elasticity equal to ρ_r. Instead of using Y_t and Y_{t-1} as the aggregate output in the typical Taylor rule, we use GDP_t and GDP_{t-1} in this advanced model, as it contains two markets. Production in both

[7] The most popular way to set parameter θ_π is to assume that $\theta_\pi = 0.75$, as this will assure that the average life of final goods price is 1 year.

markets Y_t and IH_t are the components of the overall GDP_t, as shown in Eq. 7.41. Because the intermediate good $k_{b,t}$ is utilized in the production of new housing IH_t, as shown in Eq. 7.23, it must be subtracted from Y_t. The real value of production of housing is $p_{h,t}IH_t$.

$$GDP_t = Y_t - k_{b,t} + p_{h,t}IH_t \tag{7.41}$$

7.1.5 *General Equilibrium*

As discussed previously, the advanced model contains two markets: housing market and goods market (known as non-housing market). Intuitively, the housing market is where the demand and supply of real estate meet and the goods market produces household consumption, business investment and intermediate goods required in the production of housing. Therefore, the equilibrium of the advanced model calls for market clearing in both markets, as shown in Eqs. 7.42 and 7.43.

$$C_t + Ikc_t + Ikh_t + k_{b,t} = Y_t \tag{7.42}$$

$$H_t - (1 - \delta_h)H_{t-1} = IH_t \tag{7.43}$$

The aggregate consumption is the sum of the consumption of four groups of households, meaning that $C_t = c_{cw,t} + c_{rw,t} + c_{bh,t} + c_{lh,t}$. H_t is the real estate stock hold by both household borrowers ($h_{bh,t}$) and household lenders ($h_{lh,t}$), meaning that $H_t = h_{bh,t} + h_{lh,t}$. The definitions of investment in goods market (Ikc_t) and in housing market (Ikh_t) are $Ikc_t = k_{c,t} - (1 - \delta_{kc})k_{c,t-1}$ and $Ikh_t = k_{h,t} - (1 - \delta_{kh})k_{h,t-1}$. Therefore, the expression $Ikc_t + Ikh_t$ is the total business investment. δ_{kc} and δ_{kh} are the depreciation rates of capital in goods market and housing market, respectively.

Land plays a key role in the production of housing. Its value accounts for the major part of the total value of the property.[8] As we have introduced in the housing production function 7.23, land is explicitly involved. On the other hand, the supply of land is quite unique and is far different from that of other production inputs such as fixed capital ($k_{c,t}$ and $k_{h,t}$). This results from the fact that land supply is strictly restricted by many objective

[8] According to Davis and Heathcote [9], who quantitatively analyse the quarterly data in the United States from 1952:1 to 2007:4, housing price fluctuations are mainly determined by the change of the land price.

aspects such as geographic factors and political issues, which cannot be easily modified in the short term. The most common factors include the availability, accessibility, land ownership and so forth. It becomes more restricted in urban regions as the land stock in these areas is nearly fixed. In this part of the book, we focus on the real estate in the urban area, because the properties in rural parts in the emerging markets are minor in value and limited in marketability. In other words, the total land supply grows very slowly due to many restrictions. After considering the growth of population, the per capita land growth is close to zero.[9] Therefore, we adopt the assumption of land supply as in the models of Iacoviello [6], Iacoviello and Neri [3], Liu et al. [10], and Davis and Heathcote [9]: total land supply is fixed and normalized to one. This is shown in Eq. 7.44.

$$l_t = 1 = l^{ss} \tag{7.44}$$

Another important equality in equilibrium is the identity between loan demand ($L_{bh,t}$) and loan supply ($L_{lh,t}$), $L_{bh,t} = L_{lh,t}$, this is consistent with Walras' law.[10]

As we have introduced in the basic model, in order to complete the construction of a DSGE model, we need to compute the equilibrium values of all variables included in the model. Otherwise, it is impossible to solve for the empirical results. The methodology adopted in this chapter to find the steady-state values is same as that in the basic model. Firstly, certain assumptions are proposed to set values for a small group of variables, such as the equilibrium working hours and the target inflation rate. Then, the steady-state values of the rest of variables are solved using the 'great ratio' method. More specifically, we assume that the equilibrium price level and inflation is 1, $\pi^{ss} = 1$; this is to simplify the computation. Secondly, we assume that on average both household lenders and borrowers work 8 hours per day, $n_{lh}^{ss} = n_{bh}^{ss} = \frac{1}{3}$, and rural workers 12 hours per day, $n_{cw}^{ss} = n_{rw}^{ss} = \frac{1}{2}$. This assumption is consistent with the economic realities in emerging market economies, in which people from lower level social classes need to work more than those

[9] For details, see Davis and Heathcote [9].

[10] The detailed explanation of Walras' Law can be found in the work of Tsiang [11].

from the higher level.[11] After setting these variables, the corresponding parameters, ψ_{lh}, ψ_{bh}, ψ_{rw}, and ψ_{cw}, are no longer free. We need to solve for the values of these parameters.

Similar to the basic model, the capital supply curve at the steady state derives the equilibrium capital return rate. The only difference is that two kinds of capital are involved. Thus, there are two physical capital supply curves, Eqs. 7.19 and 7.20, and there are two steady-state rental rates, r_c^{ss} and r_u^{ss}, respectively. Cancelling the equal terms at both sides of capital supply curves, we can compute the steady-state capital return rates:

$$r_c^{ss} = \frac{1}{\beta_{lh}} + \delta_{kc} - 1 \tag{7.45}$$

$$r_u^{ss} = \frac{1}{\beta_{lh}} + \delta_{kh} - 1 \tag{7.46}$$

These two equations have the same format as Eq. 6.32 in the basic model. Their economic meanings are similar as well: equilibrium capital return rate should completely compensate for the discount effect and depreciation, δ_{kc} for non-housing goods production and δ_{kh} for capital in housing production. Similarly, we can compute the steady-state real price of intermediate goods, $p_b^{ss}=1$, using 7.18. In steady state, land supply curve, Eq. 7.17, solves the relationship between the equilibrium land price, p_l^{ss}, and land rental rate, r_l^{ss}, as shown in 7.47. It is obvious that equilibrium real land price and the real land rental rate are positively correlated; the higher level of steady state land price is coupled with a higher level of steady state-land rental rate. This is consistent with our economic intuition, especially considering the limited supply of land.

$$r_l^{ss} = \frac{1 - \beta_{lh}}{\beta_{bh}} p_l^{ss} \tag{7.47}$$

[11] Although some may argue that, even in emerging market economies such as Brazil, India and China, workers are protected by law with maximum working hours up to 8. But the actual situation is far more complicated. This kind of regulation is not completely executed in emerging market economies. What is more, people in the lower level of social classes in these countries are willing to work additional hours to gain more income. As shown in the empirics of Messenger et al. [12], Harriss [13], Spector et al. [14], Hu et al. [15], Wong et al. [16], and many others, empirical evidence indicates that a large portion of workers, especially in construction and labour-intensive manufacture industries, in emerging market economies like Brazil, India and China, tend to work 10–14 hours per day; the evidence strongly supports this assumption.

An important feature of this advanced model is that it contains loans between household lenders and borrowers, using property assets as collateral. On the loan supply side, the loan supply curve described in 7.21 gives us the steady-state value of interest rate, r^{ss}, as shown in Eq. 7.50. The economic meaning of this equation is that in the steady state, the interest rate should fully compensate for the discount in household lenders' utility. This is so because the utility of current consumption should be equal to the utility of postponing that amount of consumption and using it as property loans granted to household borrowers, getting interest income and consuming it in the next period.[12] There is an inverse relationship between household lenders' discount factor, β_{lh}, and the steady-state real interest rate: the less household lender values the future the higher the interest rate should be to compensate for such discount effect

$$r^{ss} = \frac{1}{\beta_{lh}} \tag{7.48}$$

Housing assets are directly introduced into households' utility function as shown in Eqs. 7.7 and 7.8. Therefore, we find the first order condition of housing for both household lenders and borrowers—the housing demand curves shown in Eqs. 7.15 and 7.15. After substituting variables with their steady-state values we get

$$\frac{1}{h_{bh}} + u_c^{bh,ss} m p_h^{ss} \frac{1}{r^{ss}} + \beta_{bh} u_c^{bh,ss} p_h^{ss}(1 - \delta_h) = u_c^{bh,ss} p_h^{ss} + \beta_{bh} u_c^{bh,ss} p_h^{ss} \tag{7.49}$$

and

$$\frac{1}{h_{lh}} + \beta_{lh} u_c^{lh,ss} p_h^{ss}(1 - \delta_h) = u_c^{lh,ss} p_h^{ss} \tag{7.50}$$

[12] In fact, it is a natural result of the assumption implied in this advanced model, in which mortgage collateralized by property is fully settled without default (the Walras' Law). We do not introduce the possibility of default in property loans because of three reasons. Firstly, we want to focus on the dynamics between interest rate, housing market price movements and business cycles. Secondly, household loans collateralized by real estate are of lower possibility of default than that of entrepreneur loans (in the full model, the possibility of default of entrepreneur loans and thus bankruptcy rate will be considered). Thirdly, laws and regulations of bankruptcy of individuals are not fully installed in emerging market economies, making it difficult to consider such cases. In conclusion, this simplification does not change the major mechanism we wish to analyse.

Now, we move on to the production sector in this model economy to complete the view of the steady state. In previous parts of this subsection, we demonstrate that the first order conditions of production derive the demand curves for labour, land, intermediate goods, and capital. By substituting the relevant variables, we get equations to solve for these steady state values. More specifically, capital demand curve, Eqs. 7.25 and 7.26, are turned into Eqs. 7.51 and 7.52 in the steady state. We can see the positive correlations between output (Y^{ss} in non-housing market and IH^{ss} in housing market), capital stocks (k_c^{ss} in non-housing market and k_h^{ss} in housing market), and capital rents (r_c^{ss} and r_h^{ss}, respectively). Additionally, higher real housing price, p_h^{ss}, is correlated with higher volume of capital used in housing market, k_h^{ss}, and its rent, r_h^{ss}. These theoretical correlations are well consistent with the economic reality in cross-country cases.

$$\alpha Y^{ss} = r_c^{ss} k_c^{ss} x^{ss} \tag{7.51}$$

$$\mu_4 p_h^{ss} IH^{ss} = r_h^{ss} k_h^{ss} \tag{7.52}$$

Similarly, producer's labour demand curves 7.27, 7.28, 7.29, and 7.30 are transformed into Eqs. 7.53, 7.54, 7.56, and 7.55 in the steady state.

$$\mu_1 p_h^{ss} IH^{ss} = w_{cw}^{ss} n_{cw}^{ss} \tag{7.53}$$

$$(1-\alpha)\beta_3 Y^{ss} = w_{rw}^{ss} n_{rw}^{ss} x^{ss} \tag{7.54}$$

$$(1-\alpha)\beta_1 Y^{ss} = w_{lh}^{ss} n_{lh}^{ss} x^{ss} \tag{7.55}$$

$$(1-\alpha)\beta_2 Y^{ss} = w_{bh}^{ss} n_{bh}^{ss} x^{ss} \tag{7.56}$$

These equations indicate that producers' demand for labour provided by one particular group of households and the corresponding real wage is positively correlated with its labour share in production (μ_1 for rural construction workers, $(1-\alpha)\beta_3$ for rural migrant workers, $(1-\alpha)\beta_1$ for household lenders, and finally $(1-\alpha)\beta_2$ for household borrowers) and the aggregate outputs (Y^{ss} in non-housing market and IH^{ss} in the housing market). It follows that the more important and productive the labour is, the higher demand for such labour, leading to higher level of real wage to that labour. Additionally, the real wage of rural construction workers, w_{cw}^{ss}, and producer's demand for such labour, n_{cw}^{ss}, is positively correlated with real housing price, p_h^{ss}. This is so in that if housing price increases developers tend to hire more labour with higher real wage.

Same conclusion can be drawn for land. As shown in Eq. 7.57, the steady-state land demand equation is derived from Eq. 7.32.

$$\mu_3 p_h^{ss} I H^{ss} = r_l^{ss} l^{ss} \tag{7.57}$$

This equation indicates that the steady-state values of land rent and demand for land increase as housing price and/or housing output increases. Moreover, the demand for land and land rental rate become larger as the importance of land in housing production enhances. In conclusion, by using the equations describing equilibrium conditions on both demand and supply sides, we can compute the steady-state values of all variables included in the model economy.[13]

7.1.6 Unexpected Shocks

In order to quantitatively analyse the dynamics of the advanced model, we introduced a series of shocks. In the production process (described in Eqs. 7.22 and 7.23), two technological shocks are introduced to goods production ($A_{c,t}$) and housing production ($A_{h,t}$). Housing is explicitly introduced into the utility functions of urban households. It is an asset that provides positive utility for both household lenders and borrowers. Therefore, all other things unchanged, households prefer possessing higher level of housing assets. In such sense, households' attitude towards housing directly influences their demand for housing. In order to capture the dynamics of housing preference change with other economic variables, we introduce the housing preference shock. The shock of housing preference to both household borrowers and household lenders is j_t. These shocks follow AR(1) process as:

$$\begin{aligned} \ln A_{c,t} &= \rho_{Ac} \ln A_{c,t-1} + eAC \\ \ln A_{h,t} &= \rho_{Ah} \ln A_{h,t-1} + eAh \\ \ln j_t &= \rho_j \ln j_{t-1} + ej \end{aligned} \tag{7.58}$$

As shown in Eqs. 7.39 and 7.40, the inflation innovation ($\varepsilon_{\pi,t}$) and the monetary policy shock ($\varepsilon_{r,t}$) are introduced to represent the unexpected

[13] Unfortunately, there is hardly a paper-pencil solution for this group of equations. MATLAB helps us to solve for these values using numerical methods. The details of solving steady-state values for the advanced and the full models are demonstrated in the following parts of this book.

innovations to the rates of inflation and real interest. $\varepsilon_{\pi,t}$ and $\varepsilon_{r,t}$ are i.i.d. white noises with variances σ_{π}^2 and σ_r^2. Similarly, eAc, eAh and ej in Eq. 7.58 are i.i.d. white noises as well, and their variances are σ_{eAc}^2, σ_{eAh}^2 and σ_{ej}^2, respectively.

7.2 Theoretical Summary and Testable Hypotheses

This advanced model is based on the basic model discussed in the previous chapter. It expands the model economy structure by adding many valuable economic qualities, such as two sectors in production (housing and non-housing sectors), nominal rigidities in consumption goods market (following the Colvo [5] pricing mechanism), and loans among household lenders and household borrowers with real estate as collateral. The general structure of this advanced model is shown in Fig. 7.1. Housing market has been explicitly introduced into the model economy and housing is directly included in households' utility functions. Additionally, we further expand the basic model by introducing more sophisticated heterogeneities in the household sector: four exclusive groups of households are installed in this model—household lenders, household borrowers, rural immigrant workers,[14] and rural migrant construction workers.[15] This feature is to capture the economic characteristics in emerging market economies, where there is a layered social structure and thus a lack of representative middle-class households. In order to better examine the differences among these four groups of households, each of them has been modelled with economic features according to their real-world condition. Only household lenders and borrowers are assumed to hold marketable real estate assets. This is to match the reality in emerging market economies that people living in rural areas or slums and a large portion of urban workers coming from the

[14] More specifically, this group of household includes people who live and work in urban areas but with insufficient ability to buy property. They either rent accommodation or live in properties with negligible market value. These people may not come from rural areas. In our model, we still include them as rural migrant workers since they share common economic features with rural migrant workers.

[15] More generally, the definition of 'urban' and 'rural' in this model are not necessarily restricted in their geographic conception. They can be conceived or explained as more developed and less developed areas as well. Thus, this model can be used in the analysis of economies with material gap between geographic areas and/or social classes, each of which represents a non-negligible part of the whole population.

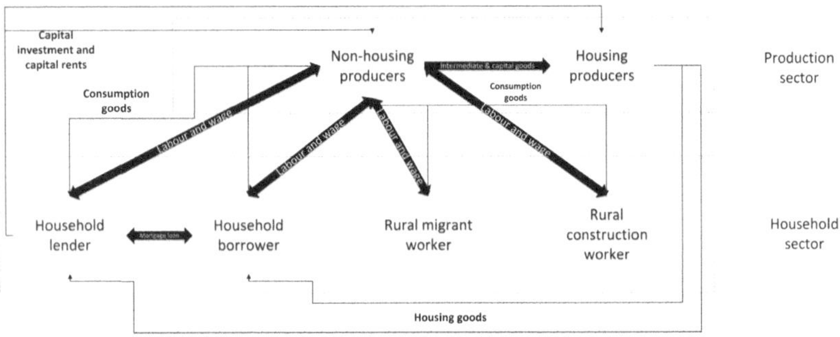

Fig. 7.1 The structure of the advanced model

less developed areas of the economy do not have property assets.[16] As a result, it is natural to assume that loans are only made between household lenders and household borrowers. Additionally, we assume that this kind of loan, as in the real world, is made against real estate assets as collateral. The loan-to-value ratio, the value of parameter m in Eq. 7.12, differs in different economies according to regulation and economic tradition. We will calibrate this parameter for different countries in the empirical analysis.

The price of real estate plays a very important role in the dynamics of this model, since its changes give rise to fluctuations of not only variables in the housing market like housing demand and investment in housing production but also other real economic variables such as consumption, real wages, and the aggregate output. It is very clear that this advanced model implies the positive correlation between real housing prices and the aggregate GDP. Additionally, mortgage loans are positively correlated with the aggregate output as well. One of the most straightforward effects can be seen in the consumption of rural construction workers. Those households' major income resource is their wage in the housing market. As output and demand for labour are positively correlated with housing prices, real wages for construction workers rise when housing prices go up and drop when they go down. Therefore, we expect the co-movement of housing prices and rural construction workers' consumption. We also expect the positive

[16] Even some of them may have real estate assets, their property assets are either unmarketable as the situation in China, where most of real estate assets in rural area can not be traded, or the value of their property assets is negligible, as the properties in slums.

relationships between housing prices and consumption made by household lenders and rural migrant workers, as the increase of housing prices provides more budgets for household lenders and pushes up their consumption demand. This implies that rural migrant workers' real wages and working hours move in the same direction with housing prices. The effect of housing prices changing household borrower's consumption is complex, as it contains components of opposite directions. On one hand, the increase of real estate price pushes up the investment and aggregate consumption, and thus leads to a higher level of real wage of household borrowers. On the other hand, the higher level of housing prices increase borrowers' interest repayment burden, bringing negative effect on borrowers' consumption. As a result, the overall effect depends on the joint impact of both effects.

The correlation between the real housing prices and the real land prices are hypothesized to be positive. The economic logic behind this hypothesis lies in the fact that land is one of the major input components in housing production. Higher level of housing prices induces an increase in the demand for land and thus pushes up the real land prices and land rents. Based on a similar logic, real land prices and household borrower's housing demand are negatively correlated.

As in the basic model, in which physical capital is possessed by urban households, only household lenders in the advanced model own physical capital assets (because there are non-housing and housing production sectors, physical capital assets also include capital assets used in the non-housing sector, $k_{c,t}$, and in the housing sector, $k_{h,t}$). The corresponding rental rates of these two kinds of capital assets are $r_{c,t}$ and $r_{h,t}$, respectively, both of which are also transferred to household owners eventually. Therefore, household lenders can be treated as the capital providers, since they provide not only loans to household borrowers but also physical capital assets to producers. Since we consider the heterogeneities in households and explicitly introduce the housing market into this model, more dynamics and relationships that are not captured in the basic model can be examined. In conclusion, household lenders have the most multiple resources of income: real wage, $w_{lh,t}$, capital rental income, $r_{c,t}$ and $r_{h,t}$, dividends from the non-housing market with monopoly profit, div_t, land rental income, $r_{l,t}l_t$, and loan interest income, $L(lh,t)r_t$. As a result, they value the future with the highest discount rate: $\beta_{lh} > \beta_{bh} > \beta_{rw} \geq \beta_{cw}$. Additionally, because household lenders own all the physical capital assets and land and lend loans to household borrowers, they are more sensitive to changes in interest rates and other economic innovations than other groups of households. We also expect that the consumption of rural migrant workers and construction workers are directly positively correlated with their real wages and demand for their labour, as real wages are their major source of income. Household borrowers need loans to support their purchase of properties. Therefore, it is reasonable to expect that the increase of interest rate will lead to a lower level of housing demand, as it increases their mortgage repayment burden. Since more property held by household borrowers increases their loan repayment, a negative relationship between household borrower's housing and their consumption emerges. An interesting hypothesis can be made that the increase of interest rates decreases the housing demand and thus the real wage for construction workers, leading to a lower level of consumption of construction workers whose major income resource is their real wage in housing production.

Another quality of the advanced model is that it contains short-run price rigidity in consumption (non-housing) market. We have not introduced this kind of rigidity in the housing market in that unlike purchasing consumption goods, real estate transactions normally take much longer time for both sides of that transaction to negotiate. Thus, the final prices can be adjusted, making it reasonable to assume that housing price has no rigidity. As for the price rigidity in the consumption market, it is installed in this model via the Calvo pricing mechanism. Using the assumptions of wholesale producers, who work in a fully competitive market, and retailers, who are in a monopolistic competitive market, and as such they have the ability to set price for profit maximization, we get the Philips curve of non-housing market as shown in Eq. 7.39.

In conclusion, the advanced model expands the basic model, and there are four groups of households and two markets in the model economy. Certain similar expected correlations can be drawn in the advanced model as in the basic one. For example, consumption, real wages, and investment are still expected to be pro-cyclical variables in the advanced model. Capital rents are positively correlated with aggregate output too. As more economic agents are included in the advanced model, more dynamics and relationships are modelled and analysed. To better demonstrate these theoretical hypotheses, we summarize the theoretical hypotheses in Table 7.1.

In the basic model, only productivity shock is included to quantify the dynamics between economic variables and exogenous shocks. As we discussed above, the advanced model is advanced partially in that it contains a wider range of shocks than the basic model. In fact, shocks of productivity in both housing and non-housing production are introduced

Table 7.1 Theoretical hypotheses of correlations in the advanced model

Economic factors	*Hypothesized correlations*
Aggregate consumption, GDP	Positive
Investment in fixed capital, GDP	Positive
Real wages, GDP	Positive
Inflation, GDP	Positive
Housing prices, GDP	Positive
Housing prices, Consumption	Positive
Housing prices, Investment	Positive
Housing prices, Mortgage loans	Positive
Mortgage loans, GDP	Positive

in the advanced model. Additionally, unexpected monetary shock in terms of interest rate changes is also introduced into this model. Since housing assets explicitly enters the household's utility functions, we use housing preference shocks to capture the possible changes of household's attitude towards housing assets (put it in another way, the housing demand shock). Based on our theoretical inference of this advanced model, we summarize the impulse responses of economic variables against these exogenous shocks in Tables 7.2, 7.3, and 7.4.

Table 7.2 summarizes the hypothesized impulse responses against productivity shocks, $A_{c,t}$ and A_h. The direct effect of a positive productivity shock in the non-housing market is the increase of aggregate output, y_t and GDP_t. What is more, the investment in physical capital assets, int_t, increases instantly in response to the positive productivity shock. Secondly, a positive productivity shock leads to a higher level of labour demand ($n_{lh,t}$, $n_{bh,t}$, and $n_{rw,t}$) and real wages for households ($n_{lh,t}$, $n_{bh,t}$, and $n_{rw,t}$). This increase of income will push up housing demand, $h_{lh,t}$ and $h_{bh,t}$. Thus, the construction of new housing, IH_t, and real wage of construction workers, $w_{cw,t}$, increase. Then, it is safe to expect that capital rents in both markets and land rental rate ($r_{c,t}$, $r_{h,t}$, and $r_{l,t}$) increase as well. The increased level of housing demand leads to the higher level of housing prices, $p_{h,t}$. Additionally, because the real income of all households increases, the aggregate consumption ($c_{lh,t}$, $c_{bh,t}$, $c_{rw,t}$, and $c_{cw,t}$) is sure to rise, and thus the inflation rate, π_t, will increase too. On the other hand, according to the monetary policy rule, the increase of real GDP and inflation rate is followed by an increase of the real interest rate, r_t, worsening the

Table 7.2 Theoretical hypotheses of the advanced model: Impulse Responses to productivity shocks

Economic variables	*Exogenous shocks (positive)*	*Hypothesized responses*
GDP_t	Productivity shock, $A_{c,t}$	Gradually rise to a new level
Investment	Productivity shock, $A_{c,t}$	Instantly rise and gradually descend to a new level
Consumption	Productivity shock, $A_{c,t}$	Gradually rise to a new level
Real wages	Productivity shock, $A_{c,t}$	Gradually rise to a new level
GDP_t	Productivity shock, $A_{h,t}$	Instantly small rise and gradually descend to a new level
Investment	Productivity shock, $A_{h,t}$	Small decrease and gradually rise to a new level
Consumption	Productivity shock, $A_{h,t}$	Instantly small increase and gradually descend to a new level
Real wages	Productivity shock, $A_{h,t}$	Instantly small increase and gradually descend to a new level
Inflation	Productivity shock, $A_{c,t}$	Rise and then return to the original level
Real interest rate	Productivity shock, $A_{c,t}$	Instantly rise and gradually descend to the original level
Real housing price	Productivity shock, $A_{c,t}$	Gradually rise to a new level
Inflation	Productivity shock, $A_{h,t}$	Instantly rise and gradual return to the original level
Real interest rate	Productivity shock, $A_{h,t}$	Instantly rise and gradually descend to the original level
Real housing price	Productivity shock, $A_{h,t}$	Instantly drop and gradually return to a new level

interest repayment burden of household borrowers. Therefore, the demand for housing decreases and consumption goes down, since households need to pay more for the loan interest repayments. In general, higher levels of the real rental rate and prices in both markets rise in relation to the decrease of capital demand and demand for consumption and housing. This process is repeated for a certain period of time until the negative effects of increased interest rate and higher level of real rents grow and offset this positive feedback cycle. Finally, the whole economy arrives at a new equilibrium condition, where all impacts of positive productivity shocks cancel out each other.

Similar dynamics are expected in the case of a positive productivity shock in the housing market. On one hand, the first direct impact of such shock is the growth of housing production, IH_t, and thus the real wages of construction workers, $w_{cw,t}$ and their working hours, $n_{cw,t}$, rise. On the

Table 7.3 Theoretical hypotheses of the advanced model: Impulse Responses to housing preference shocks

Economic variables	*Exogenous shocks* (positive)	*Hypothesized responses*
GDP_t	Housing demand, j_t	Increase and then return to the original level
Investment	Housing demand, j_t	Instantly rise and gradually descend to the original level
Consumption	Housing demand, j_t	Instantly increase and gradually descend to the original level
Real wages	Housing demand, j_t	Instantly increase and gradually descend to the original level
Inflation	Housing demand, j_t	Gradually rise to the original level
Real interest rate	Housing demand, j_t	Instantly rise and gradually descend to the original level
Real housing prices	Housing demand, j_t	Instant increase and gradually descend to the original level

Table 7.4 Theoretical hypotheses of the advanced model: Impulse Responses to interest-rate shocks

Economic variables	*Exogenous shocks (positive)*	*Hypothesized responses*
GDP_t	Interest rate, $e_{r,t}$	Sharply drop and gradually rise to the original level
Investment	Interest rate, $e_{r,t}$	Sharply drop and gradually rise to the original level
Consumption	Interest rate, $e_{r,t}$	Sharply drop and gradually rise to the original level
Real wages	Interest rate, $e_{r,t}$	Sharply drop and gradually rise to the original level
Inflation	Interest rate, $e_{r,t}$	Rise and then descend to the original level
Real housing prices	Interest rate, $e_{r,t}$	Instantly sharp drop and gradually return to the original level

other hand, the higher level of housing supply temporally decreases the real housing prices, $p_{h,t}$, which goes up in the later periods. This decrease in housing prices is normally followed by greater demand for housing, pushing up housing prices. Additionally, the increase of real wages of construction workers leads to the growth of their consumption, $c_{cw,t}$. Thus, the aggregate output, y_t and GDP_t, increases as the aggregate demand increases, raising the price level in the consumption market, p_t, and thus the inflation rate, π_t. In general, when aggregate demand and output begin to rise, the household's working hours ($n_{lh,t}$, $n_{bh,t}$, and $n_{rw,t}$) and real wages ($w_{lh,t}$, $w_{bh,t}$, and $w_{rw,t}$) of households who working in the non-housing market grow and thus their consumption and demand for housing, $h_{lh,t}$ and $h_{bh,t}$, increase as well. Because of the rise of aggregate output in both non-housing and housing markets, the capital rents in these two markets, $r_{c,t}$ and $r_{h,t}$, increase accordingly. The increased capital rental rates and real interest rate cast downward pressure on capital and housing demands. Moreover, the tightening monetary policy in terms of a higher level of the real interest rate decreases household borrowers' demand for housing, as it makes their interest repayment burden heavier. Additionally, the higher level of real prices in both consumption and housing markets decreases households' demand for consumption and housing goods. The above process is repeated for a period of time until the whole economy finds its new equilibrium condition, when the effects of two opposite directions offset with each other. As we have discussed in the theoretical framework, since the production of housing is much less sensitive to productivity shocks than in the non-housing market, the impulse responses to the housing productivity shocks are expected to be much minor than those to the non-housing productivity shocks.

Table 7.3 hypothesizes the outcomes of a positive housing preference shock (i.e. the housing demand shock). As housing assets have been explicitly installed in urban households' utility function, higher level of households' housing means more utility for those households. Therefore, as shown in Eqs. 7.7 and 7.8, a positive housing preference shock pushes up the housing demand of both the household lender, $h_{lh,t}$, and the household borrower, $h_{bh,t}$. Quite naturally, this increase of housing demand increases the housing prices, $p_{h,t}$ and housing production, IH_t. Together with the growth of housing supply, investment in the capital of housing production, Ikc_t, rises as well. Because housing production is counted as a significant component of overall output, GDP_t also increases. Therefore, according to the monetary rule, real interest rate tends to rise, reducing household borrower's ability to purchase more housing assets. Additionally, to produce more housing, developers need more intermediate goods and capital (including land as it is one of the most important input in housing production). Thus, investment in the capital of the non-housing market, Ikc_t, begins to rise; then real prices and rents of capitals and land ($r_{c,t}$, $r_{h,t}$, $r_{l,t}$, and $p_{l,t}$) also rise. As a result, we expect the aggregate output and investment in physical capital assets to increase at the first stage and then to drop as demand shrinks. The growth of housing production leads to the higher level of real wages, $w_{cw,t}$, and more working hours, $n_{cw,t}$, of construction workers. In turn, these construction workers purchase more consumption goods, $c_{cw,t}$ increase. On the other hand, because household borrowers and lenders spend more on housing than they used to, their spending on consumption goods, $c_{lh,t}$ and $c_{bh,t}$, shrinks. What is more, a higher level of housing asset increases the loan repayment burden on household borrowers, casting downward pressure on their demand for consumption goods. As we have discussed previously, the direction of the change of household lenders' consumption depends on the overall effects, as they possess multiple sources of income. Likewise, the movement of working hours and real wages of households working in the non-housing market is determined by several aspects of two opposite directions. Firstly, the increase of demand for intermediate goods in housing production gives rise to a higher level of working hours and real wages. On the contrary, the effect of purchasing more housing assets decreases household lenders' and borrowers' expenditure on consumption and thus worsens aggregate demand. In conclusion, the new equilibrium condition can be achieved only when both consumption and housing markets clear properly.

Finally, Table 7.4 demonstrates the dynamics of a positive interest-rate shock in the advanced model. As discussed before, an unexpected hike of real interest rate seriously undermines household borrowers' ability and willingness to invest in housing assets, since it worsens the loan repayment burden. Therefore, the household borrowers' housing demand, $h_{bh,t}$, tends to shrink. The direct consequence of such case is the decrease of intermediate goods in housing production, $k_{b,t}$. Additionally, as housing demand drops, construction workers' working hours and real wages become lower, together with their spending on consumption goods, c_{cw}. Additionally, household borrowers' consumption, $c_{bh,t}$, suffers from higher interest rates, which lead to more loan repayment, $L_{bh,t}r_t$. Although the increase of the rate of interest provides for household lenders more interest rate return on loans, the aggregate consumption decreases as the marginal propensity to consume is lower for household lenders than for other household groups. The falling of aggregate demand in both markets gives rise to the lower level of aggregate outputs in both markets (y_t for non-housing market, IH_t for housing market, and GDP_t for the overall aggregate output) and investment in physical capital assets, Ikc_c and Ikh_t. Additionally, households' working hours ($n_{lh,t}$, $n_{bh,t}$, and $n_{rw,t}$) and real wages

($w_{lh,t}$, $w_{lh,t}$, and $w_{lh,t}$) also suffer from the decrease of the aggregate demand. This further worsens the aggregate demand for housing and consumption goods. Therefore, at the first stage, a positive real interest rate shock leads to the slowdown of the economy in that households' aggregate demand for both consumption and housing goods, and to the decline in producers' demand for physical capital. Price levels in both housing and consumption markets (p_t, $p_{h,t}$, and land price, $p_{l,t}$) and capital rents ($r_{c,t}$ and $r_{h,t}$) are expected to descend as well. Later, this slowdown of the economy gives rise to the falling real interest rate, according to the Taylor rule. This stimulates the economy in the following periods. What is more, a lower level of capital rental rents stimulates producers to utilize more physical capital assets, and the lower level of prices encourages households' to consume more. All these effects push the economy to an equilibrium.

References

1. Bouakez, H., Cardia, E., & Ruge-Murcia, F. (2005). Habit formation and the persistence of monetary shocks. *Journal of Monetary Economics, 52*(6), 1073–1088.
2. Bernanke, B., Gertler, M., & Gilchrist, S. (1999). The financial accelerator in a quantitative business cycle framework. *Handbook of Macroeconomics, 1*, 1341–1393.
3. Iacoviello, M., & Neri, S. (2010). Housing market spillovers: Evidence from an estimated DSGE model. *American Economic Journal: Macroeconomics, 2*(2), 125–164.
4. Christiano, L., Eichenbaum, M., & Evans, C. (2005). Nominal rigidities and the dynamic effects of a shock to monetary policy. *Journal of Political Economy, 113*(1), 1–45.
5. Calvo, G. (1983). Staggered prices in a utility-maximizing framework. *Journal of Monetary Economics, 12*(3), 383–398.
6. Iacoviello, M. (2005). House prices, borrowing constraints, and monetary policy in the business cycle. *American Economic Journal: Macroeconomics, 95*(3), 739–764.
7. Barsky, R., House, C., & Kimball, M. (2007). Sticky-price models and durable goods. *The American Economic Review, 97*(3), 984–998.
8. Dixit, A. K., & Stiglitz, J. E. (1977). Monopolistic competition and optimum product diversity. *The American Economic Review, 67*(3), 297–308.
9. Davis, M. A., & Heathcote, J. (2007). The price and quantity of residential land in the United States. *Journal of Monetary Economics, 54*(8), 2595–2620.
10. Liu, Z., Wang, P., & Zha, T. (2013). Land-price dynamics and macroeconomic fluctuations. *Econometrica, 81*(3), 1147–1184.

11. Tsiang, S. C. (1966). Walras' Law, Say's Law and liquidity preference in general equilibrium analysis. *International Economic Review, 7*(3), 329–345.
12. Messenger, J., Lee, S., & McCann, D. (2007). Working time around the world: Trends in working hours, laws and policies in a global comparative perspective. *Indian Journal of Physiology & Pharmacology, 58*(2), 182–183.
13. Harris, W. (2003). *India working: Essays on society and economy.* Cambridge: Cambridge University Press.
14. Spector, P., Cooper, C., Poelmans, S., Allen, T., O'Driscoll, M., Sanchez, J., et al. (2004). A cross-national comparative study of work-family stressors, working hours, and well-being: China and Latin America versus the Anglo world. *Personnel Psychology, 57*(1), 119–142.
15. Hu, Z., & Khan, M. (1997). Why is China growing so fast? *International Monetary Fund Staff Papers, 44*(1), 103–131.
16. Wong, K., Fu, D., Li, C. Y., & Song, H. X. (2007). Rural migrant workers in urban China: Living a marginalised life. *International Journal of Social Welfare, 16*(1), 32–40.

CHAPTER 8

The Full Model

8.1 Theoretical Framework

8.1.1 Household Sector

In the economy of this full model, households are divided into four groups. This model structure accords well with the economic realities in emerging market economies, which are characterized by evident social stratification. Multiple social classes with distinct economic characteristics are dynamically connected, each makes up a large section of the population. In this model economy, they are rural construction workers (cw), who provide labour, $n_{cw,t}$, in the housing market to produce new housing, rural migrant workers (rw), who work, $n_{rw,t}$, in the goods market, urban household borrowers and urban household lenders, both of which live in the urban area and have full access to the housing market and the financial system. Such social stratification in the household sector is similar to that in the advanced model. The major difference between rural households, including rural construction workers and migrant workers, and the urban households is that only urban households (both household borrowers and household lenders) possess marketable real estate assets. The utility functions of urban and rural households are derived as follows.

D. L. Jia, *Dynamic Macroeconomic Models in Emerging Market Economies*, https://doi.org/10.1007/978-981-15-4588-7_8

The rural households' construction workers and rural migrant workers maximize their utility functions 8.1 and 8.2, respectively.

$$maxE_t \sum_{t=0}^{\infty} (\beta_{cw}^t (\ln(c_{cw,t} - b_{cw}c_{cw,t-1}) - \psi_{cw} \frac{n_{cw,t}^{(1+\eta_{cw})}}{1+\eta_{cw}}) \tag{8.1}$$

$$maxE_t \sum_{t=0}^{\infty} (\beta_{rw})^t (\ln(c_{rw,t} - b_{rw}c_{rw,t-1}) - \psi_{rw} \frac{n_{rw,t}^{1+\eta_{rw}}}{1+\eta_{rw}}) \tag{8.2}$$

The economic meanings of the parameters in these equations are similar to the ones in the advanced model. β_{cw} and β_{rw} are the discount factors with respect to two kinds of households. Terms $\ln(c_{cw,t} - b_{cw}c_{cw,t-1})$ and $\ln(c_{rw,t} - b_{rw}c_{rw,t-1})$ explain the utility of consumption with habit formation features. The disutility of working are depicted as $-\psi_{cw}\frac{n_{cw,t}^{(1+\eta_{cw})}}{1+\eta_{cw}}$ and $-\psi_{rw}\frac{n_{rw,t}^{1+\eta_{rw}}}{1+\eta_{rw}}$. Larger values of ψ_{cw} and ψ_{cw} lead to the greater disutility of working and thus less willingness to work. It is obvious that both utility functions exhibit similar format in that the utility of rural households contains only two components, the positive utility of consumption and the negative utility of working (sacrificing leisure time). The major difference between construction workers and rural migrant workers lies in that they provide labour in different markets: construction workers work ($n_{cw,t}$) in the housing market to produce real estate products, while the rural migrant workers work ($n_{rw,t}$) in the non-housing (manufacturing) market to produce consumption goods, intermediate goods and business investment. In view of these two kinds of households that are assumed to possess no marketable real estate assets and have limited access to the financial market, their budget constraints are quite simple: they work to get wage to pay for their consumption expenditure, meaning that their only source of income is their working wage ($w_{cw,t}$ and $w_{rw,t}$). Equations 8.3 and 8.4 are the budget constraints for rural construction workers (cw) and rural migrant workers (rw), respectively.

$$c_{cw,t} = w_{cw,t}n_{cw,t} \tag{8.3}$$

$$c_{rw,t} = w_{rw,t}n_{rw,t} \tag{8.4}$$

As for household borrowers and lenders, their utility functions are more complicated than those of rural households, because housing is explicitly included in their utility functions. As shown in Eqs. 8.5 and 8.6, household borrowers and household lenders try to maximize their lifelong utility under the following budget constraints.

$$maxE_t \sum_{t=0}^{\infty} (\beta_{lh})^t (\ln(c_{lh,t} - b_{lh} c_{lh,t-1}) - \psi_{lh} \frac{n_{lh,t}^{1+\eta_{lh}}}{1+\eta_{lh}} + j_t \ln h_{lh,t} \quad (8.5)$$

$$maxE_t \sum_{t=0}^{\infty} (\beta_{bh})^t (\ln(c_{bh,t} - b_{bh} c_{bh,t-1}) - \psi_{bh} \frac{n_{bh,t}^{1+\eta_{bh}}}{1+\eta_{bh}} + j_t \ln h_{bh,t} \quad (8.6)$$

Housing stock held by household lenders and household borrowers, $h_{lh,t}$ and $h_{bh,t}$, is explicitly introduced into the utility functions as $j_t \ln h_{lh,t}$ and $j_t \ln h_{bh,t}$, where j_t is the housing preference shock. Quite intuitively, a positive housing preference shock adds to the importance of housing in the overall household utility and thus leads to the increase of housing demand. Therefore, we expect an increase in housing stock and housing price after a positive housing preference shock and vice versa.

Like construction workers and rural migrant workers, household borrowers work (providing labour input $n_{bh,t}$ in the goods production process) to get wages (in real term, $w_{bh,t}$). But the application of this wage is more comprehensive as they need to repay their mortgage loan ($L_{bh,t}$) collateralized against their housing stock ($h_{bh,t}$). As a result, the budget constraint of household borrowers is shown in Eq. 8.7.

$$c_{bh,t} + p_{h,t} h_{bh,t} + L_{bh,t-1} r_t = w_{bh,t} n_{bh,t} + (1-\delta_h) p_{h,t} h_{bh,t-1} + L_{bh,t} \quad (8.7)$$

The assumption behind this mortgage loan of household borrowers is similar to that in the advanced model. Household borrowers use their current housing holdings ($h_{bh,t}$) as collateral to get a mortgage loan from the loan provider (household lenders), with the loan amount equal to $L_{bh,t} = mE_t(p_{h,t} h_{bh,t} \frac{p_{t+1}}{p_t})/r_t$. The real working wage for household borrowers in period t is $w_{bh,t} n_{bh,t}$. Therefore, the economic meaning of Eq. 8.7 is clear: the left side of this equation summarizes household borrowers' spending, while the right-hand side represents all the resources of household borrowers. The term $L_{bh,t-1} r_t$ on the left side represents the mortgage repayment in period t, and the term $L_{bh,t}$ is the mortgage loan the household borrowers get in period t. Intuitively, $p_{h,t} h_{bh,t}$ is the real value of current holding of housing assets in period t, and $(1 - \delta_h) p_{h,t} h_{bh,t-1}$ is the current real value of housing stock after considering depreciation (at the depreciation rate of δ_h). The difference between these two terms is the household borrowers' investment (or expenditure) in housing assets.

Household lenders work in the non-housing market provide labour, $n_{lh,t}$. Their wage, in real term, is $w_{lh,t}$. Additionally, they are owners of capital assets in both goods and housing markets ($k_{c,t}$ and $k_{h,t}$) and land (l_t). They rent capital ($k_{h,t}$) and land (l_t) to firms working in the housing market to produce housing and rent capital ($k_{c,t}$) to firms in the goods market to produce consumption goods (c_t), business investments (Inv_t) and intermediate goods ($k_{b,t}$). The firms working in these two markets are assumed to be ultimately owned by household lenders as well. Therefore, the profit of retailers in goods market ($\frac{x_t-1}{x_t}Y_t$) is distributed among household lenders.

As we have introduced at the beginning of this chapter, a financial market that links loan seekers and providers is explicitly installed in the FHSAM model economy. The basic assumption of this financial market is that there are, on the one hand, some loan providers who have a surplus in capital restored in the banks as deposits and, on the other hand, firms who need such loans to pay out their working capital expenditures. This loan creation process is undertaken within the financial market using financial institutes, banks for example, as intermediaries: banks accept deposits from households and use them to make loans to firms in both the goods and the housing markets. This assumption is consistent with the structure of the banking systems in the real world. The details of the financial markets in this full model is discussed in the following parts of this section, so here we focus on the supply of deposits. In this full model, we assume that household lenders are deposit providers in that they possess capital surplus and restored it in banks as deposits, $D_{lh,t}$. Some may argue that household borrowers, construction workers and rural migrant workers make deposits in the banking system as well. But first of all, household borrowers are not deposit suppliers when we consider the overall net deposits. They may have deposits in banks but after considering their borrowing from banks (their mortgage loans), they are no longer deposit suppliers. Secondly, we do admit that construction workers and rural migrant workers may deposit their savings in banks but the volume of these deposits is smaller compared with that of household lenders. Additionally, they have limited access to the financial market as discussed previously and their major economic activities in the model economy are providing labour in both markets and consuming in the goods market. Therefore, we maintain that household lenders are the ultimate net suppliers of loans including mortgages to household borrowers, who borrow to purchase housing assets, and loans to firms that use credits to pay their working capital expenditure.

In conclusion, the budget constraint of household lenders is shown in Eq. 8.8.

$$\begin{aligned}&c_{lh,t} + p_{h,t}h_{lh,t} + L_{lh,t} + D_{lh,t} + k_{c,t} + k_{h,t} + k_{b,t} + p_{l,t}l_t = \\&w_{lh,t}n_{lh,t} + (1-\delta_k)p_{h,t}h_{lh,t-1} + (1-\delta_h)p_{h,t}h_{lh,t-1} + L_{lh,t-1}r_t/\pi_t + c \\&+ (r_{c,t} + 1 - \delta_{kc})k_{c,t-1} + (r_{h,t} + 1 - \delta_{kh})k_{h,t-1} + p_{b,t}k_{b,t} + (p_{l,t} + r_{l,t})l_{t-1}\end{aligned} \tag{8.8}$$

The left-hand side is the spending and the right-hand side summarizes all the economic resources of household lenders. The real working wage for household lenders in period t is $w_{lh,t}n_{lh,t}$. Like household borrowers, $p_{h,t}h_{lh,t}$ and $(1-\delta_h)p_{h,t}h_{lh,t-1}$ are the real value of housing assets held by household lenders and the current real value of household lenders' housing assets in the previous period after consideration of depreciation (at the rate of δ_h). The difference between these two items yields the household lenders' spending (or investment) in housing assets. Capital in both goods and the housing markets ($k_{c,t}$ and $k_{h,t}$ respectively) are owned by the household lenders who rent to the firms in these two markets. The rental incomes are $r_{c,t}$ for $k_{c,t}$ and $r_{h,t}$ for $k_{h,t}$. The capital depreciation rates in goods and housing markets are δ_{kc} and δ_{kh}, respectively. Therefore, the difference between $k_{c,t}$ ($k_{h,t}$) and $(1-\delta_{kc})k_{c,t}$ ($(1-\delta_{kh})k_{h,t}$) is the capital investment in goods (housing) market. The real price of land is denoted as $p_{l,t}$, and the rental rate of land is $r_{l,t}$. Therefore, $(p_{l,t} + r_{l,t})l_{t-1}$ is the sum of real value and rental income of land in period t. As we have introduced previously, household lenders make mortgage loans, $L_{lh,t}$, to household borrowers and get interest income, $L_{lh,t-1}r_t/\pi_t$. Additionally, they deposit their capital surplus in banks, $D_{lh,t}$. The interest income of these deposits is $D_{lh,t}r^d_{t-1}/\pi_t$. Here we assume that the real interest rate of bank deposit is r^d_t, which is set by the central bank. This is the baseline risk-free rate based on which the loan rate is determined by adding a certain premium. This assumption is consistent with the interest-rate determination mechanism in the real world. This is discussed in greater details in the section of the financial market. Again, all entries in Eq. 8.8 are in real terms.

In summary, the assumptions of households stratification in the economy of the full model are similar to those in the advanced model. The classification of four household groups has been kept, and the basic economic behaviours of each household group remain unchanged except for the fact that we allow household lenders to make deposits in banks and receive the corresponding interest income. Similar to the advanced model, the labour supply equations and capital, land, intermediate goods, mortgage and deposit supply functions can be derived using the utility functions and budget constraints of households. This is demonstrated in the following sections.

8.1.2 Production and Nominal Rigidities

As in the advanced model, two markets are also explicitly installed in this full model. Firms in goods markets produce consumption goods ($c_t = c_{cw,t} + c_{rw,t} + c_{bh,t} + c_{lh,t}$), intermediate goods ($k_{b,t}$), and business investments ($Inv_t = Ikc_t + Ikh_t$). The inputs of this production process are labour conducted by all households ($n_{cw,t}$, $n_{rw,t}$, $n_{bh,t}$, and $n_{lh,t}$), capital ($k_{c,t-1}$). Such production can be explained by Eq. 8.9. In this equation, the parameters $\beta_i, i = 1, 2, 3$ are the share ratios of contribution in the production process according to the importance and contribution of each labour, meaning that the larger β_i the more important the corresponding labour. The definition of parameter α is similar to that in the standard Cobb–Douglas production function. The values of these parameters are discussed in the following part where empirical analysis is undertaken.

$$Y_t = A_{c,t}((n_{lh,t}^{\beta_1} n_{bh,t}^{\beta_2} n_{rw,t}^{\beta_3}))^{1-\alpha} k_{c,t-1}^{\alpha},$$
$$\beta_i \geq 0 \; for \; all \; i = 1, 2, 3, \; and \; \beta_1 + \beta_2 + \beta_3 = 1 \tag{8.9}$$

On the other side, firms in the housing market produce real estate to households by using land (l_{t-1}), labour of construction workers ($n_{cw,t}$), intermediate goods ($k_{b,t}$) produced in the goods markets and capital ($k_{h,t}$). This is shown in Eq. 8.10. The economic meanings of parameters $\mu_i, i = 1, 2, 3$ are similar to the parameter α in the standard Cobb–Douglas production equation, capturing the contribution shares of each factor in production. Like parameters in Eq. 8.9, the determination of the values of these parameters are discussed in the empirical analysis chapter.

$$IH_t = A_{h,t} n_{rw,t}^{\mu_1} k_{b,t}^{\mu_2} l_{t-1}^{\mu_3} k_{h,t-1}^{\mu_4},$$
$$\mu_i \geq 0 \; for \; all \; i = 1, 2, 3, 4 \; and \; \mu_1 + \mu_2 + \mu_3 + \mu_4 = 1 \tag{8.10}$$

In order to install short-term nominal rigidity in this full model, we adopt the assumption of the Calvo pricing mechanism that has been used in the advanced model. Retailers in the goods market enjoy certain freedom to adjust their price to get maximum profit under the Calvo pricing mechanism constraints: in each period, only a fraction, $1 - \theta_\pi$, of retailers can do this. Due to the unique characteristics of housing market transactions that have been discussed in the advanced model chapter, no price rigidity in the housing market has been installed in our full model. Two types of firms are included in the goods market: the wholesale producers who use labour and capital input to produce consumption goods, business investments and intermediate goods, and the retailers who are involved with wholesale products on a completely competitive market and repack these products into final goods. For simplicity, this process is assumed to be costless. The market in which retailers work is monopolistic and thus retailers face the downward sloping demand curve of the final goods. Retailers repackage wholesale goods into final goods using the Dixit–Stiglitz aggregator, which is of the Constant Elasticity Substitution (CES) type. This repacking activity can be summarized in Eq. 8.11.

$$Y_t = (\int_0^1 Y_t(i)^{\frac{\epsilon_p - 1}{\epsilon_p}} di)^{(\frac{\epsilon_p}{\epsilon_p - 1})} \tag{8.11}$$

Therefore, the profit maximization of retailers leads to Eq. 8.12.

$$\max_{Y_t(i)} \int_0^1 p_t(i) Y_t(i) di - p_{y,t}^{wholesale} Y_t \tag{8.12}$$

Together with Eq. 8.11, we find the profit maximization of the retailers as shown in Eq. 8.13.

$$\max_{Y_t(i)} \int_0^1 p_t(i) Y_t(i) di - p_{y,t}^{wholesale} (\int_0^1 Y_t(i)^{\frac{\epsilon_p - 1}{\epsilon_p}} di)^{(\frac{\epsilon_p}{\epsilon_p - 1})} \tag{8.13}$$

In view of the assumption that retailers purchase wholesale goods in a perfectly competitive market, their demand for wholesale goods can be derived from the first order condition of the retailers' profit maximization process. This is summarized in Eq. 8.14.

$$p_{y,t}^{wholesale} \frac{\epsilon_p - 1}{\epsilon_p} (\int_0^1 Y_t(i)^{\frac{\epsilon_p - 1}{\epsilon_p}} di)^{\frac{\epsilon_p}{\epsilon_p - 1} - 1} \frac{\epsilon_p}{\epsilon_p - 1} Y_t(i)^{\frac{\epsilon_p - 1}{\epsilon_p} - 1} = p_t(i) \tag{8.14}$$

As a result, based on the theoretical deductions shown in the advanced model, the Philips curve can be written as Eq. 8.15.

$$\ln \pi_t - \rho_\pi \ln \pi_{t-1} = \beta_{lh}(E_t(\ln \pi_{t+1}) - \rho_\pi \ln \pi_t) - \frac{(1-\theta_\pi)(1-\beta_{lh}\theta_\pi)}{\theta_\pi} \ln \frac{x_t}{x_{ss}} + \varepsilon_{\pi,t} \quad (8.15)$$

8.1.3 Financial Market and the Optimal Debt Contract

In the advanced model, due to the absence of financial frictions in the economy, there is only one single interest rate r_t, which is set by the central bank using the Taylor rule mechanism. Economic structure in this full model becomes more comprehensive and more consistent with the real-world situation, in that we explicitly introduce financial frictions into the model economy. Because of the frictions in the financial markets, deposit rate (r_t^d) received by the depositors and loan rate (r_t^l) paid by the loan seekers are different. The loan rate r_t^l is the sum of baseline risk-free interest rate r_t^d and some premium reflecting the features of the loan. Because the risk-free interest rate r_t^d is the baseline factor in interest-rate determination mechanism and it is the popular instrument tool of central banks to adopt their monetary policy, we start this section by discussing r_t^d.

If we briefly review the history of macroeconomics, we can find that different scholars from different schools of economics tend to bear different views on the determination of interest rates. For example, members of the Austrian School of Economics, as represented by the Neoclassical economist Eugen von Böhm-Bawerk and Friedrich A. Hayek, emphasize the importance of capital in production and time in the determination of interest rates. Original Keynesian economists believe that liquidity-preference plays a key role in the determination of interest rates. The discussion of the nature of interest rate is beyond the reach of this thesis,[1] so we adopt the most widely accepted opinion on interest rate: it is the percentage rate paid on deposits. In our thesis, banks cannot be bankrupted and thus deposits and the corresponding interest rate paid to the depositors is always fully delivered. Therefore, this interest rate (r_t^d) paid on deposits is a risk-free rate.

[1] For details of the discussion on the nature of interest rates, see Böhm-Bawerk and Smart [1], Keynes [2], Hayek [3] and Woodford [4].

As in the advanced model, central banks adopt the Taylor rule to adjust this risk-free rate as their major monetary policy tool. The mechanism of this monetary policy can be summarized in Eq. 8.16.

$$r_t^d = (1 - \rho_r) r^{ss} + \rho_r r_{t-1}^d + (1 - \rho_r)(\rho_{\pi,r}(\pi_t - \pi^{ss})) + \rho_{GDP}(\ln GDP_t - \ln GDP_{t-1}) + \varepsilon_{r,t} \tag{8.16}$$

In this mechanism, central banks adjust their interest rate according to its steady-state value (r^{ss}), the interest rate in the previous period (r_{t-1}^d), the difference between the inflation rate and its long-run target value ($\pi_t - \pi^{ss}$)), and the difference between the overall output and its previous value ($\ln GDP_t - \ln GDP_{t-1}$). Parameters ρ_r, $\rho_{\pi,r}$, and ρ_{GDP} capture the elasticities of each factor in the determination of the rate of interest.

So far, financial frictions are still not considered. All the elements are similar to those in the advanced model. We introduce financial frictions in our model based on the baseline risk-free interest rate. The importance of financial markets has been widely accepted by both industry and academia. A lot of effort has been undertaken to make a fuller description of the economy with consideration of the financial markets. Modern DSGE literature contains financial frictions; this is undertaken in both the relevant theoretical frameworks and empirical models on the assumption of Costly State Verification (CSV), which has been developed in the field of corporate finance.[2] The basic thinking behind the CSV assumption is the asymmetric information between financial intermediates who grant loans, usually banks, and the corresponding loan seekers, usually the entrepreneurs, in a standard debt (bank loan) contract. Unlike banks, entrepreneurs are assumed to be exposed to the risk of bankruptcy. Therefore, if the entrepreneur goes bankrupt (its remaining value is less than its outstanding debt to the banks), the bank will suffer from loan losses, as only part of the loan can be reclaimed. The risk uniquely connected with a project conducted by the entrepreneurs is called the idiosyncratic risk. The borrowers have the fuller information of this idiosyncratic risk than banks and provide only partial information of this risk to the banks when applying for bank loans. Thus the asymmetric information and the conflicts between the two sides of the loan lead to the moral hazard; this is a principal–agent problem and unbalanced risk-return scheme for financial intermediates who are loan makers.

[2] For more details on CSV, see the contributions proposed by Townsend [5], Boyd and Smith [6] and Winton [7].

In order to solve this dilemma, banks need to take efforts to monitor and assess the validity and quality of the entrepreneurs who are appealing for credits. Within the CSV mechanism, this monitoring and verifying process is undertaken by banks with explicit costs. According to the standard CSV assumption, this cost is proportional to the overall volume of the loan.

One of the most influential general equilibrium models with explicit financial frictions is the financial acceleration model developed by Bernanke et al. [8]. By incorporating the CSV mechanism into the traditional NCM/DSGE model, they develop a FAM-NCM/DSGE model (widely known as the BGG model), emphasizing the dynamics between the credit market and business cycles. Their findings are well consistent with theoretical hypotheses and the economic reality that the cyclical movements of the economy are tightly connected with the changes in the credit market. More specifically, in the period of recession, credit markets deteriorate as the insolvency rate sharply increases with the higher level of bankruptcy risk, asset prices collapse, and thus banks, suffer from severe challenges of soaring bad debt ratio. Therefore, the interest rate on loans from banks and other loan-making financial intermediates tends to increase accordingly in such a recession period and to decrease accordingly when the economy is in its prosperity. As shown in the first part of this book, although some economists question the role played by the financial markets. (for example, neoclassical macroeconomic models, such as the real business cycle model, are based on the assumptions in Modigliani–Miller theorem,[3] implying that structural changes in the financial markets are irrelevant to the fluctuations of the real economic activity, or, to put it in another way, the real economy is neutral to the financial market structural changes.) More and more scholars believe that changes in the financial market are not solely the passive reflection of the fluctuations in the real sectors, but one of the major driving forces of the economy's cyclical movements. For example, according to the work of Fisher [10], who develops the 'Debt-Deflation Theory' to quantify the contribution of increased debt burden to the severity of real economic outcomes, adverse financial market conditions and the following deteriorating debt burden partially resulted in the severity of the Great Depression in the early 1930s. The same conclusion can be witnessed in the works of Bernanke [11], Bernanke and Blinder [12], Bernanke and Gertler [13], and Bernanke et al. [14]. The lessons from the most recent global financial

[3] For details of the Modigliani–Miller theorem, see the work proposed by Modigliani and Miller [9].

crisis that started in August 2007 and the GR that followed, give more supporting evidence that the failure of the intermediation service provided by the financial market could be the vital factor leading to globally systematic contraction of the real economic outcomes.[4] Besides such literature with a focus on developed economies, especially the United States, research in emerging market economies indicates similar results; namely, that financial intermediation plays a key role in the connection between financial crises and their adverse real economic effects. Further examples can be found in Latin America,[5] South Korea,[6] and a group of Asian economies.[7]

Based on these theoretical propositions and empirical evidence, we build this full model with explicit financial frictions using the assumptions similar to those in the financial accelerator model: asymmetric information between the loan providers and the loan seekers and the corresponding costs to verify the state of a loan seeker. Under such conditions, both real and nominal shocks can be significantly amplified by the financial market through its credit creation process. This amplification effect between real economic outputs and financial markets stems from the mechanism that firms need external finance to support their business development and their capacity to borrow from banks; this highly depends on the market value of their net worth as the collateral for the bank loans. As a result, the decrease in asset prices (and thus the market value of the firm's net worth) deteriorates the balance sheet of firms, leading to less bank loans to support future business investment as the value of collateral drops. This feedback cycle of falling asset prices, deteriorating balance sheets, tightening bank credit and declining economic activities may move in circles to amplify the original shock (either nominal or real) to a significant level. This is the mechanism of 'Financial Accelerator'.

In the first place, let us focus on the relationship between a specific firm and a bank to derive the optimal loan contract under the CSV assumptions and then move to the aggregate level. If the net worth of the firm at time t is N_t, and it faces an opportunity to a project with an expected return rate of R^k subject to an idiosyncratic shock ω, the total expected return of this

[4] For relevant literature on this issue, see the studies conducted by Diamond and Rajan [15], Bernanke [16, 17] and Iyer et al. [18].

[5] See the works of Sachs et al. [19] and Peek and Rosengren [20].

[6] See the work proposed by Borensztein and Lee [21].

[7] See the work of Chanlau and Chen [22].

project is $\omega(1+R^k)$. By definition, the idiosyncratic shock ω is non-negative and can only be observed by the entrepreneur. Therefore, it is the source that causes the CSV mechanism, as the bank needs to sacrifice a certain cost to observe the true state of the entrepreneur asking for loan to support the relevant project. According to the assumption of the loan contract, the firm gets the loan from the bank, using its net asset as collateral. At the end of the loan contract, there are two possible outcomes: the firm may pay all the interest and principal due or fail to fulfil its obligation and thus go bankrupt. In the latter case, the bank needs to pay the monitoring cost and takes everything left of the defaulting firm.

If we denote the loan from the bank as B_t, the total value of the firm, A_t, can be written as

$$A_t = N_t + B_t \tag{8.17}$$

Intuitively, the leverage level of the firm is

$$L_t = \frac{A_t}{N_t} \tag{8.18}$$

The firm is able to repay the loan contract in full only when its total return is equal to or greater than the loan interest payment. This relation means that the realized ω should be equal to or larger than certain critical value—the cutoff value, ϖ, as shown in Eq. 8.19, where the loan rate is Z_t.

$$\varpi(1 + R^k)A_t = Z_t B_t \tag{8.19}$$

It is clear that if the realized ω falls below this critical value ϖ, the firm goes bankrupt and loses everything to the bank as its total asset is less than the principal and interest payments owed to the bank. By contrast, if the realized value of ω is larger than ϖ, the firm earns its profit after repaying both the principal and interest of the loan. Therefore, Eq. 8.19 can be rewritten as

$$\varpi = \frac{Z_t B_t}{A_t(1 + R_t^k)} = \frac{Z_t}{(1 + R_t^k)} \frac{\frac{B_t}{N_t}}{\frac{A_t}{N_t}} \tag{8.20}$$

Equations 8.17, 8.18, and 8.20 lead to

$$\varpi = \frac{Z_t}{(1 + R_t^k)} \frac{\frac{A_t - N_t}{N_t}}{\frac{A_t}{N_t}} = \frac{Z_t}{(1 + R_t^k)} \frac{L_t - 1}{L_t} \tag{8.21}$$

In Eq. 8.21, we can see that if the leverage is zero ($L_t = 1$) the critical value ϖ equals to zero too, as there is no borrowing from banks. The value of ϖ grows as the leverage level L_t increases, and the maximum value of ϖ is $\frac{Z_t}{(1+R_t^k)}$ when $L_t \to \infty$.

After we get the relationship between a firm's leverage ratio, L_t, and the critical value ϖ, we need to derive the demand for external finance by considering the firm's utility. In general, the utility of a firm can be expressed as the expected return over the opportunity cost, as shown in Eq. 8.22, in which $F(\omega)$ represents the cumulative distribution function of the idiosyncratic risk ω.

$$\frac{\int_{\varpi}^{\infty}[\omega(1+R_t^k)A_t - Z_t B_t]dF(\omega)}{N_t(1+R_t^d)} \tag{8.22}$$

The denominator of Eq. 8.22 is the opportunity cost for the firm in that it is the amount the firm can get if it deposits that amount in the bank. The nominator represents the expected payoff after deducting the loan repayment ($Z_t B_t$). Combining Eqs. 8.19 and 8.22, we have

$$\begin{aligned}
\frac{\int_{\varpi}^{\infty}[\omega(1+R_t^k)A_t - Z_t B_t]dF(\omega)}{N_t(1+R_t^d)} &= \frac{\int_{\varpi}^{\infty}[\omega(1+R_t^k)A_t - \varpi(1+R^k)A_t]dF(\omega)}{N_t(1+R_t^d)} \\
&= \int_{\varpi}^{\infty}(\omega-\varpi)dF(\omega)\frac{(1+R_t^k)A_t}{N_t(1+R_t^d)} \\
&= \int_{\varpi}^{\infty}(\omega-\varpi)dF(\omega)\frac{(1+R_t^k)}{(1+R_t^d)}L_t
\end{aligned} \tag{8.23}$$

From Eq. 8.23 we can draw that given the risk-free rate R_t^d, the critical value ϖ and the distribution of the idiosyncratic risk ω, a firm's expected payoff is positively correlated with the leverage ratio L_t. As a result, firms tend to get as much loan from the bank as they can, given other factors are unchanged. Together with the loan supply determined by the profit maximization of banks, we can find the optimal condition of bank loans in the credit markets.

In line with reality, banks are assumed to absorb deposits from households (in this chapter, household lenders) with interest rate R_t^d, and make loans to firms with loan rate Z_t. The monitoring cost of making a loan to a firm is $\mu\omega(1+R_t^k)A_s$, in which μ is a cost parameter depicting the ratio of monitoring cost to the realized return $\omega(1+R_t^k)A_s$. As we have mentioned before, if the realized value of ω falls below the critical value ϖ, the firm goes bankrupt and the bank takes away all the remaining value after paying out the monitoring cost. Therefore, the expected payoff of the bank can be written as

$$\int_{\varpi}^{\infty} \omega(1+R_t^k)A_t dF(\omega) + (1-\mu)\int_0^{\varpi} \omega(1+R_t^k)A_t dF(\omega) \quad (8.24)$$

The first component of Eq. 8.24 is the expected return for banks on the loans to the fraction of firms, which can carry out their full obligation, that is to say $\omega \geq \varpi$; and the second component is the expected return for banks on the other fraction of firms, which fail to fulfil their obligations in full, or equivalently speaking $\omega < \varpi$. The market-clearing condition in the financial market can be achieved when the expected return is equal to the cost of loans $(1+R_t^d)B_t$. Therefore, we have Eq. 8.25.

$$\int_{\varpi}^{\infty} \omega(1+R_t^k)A_t dF(\omega) + (1-\mu)\int_0^{\varpi} \omega(1+R_t^k)A_t dF(\omega) = (1+R_t^d)B_t \quad (8.25)$$

This market-clearing condition for banks can be rewritten as

$$(1-F(\varpi))Z_t B_t + (1-\mu)\int_0^{\varpi} \omega(1+R_t^k)A_t dF(\omega) = (1+R_t^d)B_t \quad (8.26)$$

and

$$1+R_t^d = \frac{(1-F(\varpi))Z_t B_t + (1-\mu)\int_0^{\varpi} \omega(1+R_t^k)A_t dF(\omega)}{B_t} \quad (8.27)$$

Equation 8.27 simply means that the average return of loans from all firms should be equal to the risk-free return $1+R_t^d$. The loan supply function can be written as

$$L_t = \frac{1}{1-\frac{(1+R_t^k)}{(1+R_t^d)}(\Gamma(\varpi)-\mu G(\varpi))} \quad (8.28)$$

Now the utility function of firms can be written using loan supply determined by the market clearing condition for banks, as shown in Eq. 8.29.

$$\begin{aligned}
&\textit{The utility of firm with leverage}(U) \equiv \int_{\varpi}^{\infty}(\omega-\varpi)dF(\omega)\frac{(1+R_t^k)}{(1+R_t^d)}L_t \\
&= \int_{\varpi}^{\infty}(\omega-\varpi)dF(\omega)\frac{(1+R_t^k)}{(1+R_t^d)}\frac{1}{1-\frac{(1+R_t^k)}{(1+R_t^d)}(\Gamma(\varpi)-\mu G(\varpi))} \\
&= (1-\Gamma(\varpi))\frac{(1+R_t^k)}{(1+R_t^d)}L_t
\end{aligned} \tag{8.29}$$

In Eqs. 8.29 and 8.28, $\Gamma(\varpi) = \varpi(1 - F(\varpi)) + G(\varpi)$ and $G(\varpi) \equiv \int_{\varpi}^{\infty} \omega dF(\omega)$, both of which are the functions of variable ϖ. Therefore, the optimal loan contract between the financial intermediary and the firm is a function of the critical value ϖ and the leverage level L_t. It is the optimal condition in that it leads to the maximization of both firm's and banks' utility. Mathematically, the critical value ϖ should be uniquely solved from Eq. 8.30.

$$\frac{d\ln U}{d\varpi} = -\frac{1-F(\varpi)}{1-\Gamma(\varpi)} + \frac{\frac{(1+R_t^k)}{(1+R_t^d)}(1-F(\varpi)-\mu\varpi F'(\varpi))}{1-\frac{(1+R_t^k)}{(1+R_t^d)}(\Gamma(\varpi)-\mu G(\varpi))} = 0 \tag{8.30}$$

According to Eq. 8.30, we get

$$\frac{1-F(\varpi)}{1-\Gamma(\varpi)} = \frac{\frac{(1+R_t^k)}{(1+R_t^d)}(1-F(\varpi)-\mu\varpi F'(\varpi))}{1-\frac{(1+R_t^k)}{(1+R_t^d)}(\Gamma(\varpi)-\mu G(\varpi))} \tag{8.31}$$

The loan rate spread can be defined as the premium over the risk-free deposit rate, $\frac{Z_t}{1+R_t^d}$. Using the critical value solved in Eq. 8.31 and the corresponding leverage ratio L_t solved in Eq. 8.28, we can calculate the loan rate spread as shown in Eq. 8.32.

$$\frac{Z_t}{1+R_t^d} = \frac{(1+R_t^k)}{(1+R_t^d)}\varpi\frac{L_t}{L_t-1} \tag{8.32}$$

Given the distribution of idiosyncratic risk ω, we can solve the critical value ϖ using Eq. 8.30. Then, the optimal leverage level, L_t, can be determined under the relationship described in Eq. 8.28. Finally, the loan spread is derived using Eq. 8.32 when both the critical value ϖ and the leverage level L_t are known. The popular assumption of the distribution of ω in the DSGE literature with financial accelerator or similar features is a log-normal distribution.

To decently model financial frictions in the economic system, we adopt the principles implied by the financial accelerator models, with certain modification and extension. First of all, we assume that firms use bank loans (BC_t) to support their working capital expenditure WC_t, which contains all the real wage for all kinds of labour inputs ($n_{cw,t}, n_{rw,t}, n_{bh,t}, n_{lh,t}$). This is shown in Eq. 8.33. Such an assumption is the application of the CIA constraints, as shown in the second part of this book, in the full model economy. Empirical and theoretical analysis has proven that it is an effective way to model the financial market in a dynamic system. Secondly, the ratio to the loan for banks to monitor the true state of the loan seekers is fixed as κ, similar to parameter μ in Eq. 8.24. Therefore, the profit of banks can be written as Eq. 8.34.

$$BC_t = WC_t = n_{cw,t}w_{cw,t} + n_{rw,t}w_{rw,t} + n_{bh,t}w_{bh,t} + n_{lh,t}w_{lh,t} \tag{8.33}$$

$$\max_{R_t^l} R_t^l(1 + \Psi(R_t^d))BC_t - R_t^d BC_t - \kappa BC_t \tag{8.34}$$

In Eq. 8.34, $\Psi(R_t^d)$ represents the loan spread caused by financial frictions. It has a similar economic meaning of spread as in Eq. 8.32, reflecting the similar mechanism in the financial accelerator model we have just derived. Function $\Psi(R_t^d)$ depicts the effects of adverse changes in the interest rate R_t^d on firms' balance sheet. This function has features in accordance with the propositions made above. First of all, $\Psi(R_t^d) \in [0, 1]$. Secondly, the first-order derivative is strictly non-negative, $\Psi'(R_t^d) \geq 0$, consistent with the properties described in Eq. 8.32.[8] In the full model, this function is written as Eq. 8.35.

$$\Psi(R_t^d) = \iota(R_t^d)^2 \quad \forall t \quad \iota > 0 \tag{8.35}$$

Under zero profit assumption, this leads to Eq. 8.36. It is clear that this full model becomes financially frictionless when both ι and κ are zero.

[8] For details on the description of function $\Psi(R_t^d)$, see the work of Chowdhury et al. [23].

This feature facilitates us to compare the performance of models with and without financial frictions.

$$R_t^l(1 + \Psi(R_t^d)) = R_t^d + \kappa \quad (8.36)$$

In conclusion, we introduce financial frictions into the full model based on the fact that loan seekers and loan makers possess asymmetric information of entrepreneurs' true status and their realized capital return. In order to get accurate information to precisely evaluate loan seekers' actual capability to generate sufficient capital return to repay the loan, loan lenders should pay the monitoring cost up to the amount of a fixed ratio of the underlying loan value. The outcomes of entrepreneurs' business activities are not deterministic as they are in the basic and the advanced models. The realized capital return may or may not reach the investor's expected value. Thus, there is a certain degree of risk that entrepreneurs may default on loan and thus declare bankruptcy. In the case of bankruptcy, the default entrepreneur gets nothing, and the lender still needs to pay the fixed ratio of the loan value and has the right to claim on whatever left with the bankrupted borrower. Therefore, loan seekers, on the loan demand side, continue to seek more loans to expand business as long as the expected investment return is higher than the opportunity cost, which is the corresponding deposit interest rate. On the loan supply side, banks optimize their profitability by making as much loan as the loan return after considering the bankruptcy cost is higher than the cost for them to raise such funds from households. As a result, the loan demand curve can be calculated as the first order condition of entrepreneurs, and the loan supply curve, the first order conditions of banks. Based on these two curves, we can finally compute the loan rate, which is positively determined by risk-free basic interest rate, R_t^d, and the loan spread, $\Psi(R_t^d)$, as shown in 8.36. Using this conclusion together with equations of households and production, we can build the full model and then solve it to get a corresponding policy function.

8.1.4 General Equilibrium

In equilibrium, both supply and demand meet in all markets. In this full model, these markets are goods market, housing market, labour market, capital market and credit market. This subsection derives the relevant equations and the equilibrium conditions.

First of all, the equilibrium in the goods market means that goods produced by wholesale firms and then repacked by retailers, are fully equal to the demand for those goods in the private sector. This can be captured in Eq. 8.37. The economic meaning of this equation is straightforward: on the left side y_t is the aggregate output produced by all the firms working in goods market and on the right side all the demand for these goods are summarized. Clearly, the total household consumption is $c_t = c_{cw,t} + c_{rw,t} + c_{bh,t} + c_{lh,t}$; and the total output is

$$y_t = c_{cw,t} + c_{rw,t} + c_{bh,t} + c_{lh,t} + Ikc_t + Ikh_t + k_{b,t} \tag{8.37}$$

The definition of capital investment in the goods market and the housing market can be derived in Eqs. 8.38 and 8.39, respectively. Thus, the total investment in physical capital is $Inv_t = Ikc_t + Ikh_t$.

$$Ikc_t = k_{c,t+1} - (1 - \delta_{kc})k_{c,t} \tag{8.38}$$

$$Ikh_t = k_{h,t+1} - (1 - \delta_{kh})k_{h,t} \tag{8.39}$$

Similarly, the equilibrium condition in the housing market is shown in Eq. 8.40, indicating that the production of new properties (IH_t) is equal to the demand for new housing assets.

$$IH_t = (h_{bh,t} + h_{lh,t}) - (1 - \delta_h)(h_{bh,t-1} + h_{lh,t-1}) \tag{8.40}$$

Therefore, we can introduce the definition of aggregate output of the economy. To better reconcile the theoretical model and real-world statistics, the aggregate output is computed using the similar gauge as it is calculated in most economies' statistics reports—named as GDP_t. As shown in Eq. 8.41, it contains two major components: firstly, the overall output in the housing market, $p_{h,t}IH_t$; secondly, the aggregate products produced in the non-housing market deducting the intermediate goods used in housing production, $y_t - p_{b,t}k_{b,t}$.[9]

$$GDP_t = p_{h,t}IH_t + y_t - p_{b,t}k_{b,t} \tag{8.41}$$

As discussed in the subsection of the financial market above, the equilibrium condition in the credit market is the equality between the demand for external financing and loan supply given the baseline interest rate r_t^d

[9] Clearly, the GDP_t is defined here in real terms.

and the corresponding business environment. In the first place, the loan supply and demand should be equal to each other as shown in Eq. 8.33. Firms seek external financing to support their working capital expenditure. Banks, on the other side, provide loans to firms using deposits made by households. In the second place, the equilibrium condition in the credit markets and the financial frictions give rise to the loan rate r_t^l displayed in Eqs. 8.36 and 8.35.

The equilibrium conditions for labour markets and capital markets can be derived via the F.O.C.s of households and firms. By finding these optimizations conducted by households and firms, we can compute the demand and supply curves of labour, physical capital, mortgage loan and land. These will be derived in detail in the following subsection with special focus on the first order conditions.

8.1.5 First Order Conditions

The first order conditions of households and firms determine the optimal equilibrium solution for labour, capital, housing and deposit. Therefore, in this subsection, we pay special attention to these first order conditions.

The labour supply of construction workers can be derived under the first order condition with respect to the labour, $n_{cw,t}$, in construction worker's Lagrangian equation. This is shown in Eq. 8.42. On the left side, $\psi_{cw} n_{cw,t}^{\eta_{cw}}$ is the marginal negative utility of providing one more unit of labour, $n_{cw,t}$. On the right side, $u_{c,t}^{cw} w_{cw,t}$ is the positive marginal utility of consumption gained by the additional wage earned by providing that extra $n_{cw,t}$ units of labour. The optimal supply of labour $n_{cw,t}$ is thus determined when these two effects offset each other.

$$\psi_{cw} n_{cw,t}^{\eta_{cw}} = u_{c,t}^{cw} w_{cw,t} \tag{8.42}$$

Similarly, the labour supply of rural migrant workers, household borrowers and household lenders can be shown in Eqs. 8.43, 8.44 and 8.45, respectively.

$$\psi_{rw} n_{rw,t}^{\eta_{rw}} = u_{c,t}^{rw} w_{rw,t} \tag{8.43}$$

$$\psi_{bh} n_{bh,t}^{\eta_{bh}} = u_{c,t}^{bh} w_{bh,t} \tag{8.44}$$

$$\psi_{lh} n_{lh,t}^{\eta_{lh}} = u_{c,t}^{lh} w_{lh,t} \tag{8.45}$$

As discussed previously, household borrowers and household lenders are the only households who possess housing assets. Thus, the first order conditions of their Lagrangian equation with respect to housing give rise to the housing demand equations for these two groups of households, as shown in Eqs. 8.46 and 8.47, respectively.

$$\begin{aligned} &\frac{j_t}{h_{bh,t}} + u^{bh}_{c,t} m p_{h,t} \frac{pi_{t+1}}{r_t} + \beta_{bh} u^{bh}_{c,t+1} p_{h,t+1}(1-\delta_h) \\ &= u^{bh}_{c,t} p_{h,t} + \beta_{bh} u^{bh}_{c,t} m p_{h,t+1} \frac{r_{t+1}}{r_t} \end{aligned} \tag{8.46}$$

$$\frac{j_t}{h_{lh,t}} + \beta_{lh} u^{lh}_{c,t+1} p_{h,t+1}(1-\delta_h) = u^{lh}_{c,t} p_{h,t} \tag{8.47}$$

Additionally, we assume, as discussed above, that capital both in the goods market and the housing market, land and firms are ultimately owned by household lenders. Therefore, the first order conditions of capital and land lead us to the equations depicting the optimal supply of capital ($k_{c,t-1}$ and $k_{h,t-1}$), land (l_{t-1}), and intermediate goods ($k_{b,t}$). These F.O.C.s are shown in Eqs. 8.48, 8.49, 8.50, and 8.51, respectively.

$$u^{lh}_{c,t} = \beta_{lh} u^{lh}_{c,t+1}(r_{c,t} + (1-\delta_{kc})) \tag{8.48}$$

$$u^{lh}_{c,t} = \beta_{lh} u^{lh}_{c,t+1}(r_{h,t} + (1-\delta_{kh})) \tag{8.49}$$

$$u^{lh}_{c,t} p_{l,t} = \beta_{lh} u^{lh}_{c,t+1}(p_{l,t+1} + r_{l,t+1}) \tag{8.50}$$

$$u^{lh}_{c,t}(p_{b,t} - 1) = 0 \tag{8.51}$$

Besides these first order conditions, the full model contains a first order condition for households, which is not included in the advanced model: F.O.C with deposit $D_{lh,t}$. This condition leads to the supply curve of deposits in this full model, as shown in Eq. 8.52.

$$u^{lh}_{c,t} = \beta_{lh} u^{lh}_{c,t} r^d_t / \pi_{t+1} \tag{8.52}$$

All the first order conditions above are those for households. Next, we derive the first order conditions for firms to get the demand equations for labour, land, intermediate goods and capital. The first order condition for retailers gives us the Philips curve, as discussed in the subsection of nominal rigidities and shown in Eq. 8.15. As we have displayed in the subsection of production and the short-term nominal rigidities, wholesale firms and housing producers use labour and other input factors, such as land and capital to produce goods and housing assets. Therefore, the first order conditions for wholesale goods producers derive the demand functions for labour, capital, land and intermediate goods accordingly. Combining Eqs. 8.9 and 8.10, both of which explain the technology used to produce goods and housing assets, with wholesale firms' profit maximization Eq. 8.53,[10] first order conditions for wholesale firms produce the demand curves for household labour (Eqs. 8.54, 8.55, 8.56, and 8.57), for capital (Eqs. 8.58 and 8.59), for land (Eq. 8.60), and finally for intermediate goods (Eq. 8.61).

$$\max \frac{y_t}{x_t}+p_{h,t}IH_t-WC_tr_t^l-r_{c,t}k_{c,t-1}-r_{h,t}k_{h,t-1}-r_{l,t}l_{t-1}-p_{b,t}k_{b,t} \quad (8.53)$$

$$\mu_1 p_{h,t}IH_t = w_{cw,t}n_{cw,t}r_t^l \quad (8.54)$$

$$(1-\alpha)\beta_3 Y_t = n_{rw,t}w_{rw,t}x_tr_t^l \quad (8.55)$$

$$(1-\alpha)\beta_2 Y_t = n_{bh,t}w_{bh,t}x_tr_t^l \quad (8.56)$$

$$(1-\alpha)\beta_1 Y_t = n_{lh,t}w_{lh,t}x_tr_t^l \quad (8.57)$$

$$\alpha Y_t = r_{c,t}k_{c,t-1}x_t \quad (8.58)$$

$$\mu_4 p_{h,t}IH_t = r_{h,t}k_{h,t-1} \quad (8.59)$$

$$\mu_3 p_{h,t}IH_t = r_{l,t}l_{t-1} \quad (8.60)$$

$$\mu_2 p_{h,t}IH_t = p_{b,t}k_{b,t} \quad (8.61)$$

8.1.6 Shocks

In order to quantitatively analyse the dynamics of the advanced model, we introduced a rich set of shocks. In the production process (depicted in Eqs. 8.9 and 8.10), two technological shocks are introduced to goods production ($A_{c,t}$) and housing production ($A_{h,t}$). Moreover, housing is explicitly introduced into household's utility function as shown in Eqs. 8.5 and 8.6. Due to the positive utility of housing, all other things unchanged, household prefer holding higher level of housing. Therefore, households' attitude towards housing will affect their demand for housing. In order to model the dynamics of such change of preference in the model economy, we

[10] The definition of WC_t is as in Eq. 8.33. The term $WC_tr_t^l$ is the wholesale firms' repayment for loan to support their working capital expenditures.

install the housing preference shock in the corresponding equations. The housing preference shock to both household borrowers and household lenders is j_t. These shocks follow AR(1) process as:

$$\begin{aligned} \ln A_{c,t} &= \rho_{Ac} \ln A_{c,t-1} + eAC \\ \ln A_{h,t} &= \rho_{Ah} \ln A_{h,t-1} + eAh \\ \ln j_t &= \rho_j \ln j_{t-1} + ej \end{aligned} \tag{8.62}$$

As shown in Eqs. 8.15 and 8.16, the inflation shock ($\varepsilon_{\pi,t}$) and the monetary policy shock ($\varepsilon_{r,t}$) are introduced in the determination of inflation and real interest rate. $\varepsilon_{\pi,t}$ and $\varepsilon_{r,t}$ are i.i.d. white noises with variances σ_π^2 and σ_r^2. Similarly, eAc, eAh and ej in Eq. 8.62 are i.i.d. white noises as well and their variances are σ_{eAc}^2, σ_{eAh}^2 and σ_{ej}^2, respectively.

8.1.7 *Steady State*

So far, we have built the full model with 39 variables and corresponding 39 equations as shown in the subsections above. The final step of completing this full FHSAM is to find the steady sate values for all variables.[11] In steady state, all the effects of shocks are zero. Therefore, we have $A_c^{ss} = 1$ and $A_h^{ss} = 1$.[12] For simplicity of calculation, we assume that the steady-state inflation rate in goods market is zero ($\pi^{ss} = 1$) and that the steady-state real price level is one ($p^{ss} = 1$).

With the aim to make our model more economically consistent with the real world, we further assume that the steady-state working hours for household borrower and lenders are 8, meaning that they work 1/3 per day ($n_{bh}^{ss} = n_{lh}^{ss} = \frac{1}{3}$). On the other hand, because, as we have discussed in the subsection on households, rural construction workers and rural migrant workers have limited wealth resources and lower working skill; as a result, they work longer than their urban counterparts, who possess superior access to a wider range of economic resources. We thereby assume they work half

[11] To avoid duplication, we only derive the steady-state values of variables for the full model. The reduced-scale solutions can be easily made to get the steady-state values for the advanced model, which is a simpler version.

[12] The upper index 'ss' is the symbol of steady-state value for the parameter to which it is attached.

day each day, meaning that $n_{cw}^{ss} = n_{rw}^{ss} = \frac{1}{2}$.[13] By doing so, we need to consider parameters ψ_{cw}, ψ_{rw}, ψ_{bh}, and ψ_{lh} as free variables, meaning that these parameters can not be calibrated.

As in the advanced model, land is assumed to be fixed and normalized to 1, that is $l_t = l^{ss} = 1$. From Eq. 8.51 we can easily conclude that $p_{b,t} = p_b^{ss} = 1$. In steady state, we have $u_{lh,t}^c = u_{lh,t-1}^c = u_{lh}^{c,ss}$. Thus, $r_c^{ss} = \frac{1}{\beta_{lh}} + \delta_{kc} - 1$ and $r_h^{ss} = \frac{1}{\beta_{lh}} + \delta_{kh} - 1$ according to Eqs. 8.48 and 8.49, meaning that the steady-state values of capital return are determined by household lenders discount factor and the depreciation rate of capitals.

Based on these values, we can solve the steady-state values for the remaining variables. Considering the growing complexity of the model, there is hardly an analytical solution as in the basic model. We need to use software to get numerical solutions for the remaining variables' steady-state values. More specifically, we use MATLAB software to get these numerical solutions based on equations from 8.63 to 8.77.[14]

The steady state in the credit market is

$$D_{lh}^{ss} = BC^{ss} \tag{8.63}$$

The steady-state values for the demand and supply of banking credit are determined by

$$w_{lh}^{ss} n_{lh}^{ss} + w_{bh}^{ss} n_{bh}^{ss} + w_{rw}^{ss} n_{rw}^{ss} + w_{cw}^{ss} n_{cw}^{ss} = BC^{ss} \tag{8.64}$$

[13] Some may argue that according to labour laws and related regulations, workers are protected from working more than 8 hours per day, but the situation in emerging market economies is tricky. Because of the ineffective administrative efforts, the absence of strong workers' union, the inferior bargaining position of employees and even the willingness of workers themselves to earn extra gain, a large portion of rural workers exceed the 8 hours per day limit. The situation gets even worse in lower-end industries like construction, in which rural workers play the majority part. For supporting evidence, see the studies conducted by Velasquez [24], Brown et al. [25], Chan and Ngai [26], Burra [27], Rocha and Debert [28] among many others. Similar conclusion concerning this issue is drawn in the advanced model. Moreover, FHSAM allows modeller to modify such steady-state values of working hour, within the range of (0, 1). Researchers can assign values to n^{ss} based on their judgement.

[14] These equations are derived using equations described in the relevant subsections above, given steady values already known. The 'great ratio' method adopted in solving steady-state values for basic model has been used as well.

The relationships derived by the 'great ratio' method are shown in Eqs. 8.65, 8.66, 8.68, and 8.76

$$\frac{\mu 1}{\mu 4}\frac{r_h^{ss}k_h^{ss}}{r^{l,ss}} = c_{cw}^{ss} \tag{8.65}$$

$$\frac{\mu 2}{\mu 4}\frac{r_h^{ss}k_h^{ss}}{r^{l,ss}} = k_b^{ss} \tag{8.66}$$

The equilibrium in goods market (non-housing market) at steady state is

$$c_{cw}^{ss} + c_{rw}^{ss} + c_{bh}^{ss} + c_{lh}^{ss} + k_c^{ss}\delta_{kc} + k_h^{ss}\delta_{kh} + k_b^{ss} = y^{ss} \tag{8.67}$$

The economic meaning of 8.67 is straightforward: all the goods produced in this market are either consumed by households (c_{cw}^{ss}, c_{rw}^{ss}, c_{bh}^{ss}, and c_{lh}^{ss}), or invested in physical capital ($Ikc^{ss} = k_c^{ss}\delta_{kc}$ and $Ikh^{ss} = k_h^{ss}\delta_{kh}$), or provided to housing production (k_b^{ss}).

$$p_h^{ss} = \frac{r_h^{ss}}{\mu_4 (n_{cw}^{ss})^{\mu_1}(k_b^{ss})^{\mu_2}(k_h^{ss})^{\mu_4 - 1}} \tag{8.68}$$

Household borrower's demand for housing asset can be derived from Eq. 8.46 as

$$\begin{aligned}&\frac{1}{h_{bh}^{ss}} + \frac{1-\beta_{bh}b_{bh}}{(1-b_{bh})c_{bh}^{ss}} m \frac{p_h^{ss}}{r^{d,ss}} + \beta_{bh}\frac{1-\beta_{bh}b_{bh}}{(1-b_{bh})c_{bh}^{ss}} p_h^{ss}(1-\delta_h)\\ &- \frac{1-\beta_{bh}b_{bh}}{(1-b_{bh})c_{bh}^{ss}} p_h^{ss} - \beta_{bh}\frac{1-\beta_{bh}b_{bh}}{(1-b_{bh})c_{bh}^{ss}} p_h^{ss} m = 0\end{aligned} \tag{8.69}$$

Similarly, Eq. 8.70 represents the steady-state household lender's demand for housing derived from Eq. 8.47.

$$\frac{1}{h_{lh}^{ss}} + \beta_{lh}\frac{1-\beta_{lh}b_{lh}}{(1-b_{lh})c_{lh}^{ss}} p_h^{ss}(1-\delta_h) = \frac{1-\beta_{lh}b_{lh}}{(1-b_{lh})c_{lh}^{ss}} p_h^{ss} \tag{8.70}$$

Equation 8.71 is household borrower's budget constraint in the steady state, and Eq. 8.72 is household lenders' one.

$$c_{bh}^{ss} + p_h^{ss}h_{bh}^{ss} + mp_h^{ss}h_{bh}^{ss} - w_{bh}^{ss}n_{bh}^{ss} - (1-\delta_h)h_{bh}^{ss}p_h^{ss} - mp_h^{ss}h_{bh}^{ss}/r^{d,ss} = 0 \tag{8.71}$$

$$
\begin{aligned}
& c_{lh}^{ss} + p_h^{ss} h_{lh}^{ss} + p_l^{ss} + k_c^{ss} + k_h^{ss} + k_b^{ss} + L_{lh}^{ss} + D_{lh}^{ss} \\
& = w_{lh}^{ss} n_{lh}^{ss} + (1 - \delta_h) p_h^{ss} h_{lh}^{ss} + (p_l^{ss} + r_l^{ss}) l^{ss} + (r_c^{ss} + (1 - \delta_{kc})) k_c^{ss} \\
& + (r_h^{ss} + (1 - \delta_{kh})) k_h^{ss} + p_b^{ss} + \frac{x^{ss} - 1}{x^{ss}} y^{ss} + L_{lh}^{ss} r^{d,ss} + D_{lh}^{ss}
\end{aligned}
\tag{8.72}
$$

In steady state, the holding of housing asset for household lenders and borrowers is stable. Thus, the production of new housing should be strictly equal to the depreciation of housing stock. This relationship derives Eq. 8.73.

$$
(n_{cw}^{ss})^{\mu_1} (k_b^{ss})^{\mu_2} (k_h^{ss})^{\mu_4} = \delta_h (h_{lh}^{ss} + h_{bh}^{ss}) \tag{8.73}
$$

$$
GDP^{ss} = p_h^{ss} \delta_h (h_{lh}^{ss} + h_{bh}^{ss}) + y_{ss} - k_b^{ss} \tag{8.74}
$$

Equation 8.74 is the equilibrium condition for overall output, GDP_t. Clearly, the first term, $p_h^{ss} \delta_h (h_{lh}^{ss} + h_{bh}^{ss})$, on the right side of this equation represents the steady-state output in housing market, which should be equal to the product of steady-state housing price, p_h^{ss}, multiplied by the new housing produced to compensate the depreciation of housing assets held by household lenders and borrowers (this is the market clearing condition of housing market at equilibrium). According to the definition of GDP, only final goods should be considered. Therefore, we subtract the intermediate goods, k_b^{ss}, from the non-housing market production, y^{ss}.

$$
L_{lh}^{ss} = m p_h^{ss} h_{bh}^{ss} / r^{d,ss} \tag{8.75}
$$

This equation examines the steady-state loan made by household lenders, equalling to the loan demand of household borrowers. This equation tells us that the equilibrium demand for loan is negatively correlated to the real interest rate and positively related with the loan-to-value ratio, m, equilibrium housing price, p_h^{ss}, and household borrower's holding of real estate assets, h_{bh}^{ss}. This is completely consistent with the economic reality.

$$
r_l^{ss} = r_h^{ss} k_h^{ss} \frac{\mu_3}{\mu_4} \tag{8.76}
$$

In terms of a theoretical perspective, the steady-state rate of land rent should be positively correlated with the steady-state capital used in housing production, k_h^{ss}, and the steady-state rental rate of such capital, r_h^{ss}, as land is a very important input in housing production, as shown in Eq. 8.76.

Additionally, the equilibrium value of the land rent is higher when its importance in housing production is higher, meaning that term, $\frac{\mu_3}{\mu_4}$, is larger.

$$p_l^{ss} = \beta_{lh} r_l^{ss} / (1 - \beta_{lh}) \tag{8.77}$$

As Eq. 7.47 in advanced model, the steady-state price of land, p_l^{ss}, is positively correlated with land rental rates in equilibrium, r_l^{ss}. MATLAB can provide numerical solutions to these equations, if parameters are properly set; we then get one set of real solutions that make economic sense.[15]

In conclusion, in these three chapters we try to build three models with gradually increasing comprehensive economic structure. Starting from the basic model with no housing and financial markets and no nominal rigidities, we then produce the advanced model with an explicit housing market and the corresponding mortgage between lenders and borrowers. Nominal rigidities in goods markets have been installed in this advanced model as well. Finally in the full model, we add financial frictions and the corresponding credit market into the model economy, making it more consistent with the economic reality. Additionally, we introduce the heterogeneities not only in firms but also in households. Four groups of households with different economic characteristics and behaviours have been installed in the advanced and full models to better capture the special features in emerging market economies with evident social stratification. Based on the models we build in these three chapters, we are able to undertake empirical analysis on Brazil, India and China in the following part.

8.2 Theoretical Summary and Testable Hypotheses

Based on the theoretical construction of the basic model and the advanced model, which contains the housing market and mortgage loans, we build this final model—the full FHSAM. This model has a wider range of economic qualities including short-run nominal rigidities in the consumption market, an explicit housing market, detailed household classification consistent with emerging market economies' social structure, mortgage loans using property as collateral and a financial sector, which creates loans to

[15] The appendix to this chapter provides the details of how to find steady-state values for all the variables in the model.

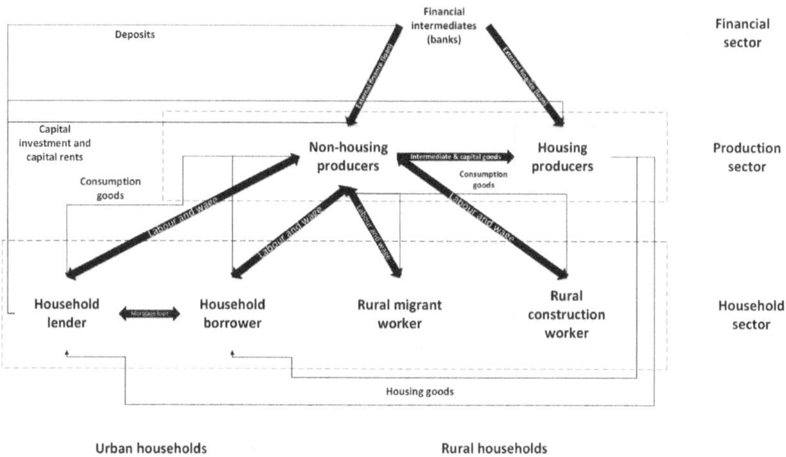

Fig. 8.1 The structure of the full model

entrepreneurs using deposits from household lenders (the ones with capital surplus). A general picture of the full model's structure is shown in Fig. 8.1.

Beyond the advanced model, we add the financial market into this full model to complete the FHSAM modelling. In this full model, financial market links capital surplus (the household lenders) and loan seekers (entrepreneurs), who need loans to satisfy their expenditure on working capital, WC_t. The financial market in this full model is not frictionless. As in the BGG model and other DSGE models such as Smets and Wouters [29], Gerali et al. [30], and Christiano et al. [31], financial frictions are resulted in the fact that loan seekers, and financial intermediates, usually the banks, have asymmetric information on the expected future outcomes of loan seekers' business. In the basic and the advanced models, all business investments are risk-free as the outcomes of their business are deterministic according to the production function; thus, there is no bankruptcy risk for entrepreneurs. But in the full model, we relax this assumption to accommodate the fact that in the real business world the outcomes of entrepreneurs' production may or may not reach their expectations when they apply for the loan. If the outcomes turn out to be less than the expected value, the loan will be defaulted and the entrepreneur is at the risk of bankruptcy. Although both financial intermediates and entrepreneurs are aware of this fact, their access to accurate information to estimate such risk is different. It is natural that loan seekers have more accurate information as they themselves operate the business and have internal information inaccessible from outside. This may lead to the emergence of 'moral hazard'. To overcome this challenge, financial intermediates need to make efforts to monitor entrepreneurs' business activities to make sure they are efficiently utilizing the loan in a proper way. And these efforts, of course, are not costless, in that financial intermediates need to pay for such monitoring activities. This is the basic idea of introducing financial intermediaries and financial frictions by assuming 'costly state verification' (CSV) mechanism. Under such assumption, financial intermediaries pay a fixed ratio of the loan value as the 'auditing cost' helping them to accurately estimate the possible future outcomes of loan seekers' business activities and their realized return on capital.[16] This assumption explains the real-world economic phenomenon that external finance without collateral is typically more expensive than internal finance and collateralized external finance. By following such approach, we can model the financial market with frictions based on the optimization behaviours of both loan seekers and lenders. On the one hand, loan seekers intend to get more loan as long as the expected return on capital is higher than the cost of external finance. Thus, entrepreneurs' optimization condition gives rise to the demand curve of loan from financial intermediaries. On the other hand, financial intermediaries try to maximize their profitability by creating as much loan as the expected return (after considering the CSV issue and the probability of loan seekers' bankruptcy) is higher than the cost of raising fund from households.[17] The optimal solution to such maximum seeking behaviour derives the loan supply curve. Therefore, the market-clearing condition for the financial market can be achieved when the loan demand curve meets the loan supply curve. Conclusively, after inferences introduced in the previous section, the financial market-clearing condition can be derived in Eq. 8.32. Using this equation, we can compute the loan rate as a function of critical value and optimal leverage. Finally, the zero profit condition of financial

[16] In particular, this cost is composed of several important economic components such as auditing, accounting and legal costs. This cost can be interpreted as bankruptcy cost, in that if entrepreneur defaults and then claim bankruptcy, financial intermediates must pay such cost and only receive the wreck value of such entrepreneur, who gets nothing.

[17] Because the cost for banks to raise such fund is the deposit rate paying to the households, the cost of loan is equal to the interest rate, r_t, which is assumed to be risk free.

intermediaries yields the loan rate determined by monitoring cost, κ, and loan rate spread, $\Psi(R_t^d)$, as shown in Eq. 8.36.

By introducing the above elements, we build the full model with four household groups (also can be explained as social layers or social classes), two real production sectors—the housing and the non-housing sectors, and the financial market. The equilibrium condition of this economy can be achieved when all these markets clear. Therefore, the first order conditions of these economic agents explain the optimization patterns in this dynamic expectation system. By solving this dynamic model using the mathematical techniques we have demonstrated previously in this chapter, we can find the solution to this model and the corresponding impulse responses of economic variables.

In general, more theoretical hypotheses are included in this full model, as it contains the financial markets and financial frictions. In the advanced model, household's working hours and real wages move in the same direction with their labour contribution in production. A similar conclusion of this full model can be drawn on the positive correlation between household's labour share in production and their labour supply. For example, the higher the value of $(1-\alpha)\beta_1$ is, the greater the contribution of household lenders' labour in production. Therefore, both the demand for such labour, $n_{lh,t}$, and the corresponding real wage, $w_{lh,t}$, will be higher. This is a realistic hypothesis in that it is consistent with our economic intuition. Additionally, the full model also yields the hypothesis that investment in physical capitals, both Ikc_t and Ikh_t, are procyclical variables to the overall output, GDP_t. And households' consumption ($c_{lh,t}$, $c_{bh,t}$, $c_{rw,t}$, and $c_{cw,t}$) is positively correlated with GDP_t as well. Therefore, the inflation rate is a procyclical variable too. This is so because products in the non-housing market are either consumed by households or used in production (including investment in physical capital and intermediate goods). According to the definition of aggregate output, GDP_t, housing products are also included as $p_{h,t} IH_t$. in 8.41. Therefore, we expect a positive correlation between housing prices, $p_{h,t}$, and the real GDP and real investment in physical capital assets, inv_t. Because both household consumption and investment in physical capitals are procyclical variables, they are expected to be positively correlated as well. More household consumption raises demand and thus calls for more capital investment and labour input to increase the supply. And the increase in real wages pushes up household consumption. As a result, household consumption, investment in physical capital, labour and real wages are all procyclical variables in this full model.

What is more, a higher level of aggregate output is typically followed by the increase of capital rental rates, $r_{c,t}$. In the housing market, the increase of household real wages increases housing demand and thus the investment in housing capital, Ikh_t. Thus, the corresponding real capital rental rate, $r_{h,t}$, is positively correlated with aggregate output, GDP_t, as well. According to the monetary policy rule, real interest rate, r_t, moves in the same direction as GDP_t and the inflation rate, π_t. These hypotheses are summarized in Table 8.1.

Since the financial market and financial frictions are included in this full model, it is possible to analyse the correlation between economic factors and factors related to financial frictions. According to the CSV assumption, financial frictions lead to the condition that loan rate is higher than the risk-free interest rate, as financial intermediaries need to pay a certain cost to get precise information of loan seekers' realized capital return. In the full model, the monitoring cost is denoted as κ, which is a fixed ratio to underlaying loan value, and the risk premium, $\Psi(R_t^d)$, as shown in Eq. 8.36. Therefore, the actual loan rate, r_t^l, is positively correlated with monitoring cost, κ, and the risk premium, $\Psi(R_t^d)$. Additionally, loan risk premium grows as the real interest rate increases, as shown in Eq. 8.35. Based on the hypotheses discussed above, the loan rate spread and the loan rate are also procyclical variables, meaning that they tend to increase when the aggregate output grows. This conclusion is consistent with the realistic economic phenomenon in that entrepreneurs need to pay higher interest rate on their loans, when the aggregate output exceeds its long-run trend. Similarly, loan rate is positively correlated with inflation rate. These hypotheses are demonstrated in Table 8.1.

Table 8.1 Theoretical hypotheses of correlations in the full model: financial frictions

Economic factors	*Hypothesized correlations*
Loan rate spread, $\Psi(R_t^d)$, and risk-free interest rate, R_t^d	Positive
Loan rate, R_t^l, and risk-free interest rate, R_t^d	Positive
Loan rate, R_t^l, and monitoring cost, κ	Positive
Loan rate, R_t^l, and aggregate output, GDP_t	Positive
Loan rate, R_t^l, and inflation rate, π_t	Positive

Table 8.2 Theoretical hypotheses of the full model: impulse responses to productivity shocks

Economic variables	*Exogenous shocks (positive)*	*Hypothesized responses*
GDP_t	Productivity shock, $A_{c,t}$	Gradually rise to a new level
Investment	Productivity shock, $A_{c,t}$	Instantly rise and gradually descend to a new level
Consumption	Productivity shock, $A_{c,t}$	Gradually rise to a new level
Real wages	Productivity shock, $A_{c,t}$	Gradually rise to a new level
GDP_t	Productivity shock, $A_{h,t}$	Instantly small rise and gradually descend to a new level
Investment	Productivity shock, $A_{h,t}$	Small decrease and gradually rise to a new level
Consumption	Productivity shock, $A_{h,t}$	Instantly small increase and gradually descend to a new level
Real wages	Productivity shock, $A_{h,t}$	Instantly small increase and gradually descend to a new level
Inflation	Productivity shock, $A_{c,t}$	Instantly rise and return to the original level
Real interest rate	Productivity shock, $A_{c,t}$	Instantly rise and gradually descend to the original level
Real housing prices	Productivity shock, $A_{c,t}$	Gradually rise to a new level
Banking credit	Productivity shock, $A_{c,t}$	Gradually rise to a new level
Inflation	Productivity shock, $A_{h,t}$	Instant rise and gradual return to the original level
Real interest rate	Productivity shock, $A_{h,t}$	Instantly rise and gradually descend to the original level
Real housing prices	Productivity shock, $A_{h,t}$	Instantly drop and gradually return to a new level
Banking credit	Productivity shock, $A_{h,t}$	Instantly rise and gradually descend to a new level

As we did in the basic and the advanced models, impulse responses of economic variables to exogenous shocks are also analysed in this full model. Because we introduce the financial market and financial frictions in the full model, certain additional hypothesized impulse responses are included in this analysis. As shown in Table 8.2, a similar conclusion can be drawn in the full model as in the advanced model. A positive productivity shock, either in the housing, $A_{h,t}$, or in the non-housing market, $A_{c,t}$, pushes up the aggregate output and thus the real wages of households. The increase of the real wages encourages households to spend more on both consumption and housing, thereby promoting further aggregate demand. As a result, capital rental rates, housing prices, land price, land rental rate and inflation rate begin to rise. According to the Taylor rule, this is followed by the

Table 8.3 Theoretical hypotheses of the full model: impulse responses to housing preference shocks

Economic variables	*Exogenous shocks (positive)*	*Hypothesized responses*
GDP_t	Housing demand, j_t	Increase and then return to the original level
Investment	Housing demand, j_t	Instantly rise and gradually descend to the original level
Consumption	Housing demand, j_t	Instantly increase and gradually descend to the original level
Real wages	Housing demand, j_t	Instantly increase and gradually descend to the original level
Inflation	Housing demand, j_t	Gradually rise to the original level
Real interest rate	Housing demand, j_t	Instantly rise and gradually descend to the original level
Real housing prices	Housing demand, j_t	Instantly increase and gradually descend to the original level
Banking credit	Housing demand, j_t	Instantly increase and gradually descend to the original level

Table 8.4 Theoretical hypotheses of the full model: impulse responses to interest-rate shocks

Economic variables	*Exogenous shocks (positive)*	*Hypothesized responses*
GDP_t	Interest rate, $e_{r,t}$	Sharply drop and gradually rise to the original level
Investment	Interest rate, $e_{r,t}$	Sharply drop and gradually rise to the original level
Consumption	Interest rate, $e_{r,t}$	Sharply drop and gradually rise to the original level
Real wages	Interest rate, $e_{r,t}$	Sharply drop and gradually rise to the original level
Inflation	Interest rate, $e_{r,t}$	Rise and then descend to the original level
Real housing prices	Interest rate, $e_{r,t}$	Instantly slump and gradually return to the original level
Banking credit	Interest rate, $e_{r,t}$	Instantly slump and gradually return to the original level

corresponding increase of the real interest rate, providing downward pressure on economic activity. In the full model, entrepreneurs need to borrow from banks to pay their working capital expenditure. Additionally, the loan rate spread is, as shown in Eq. 8.35, positively correlated with the real interest rate. As a result, this amplification effect of financial frictions gives rise to higher volatility and more instant responses of economic variables than those in the basic and advanced models. For example, investments in physical capitals react to the increase of interest rate induced by productivity shocks more quickly and in a more volatile way than it does in the basic and the advanced models.

In Table 8.3, we summarize the hypothesized impulse responses of economic variables to the exogenous housing preference shock in the full model. The basic conclusions are similar to those in the advanced model. A positive housing preference shock encourages household borrowers and lenders to purchase more housing assets, $h_{bh,t}$ and $h_{lh,t}$, respectively. Therefore, the housing production begins to increase via both renting more physical capital, $k_{h,t}$ and hiring more labour of construction workers, $n_{cw,t}$. This is typically followed by the increasing values of real wage, $w_{cw,t}$, the demand for intermediate goods, $k_{b,t}$, and the capital rental rate, $r_{h,t}$. Such an increase in the real wage of construction workers and the demand for intermediate goods and capital assets used in housing production leads to a higher level of construction workers' consumption, $c_{cw,t}$ and labour and capital demand in the non-housing market. As a result, real wages of household lenders, $w_{lh,t}$, household borrowers, $w_{bh,t}$, and rural migrant workers, $w_{rw,t}$ and capital rental rate in the non-housing market, $r_{c,t}$, begin to rise. The growth of aggregate output in both housing and non-housing market gives rise to higher level of prices in these two markets, p_t and $p_{h,t}$. The consequence is the increase in real interest rate, r_t, thereby worsening household borrowers' budget constraint. Therefore, the housing demand begins to drop. Things are still almost unchanged so far as it is in the advanced model. But after introducing financial frictions into the full model, impulse responses against housing preference shocks are more complicated and volatile, as the increase in the real interest rate drives both the loan spread and thus the loan rate up. This deteriorates the entrepreneurs' ability and willingness to get loans used to pay for their working capital expenditures. In conclusion, the financial amplification effect makes economic variables react to the housing preference shock in a more volatile and instant manner.

Finally, we summarize how economic variables react to a positive interest-rate shock in Table 8.4. Similar to the impulse response analysis of the full model shown above, economic variables react to exogenous interest-rate shocks with higher level of volatility. This is so because of the amplification effect induced by financial frictions. A positive interest-rate shock (an adverse interest-rate shock) pushes up both loan spread and the corresponding loan rate, seriously undermining the entrepreneur's willingness and capability to borrow from banks, decreasing the aggregate demand and overall output. Therefore, real wages and thus the consumption of households decreases. Additionally, the increase of the interest rate draws down household borrowers' demand for housing, $h_{bh,t}$, since it deteriorates their mortgage loan repayment burden. As a result, the aggregate output begins to shrink to a degree, which is lower than it is in the basic and the advanced models. As a result of the decrease in aggregate demand and overall production in both housing and non-housing markets, the volume of banking credit drops too. This trend will persist for a period of time until the economy reaches its new equilibrium.

Appendix

MATLAB is adopted to find the steady-state values for the full model (the solution of the advanced model can be easily achieved using a similar and simpler program). The MATLAB codes are shown as follows.

```
function y=fun(x);

y(1) = x(2)+x(3)+x(4)-x(1);
y(2) = wlhss*nlhss+wbhss*nbhss+crwss+x(12)-x(1);
y(3) = (mu1/mu4)*(rhss*x(5))/rlss-x(12);
y(4) = (mu2/mu4)*x(5)*rhss-x(6);
y(5) = x(10)+x(11)+crwss+x(12)+kcss*deltakc+x(5)*deltakh+x(6)-yss;
y(6) = rhss/(mu4*(ncwss∧ mu1)*(x(6)∧ mu2)*(x(5)∧(mu4-1)))-x(7);
y(7) = 1/x(8)+(((1-betabh*bbh)/(1-bbh))/(x(11)))*m*(x(7)/rss)
+betabh*(((1-betabh*bbh)/(1-bbh))/(x(11)))*x(7)*(1-deltah)-x(7)*
((1-betabh*bbh)/(1-bbh))/(x(11))-(betabh*
((1-betabh*bbh)/(1-bbh))/(x(11)))*m*x(7);
y(8) = 1/x(9)+(betalh*((1-betalh*blh)/(1-blh))/(x(10)))*(1-deltah)*x(7)
-x(7)*((1-betalh*blh)/(1-blh))/(x(10));
y(9) = x(11)+x(7)*x(8)*deltah+m*x(7)*x(8)+x(3)-wbhss*nbhss-m*x(7)*x
(8)/rss-x(3)*rdss;
y(10)= x(10)+x(7)*x(9)+x(15)+kcss+x(6)+x(5)+x(14)+x(2)-wlhss*nlhss
-(1-deltah)*x(7) *x(9)-(x(15)+x(16))-(rcss+(1-deltakc))*kcss
-(rhss+(1-deltakh)) *x(5)-x(6)-(xss-1)*(yss/xss)-x(14)*rss-x(2)*rdss;
y(11)= (ncwss∧ mu1)*(x(6)∧ mu2)*(x(5)∧ mu4)-deltah*(x(9)+x(8));
y(12)= x(7)*deltah*(x(9)+x(8))+yss-x(6)-x(13);
```

```
y(13)=x(3);
y(14)= x(14)-m*x(7)*x(8)/rss;
y(15)= x(16)-(mu3/mu4)*rhss*x(5);
y(16)= x(15)-betalh*x(16)/(1-betalh);

x0=[5 2 0 1 10 10 1 5 5 1 1 1 2 5 1 1];
% BC Dlh Dbh Bcb kh kb ph hbh hlh clh cbh ccw GDP Llh pl rl
options = optimset('MaxIter',1e8,'MaxFunEvals',1e8,'TolFun',1e-8);

x=fsolve(@fun,x0,options);
BCss=real(x(1));
Dlhss=real(x(2));
Dbhss=real(x(3));
Bcbss=real(x(4));
khss=real(x(5));
kbss=real(x(6));
phss=real(x(7));
hbhss=real(x(8));
hlhss=real(x(9));
clhss=real(x(10));
cbhss=real(x(11));
ccwss=real(x(12));
GDPss=real(x(13));
Llhss=real(x(14));
plss=real(x(15));
rlss=real(x(16));
```

References

1. Böhm-Bawerk, E., & Smart, W. (1890). *Capital and interest: A critical history of economical theory*. New York: Macmillan and Company.
2. Keynes, J. M. (1936). *The general theory of interest, employment and money*. London: Macmillan.
3. Hayek, F. A. (1939). *Profits, interest, and investment, and other essays on the theory of industrial fluctuations*. London: George Routledge and Sons, Limited.
4. Woodford, M. (2001). The Taylor rule and optimal monetary policy. *The American Economic Review*, *91*(2), 232–237.

5. Townsend, R. M. (1979). Optimal contracts and competitive markets with costly state verification. *Journal of Economic Theory, 21*(2), 265–293.
6. Boyd, J. H., & Smith, B. D. (1994). How good are standard debt contracts? stochastic versus nonstochastic monitoring in a costly state verification environment. *Journal of Business, 67*(4), 539–561.
7. Winton, A. (1995). Costly state verification and multiple investors: The role of seniority. *Review of Financial Studies, 8*(1), 91–123.
8. Bernanke, B., Gertler, M., & Gilchrist, S. (1999). The financial accelerator in a quantitative business cycle framework. *Handbook of Macroeconomics, 1*, 1341–1393.
9. Modigliani, F., & Miller, M. H. (1959). The cost of capital, corporation finance, and the theory of investment. *The American Economic Review, 49*(4), 655–669.
10. Fisher, I. (1933). The debt-deflation theory of Great Depressions. *Econometrica, 1*(4), 337–357.
11. Bernanke, B. (1983). Nonmonetary effects of the financial crisis in the propagation of the Great Depression. *Journal of Economics and Business, 51*(3), 215–235.
12. Bernanke, B., & Blinder, A. (2000). *Credit, money, and aggregate demand* (NBER Working Papers No. 782).
13. Bernanke, B., & Gertler, M. (1989). Agency costs, net worth, and business fluctuations. *The American Economic Review, 79*(1), 14–31.
14. Bernanke, B., Lown, C., & Friedman, B. (1991). The credit crunch. *Brookings Papers on Economic Activity, 1991*(2), 205–247.
15. Diamond, D. W., & Rajan, R. G. (2009). The credit crisis: Conjectures about causes and remedies. *The American Economic Review, 99*(2), 606–610.
16. Bernanke, B. (2010). Causes of the recent financial and economic crisis (testimony before the Financial Crisis Inquiry Commission). In H.P. Penny (Ed.), *Statements and speeches of Ben S. Bernanke* (pp. 2205–2209). Princeton: Princeton University Press.
17. Bernanke, B. (2013). *The Federal Reserve and the financial crisis.* Princeton: Princeton University Press.
18. Iyer, R., Peydro, J.-L., da Rocha-Lopes, S., & Schoar, A. (2014). Interbank liquidity crunch and the firm credit crunch: Evidence from the 2007–2009 crisis. *Review of Financial Studies, 27*(1), 347–372.
19. Sachs, J., Tornell, A., Velasco, A., Calvo, G., & Cooper, R. (1996). Financial crises in emerging markets: The lessons from 1995. *Brookings Papers on Economic Activity, 1996*(1), 147–215.
20. Peek, J., & Rosengren, E. (2000). Implications of the globalization of the banking sector: The Latin American experience. *New England Economic Review, 53*(6), 145–185.

21. Borensztein, E., & Lee, J. (2002). Financial crisis and credit crunch in Korea: Evidence from firm-level data. *Journal of Monetary Economics, 49*(4), 853–875.
22. Chanlau, J.A. & Chen, Z. (1998). *Financial crisis and credit crunch as a result of inefficient financial intermediation: With reference to the Asian financial crisis* (IMF Working Papers No. 127).
23. Chowdhury, I., Hoffmann, M., & Schabert, A. (2006). Inflation dynamics and the cost channel of monetary transmission. *European Economic Review, 50*(4), 995–1016.
24. Velasquez, M. (2002). *Business ethics: Concepts and cases.* Saddle River: Prentice Hall.
25. Brown, D. K., Deardorff, A., & Stern, R. (2004). The effects of multinational production on wages and working conditions in developing countries. In S. Holcombe (Ed.), *Challenges to globalization: Analyzing the economics* (pp. 279–330). Chicago: University of Chicago Press.
26. Chan, K. C., & Ngai, P. (2009). The making of a new working class? A study of collective actions of migrant workers in South China. *China Quarterly, 198*(1), 287–303.
27. Burra, N. (1995). Born to work: Child labour in India. *Journal of Asian Studies, 56*(2), 31–54.
28. Rocha, L., & Debert, R. (2004). Working conditions, visual fatigue, and mental health among systems analysts in Sao Paulo, Brazil. *Occupational and Environmental Medicine, 61*(1), 24–32.
29. Smets, F., & Wouters, R. (2007). Shocks and frictions in US business cycles: A Bayesian DSGE approach. *The American Economic Review, 97*(3), 586–606.
30. Gerali, A., Neri, S., Sessa, L., & Signoretti, F. M. (2010). Credit and banking in a DSGE model of the Euro area. *Journal of Money, Credit and Banking, 42*(1), 107–141.
31. Christiano, L. J., Trabandt, M., & Walentin, K. (2011). Introducing financial frictions and unemployment into a small open economy model. *Journal of Economic Dynamics and Control, 35*(12), 1999–2041.

CHAPTER 9

Solving DSGE Models

9.1 Linearizing the Non-Linear Dynamic Stochastic Models

As we previously demonstrated, a dynamic rational expectation system is usually expressed as a group of equations including first order conditions, constraints, and market clearing conditions. Based on mathematical techniques, the solution to a linear rational expectations system can be feasibly solved analytically. But things get more complicated when non-linear models are involved. One of the major challenges of the DSGE modelling lies in the fact that most of these dynamic stochastic models are, unfortunately, non-linear; and the analytical solution to them is thus difficult, if not impossible, to derive.[1] Even in the simplest non-linear rational expectations system, there is only a tiny opportunity that an analytical solution exists. Therefore, a lot of numerical efforts have been delivered to overcome this issue. These early attempts are included in the works of Kydland and Prescott [2], who try to solve the DSGE model by replacing the original problem with a linear quadratic approximation; also King et al. [3], in whose work the equilibrium conditions are linearized, and Christiano [4], who uses a value function iteration to find a solution.

Thanks to the mathematical innovation and the development of control theory, methods to solve DSGE models follow the principles of

[1] In fact, according to Fernández-Villaverde [1], DSGE models, except for a very few exceptions, cannot be solved in a 'paper and pencil' way.

D. L. Jia, *Dynamic Macroeconomic Models in Emerging Market Economies*,
https://doi.org/10.1007/978-981-15-4588-7_9

scientific computation and perturbation. The basic content of the perturbation method[2] is to replace the original model, which cannot be solved analytically, with a simpler one (in the case of DSGE solution, a linear state-space representation solution) that can be feasibly solved and use this solution of the simplified model to approximate the solution to the original model. As summarized in Judd and Guu [5], linearization can be conceived as the first-order term of perturbation. More specifically, to find the approximate solution one should calculate the Taylor expansion of the policy function about the steady state.[3] Thus, linearization is the first-order term of this Taylor expansion. As the familiarity with linearization in DSGE modelling accumulates, economists develop many methods to manually linearize the non-linear DSGE models.[4]

As shown in 9.4, the first-order Taylor expansion of variable x_t near the steady-state point x is

$$f(x_t) \simeq f(x) + f'(x)(x_t - x) \tag{9.1}$$

Additionally, the log-deviation of x_t can be expressed as

$$\widetilde{x}_t = \ln X_t - \ln X \tag{9.2}$$

Let us further denote $f(x_t) \equiv \ln X_t - \ln X$, then 9.1 becomes

$$\begin{aligned}\widetilde{x}_t &= \ln X_t - \ln X = \ln(1 + \frac{X_t - X}{X}) \\ &\simeq \frac{\partial \ln(1 + \frac{X_t - X}{X})}{\partial X_t} |_{X_t = X} (X_t - X) = \frac{1}{X}(X_t - X)\end{aligned} \tag{9.3}$$

It is clear from Eq. 9.3 that log-deviation can be approximately treated as a percentage deviation from steady state. This is an important advantage as it makes more economic sense and thus links better the theoretical model

[2] For more details of the perturbation method, see Judd and Guu [5].

[3] A typical example of Taylor expansion of variable x at point x_o can be written as

$$f(x) \simeq f(x_0) + f'(x_0)(x - x_0) + \frac{1}{2} f''(x_0)(x - x_0)^2 + Higher Order Terms \tag{9.4}$$

More details of Taylor expansion in econometrics, see Fernández-Villaverde [1].

[4] If the model is programmed in Dynare without manual linearization, it is automatically linearized by Dynare around the deterministic steady state.

with data. Then, we can transform all the variables X_t in the model into $\widetilde{x}_t$ using

$$\widetilde{x}_t \approx \frac{1}{X}(X_t - X) = \frac{X_t}{X} - 1 \tag{9.5}$$

The log-deviation expression of variables is consistent with the loglinearization method—the total differential method advocated by Galí and Monacelli [6]. The procedure of this loglinearization method starts from taking the logarithm on both sides of the equation. Then take total differential of each variable at its steady-state value. In the first step, we take logarithm on both sides of a standard Cobb–Douglas production function $Y_t = K_t^{\alpha}(A_t L_t)^{1-\alpha}$:

$$\log Y_t = \alpha \log K_t + (1-\alpha)\log A_t + (1-\alpha)\log L_t \tag{9.6}$$

Then, if we take the total differential of Eq. 9.6 in the steady state, we have

$$\frac{1}{Y}dY_t = \alpha\frac{1}{K}dK_t + (1-\alpha)\frac{1}{A}dA_t + (1-\alpha)\frac{1}{L}d\log L_t \tag{9.7}$$

By using the log-deviation introduced in Eq. 9.5, it turns into

$$\widetilde{Y}_t = \alpha\widetilde{K}_t + (1-\alpha)\widetilde{A}_t + (1-\alpha)\widetilde{L}_t \tag{9.8}$$

Therefore, a non-linear production function has been linearized in log-deviation expression using the total differential method. Another mathematical method to log-linearize the model is to use the Taylor expansion. We still use the Cobb–Douglas production function as an example. The first step of this method is the same as the total differential method, by taking logarithms on both sides of the production function. Then we use the first-order Taylor expansion at the steady state on each term in Eq. 9.6 to derive Eq. 9.9:

$$\begin{aligned}
\ln Y_t &= \ln Y + \frac{1}{Y}(Y_t - Y) \\
\ln K_t &= \ln K + \frac{1}{K}(K_t - K) \\
\ln A_t &= \ln A + \frac{1}{A}(A_t - A) \\
\ln L_t &= \ln L + \frac{1}{L}(L_t - L)
\end{aligned} \tag{9.9}$$

Plugging in Eqs. 9.6 and 9.9 can be rewritten as

$$\ln Y + \frac{1}{Y}(Y_t - Y) = \alpha[\ln K + \frac{1}{K}(K_t - K)] + (1-\alpha)[\ln A + \frac{1}{A}(A_t - A)] + (1-\alpha)[\ln L + \frac{1}{L}(L_t - L)] \tag{9.10}$$

After eliminating the steady-state values out of Eq. 9.10, we get

$$\frac{Y_t}{Y} = \alpha\frac{K_t}{K} + (1-\alpha)\frac{A_t}{A} + (1-\alpha)\frac{L_t}{L} - (1-\alpha) \tag{9.11}$$

Because Y, K, A, and L are steady-state values, they can be considered as non-negative constants. Therefore, Eq. 9.11 is the linearized expression of the Cobb–Douglas production equation. A third way to loglinearize a model is proposed by Uhlig [7]. This method is different from the above two methods in that derivatives are not involved. Rearranging Eq. 9.2, we have

$$\ln X_t = \ln X + \widetilde{x}_t \tag{9.12}$$

Then we take exceptional on both sides to find

$$X_t = e^{\ln X + \widetilde{x}_t} = Xe^{\widetilde{x}_t} \tag{9.13}$$

The method proposed by Uhlig [7] can be conducted by substituting all the variables using Eq. 9.13. After these substitutions, the model can be linearized by the following approximations.

$$\begin{aligned} e^{\widetilde{x}_t} &\approx 1 + \widetilde{x}_t \\ e^{\widetilde{x}_t + a\widetilde{y}_t} &\approx 1 + \widetilde{x}_t + a\widetilde{y}_t \\ \widetilde{x}_t\widetilde{y}_t &\approx 0 \end{aligned} \tag{9.14}$$

If we still use Cobb–Douglas production function as an example, Uhlig's method starts from substituting each variable under the rule of Eq. 9.13:

$$Ye^{\widetilde{Y}_t} = K^{\alpha}e^{\alpha\widetilde{K}_t}A^{1-\alpha}e^{(1-\alpha)\widetilde{A}_t}L^{1-\alpha}e^{(1-\alpha)\widetilde{L}_t} \tag{9.15}$$

After eliminating the steady-state values from 9.15, we have

$$e^{\widetilde{Y}_t} = e^{\alpha\widetilde{K}_t}e^{(1-\alpha)\widetilde{A}_t}e^{(1-\alpha)\widetilde{L}_t} \tag{9.16}$$

Using approximation shown in Eq. 9.14, the original Cobb–Douglas production function is linearized into

$$\tilde{Y}_t = \alpha \tilde{K}_t + (1-\alpha)\tilde{A}_t + (1-\alpha)\tilde{L}_t \tag{9.17}$$

It is evident that the linearization result of Uhlig's method is very similar to that given by log-deviation method. After linearization, the original non-linear DSGE models can be transformed into state-space representation that we discuss in the following section. In this book, we use all these three linearization methods to find the state-space representation of the original non-linear DSGE models, enhancing the reliability of our analysis.

9.2 The State-Space Representation of the DSGE Model

After linearization, a standard DSGE model can be written in matrix form:

$$\begin{pmatrix} m11 & m12 \\ m21 & m22 \end{pmatrix} \times \begin{pmatrix} x_{1,t} \\ x_{2,t} \end{pmatrix} = \begin{pmatrix} x_{1,t+1} \\ x_{2,t+1} \end{pmatrix} \tag{9.18}$$

and

$$M \equiv \begin{bmatrix} m11 & m12 \\ m21 & m22 \end{bmatrix} \tag{9.19}$$

in which matrix x_1 represents all the control variables (jump or forward-looking variables) in the DSGE model, and it contains n items. Thus, x_1 is a $n \times 1$ vector. Likewise, matrix x_2 is a $m \times 1$ vector representing all the state (predetermined) variables in the same model. The correlation matrix M, which is $(n+m) \times (n+m)$, contains all the information of the DSGE model, including the solution we are looking for: the policy rule, ϕ, under which $x_{1,t+1} = \phi \cdot x_{2,t}$. To better understand the meaning of matrix M, as in Eq. 9.18, we can further denote $m11$ and $m21$ as the $n \times n$ square matrix and $m12$ and $m22$ the $m \times m$.

From Eq. 9.18, we have

$$\begin{aligned} E_t x_{1,t+1} &= m11 \cdot x_{1,t} + m12 \cdot x_{2,t} \\ &= m11 \cdot \phi \cdot x_{2,t} + m12 \cdot x_{2,t} \\ &= C \cdot x_{2,t} \end{aligned} \tag{9.20}$$

$$\begin{aligned} E_t x_{2,t+1} &= m21 \cdot x_{1,t} + m22 \cdot x_{2,t} \\ &= m21 \cdot \phi \cdot x_{2,t} + m22 \cdot x_{2,t} \\ &= A \cdot x_{2,t} \end{aligned} \tag{9.21}$$

Therefore, $\phi \cdot A = C$. We can rewrite 9.18 as:

$$x_{1,t} = C \cdot x_{2,t-1} + D \cdot \varepsilon_{1,t} \tag{9.22}$$

$$x_{2,t} = A \cdot x_{2,t-1} + B \cdot \varepsilon_{2,t} \tag{9.23}$$

The mathematical explanation of Eqs. 9.22 and 9.23 is: the value of control variables in period t ($x_{1,t}$) is determined by the value of state variables in the previous period $t - 1$ ($x_{2,t-1}$) and the innovations in that period t ($\varepsilon_{1,t}$); similarly, the value of state variables in period t ($x_{2,t}$) is determined by the value of these state variables in previous period $t - 1$ ($x_{2,t-1}$) and the innovations in the same period t ($\varepsilon_{2,t}$). These values are connected by coefficient matrices A, B, C, and D, all of which are functions of parameters (θ) of this model. We can write the solution of this model as

$$s_t = \Phi(s_{t-1}, \varepsilon_t; \theta) \tag{9.24}$$

$$y_t = \Psi(s_t, \upsilon_t; \theta) \tag{9.25}$$

Equation 9.24 is the transition function and Eq. 9.25 the measurement function. From an econometrics perspective, s represents the state vector, containing both control and state variables, and Φ is the model's transition equation, which can be viewed as the combination of A, B, C, and D in Eqs. 9.22 and 9.23 and of course is a function of the structural parameters, θ. In Eq. 9.25, y_t is the economic observables and υ_t the shocks to these observables. In practice, to solve a dynamic rational expectations system we need to find the steady state of this model and then to use perturbation method to analyse the dynamics near this steady state. Under this linear state-space representation, DSGE models can be solved.

9.3 Blanchard–Kahn Condition

Based on the linear representation of the DSGE models in states space discussed above, we can solve for the policy function, ϕ, using certain mathematical approach. Here we introduce the use of Blanchard–Kahn method,[5] which is currently the standard method in the Dynare package.

[5] The details of Blanchard–Kahn method can be found in the contribution jointly proposed by Blanchard and Kahn [8], which is one of the most important papers in the domain of solving dynamic planning systems.

The matrix M in Eq. 9.18 can be expressed as:

$$M = \Gamma \Lambda \Gamma^{-1} \tag{9.26}$$

in which Γ is the eigenvectors matrix in columns and Γ is the diagonal eigenvalues matrix, which can be rearranged into:

$$\Lambda = \begin{pmatrix} \Lambda_1 & 0 \\ 0 & \Lambda_2 \end{pmatrix} \tag{9.27}$$

The sub-matrix Λ_1 is a $Q \times Q$ diagonal square matrix represents all the eigenvalues less than 1 and Λ_2 is a a $B \times B$ diagonal square matrix larger than 1 (quite intuitively there is $Q + B = M + N$). That is to say $|\Lambda_1| < 1$ and $|\Lambda_2| > 1$. In other words, Λ_1 represents all the stable eigenvalues and Λ_2 the unstable ones.

Therefore, we further maintain that

$$E_t x_{t+1} = M x_t = \Gamma \Lambda \Gamma^{-1} x_t = \Gamma \Lambda z_t, \; z_t \equiv \Gamma^{-1} x_t \tag{9.28}$$

If we multiply Γ^{-1} at both sides of 9.28, we have

$$E_t z_{t+1} = \Lambda z_t \tag{9.29}$$

According to the rearrangement of Λ, we can rearrange z_t to find:

$$E_t z_{t+1} = \Lambda z_t = \begin{pmatrix} \Lambda_1 & 0 \\ 0 & \Lambda_2 \end{pmatrix} \begin{pmatrix} z_{1,t} \\ z_{2,t} \end{pmatrix} \tag{9.30}$$

Because $|\Lambda_2| > 1$, then $E_t = \Lambda_2 z_{2,t} = \Lambda_2^2 z_{2,t-1} = \ldots = \Lambda_2^n z_{2,t-n+1}$. Therefore, for $z_{2,t-n+1} > 0$, $\lim_{n \to \infty} E_t z_{2,t+1} \to \infty$. Therefore, $z_{2,t}$ must be exactly zero for all time t. Using this relationship we can solve for the policy function by partition of Γ^{-1} to recover x_t. Here, we need to notice that the necessary condition to find solution is that the number of eigenvalues of the matrix M should be equal to the number of jump variables in the DSGE model. This is the so-called Blanchard–Kahn condition. If this condition is not met, Dynare cannot solve the policy function of the model.

Partition of Γ^{-1} is

$$\Gamma^{-1} = \begin{pmatrix} G_{11} & G_{12} \\ G_{21} & G_{22} \end{pmatrix} \tag{9.31}$$

By definition, G_{11} is a $Q \times N$ matrix, G_{12} a $Q \times M$, G_{21} is a $B \times N$, and G_{22} is a $B \times M$. Therefore,

$$\Gamma^{-1}\begin{pmatrix} Z_{1,t+1} \\ z_{2,t+1} \end{pmatrix} = z_{t+1} = \begin{pmatrix} G_{11} & G_{12} \\ G_{21} & G_{22} \end{pmatrix}\begin{pmatrix} x_{1,t} \\ x_{2,t} \end{pmatrix} \tag{9.32}$$

For all t, $z_{2,t} = 0$ means

$$0 = z_{2,t} = G_{21}x_{1,t} + G_{22}x_{2,t} \tag{9.33}$$

Finally, we find the decision rule of the target DSGE model as shown in Eq. 9.34. This equation tells us how control variables ($x_{1,t}$) are determined in terms of the contemporary state variables ($x_{2,t}$).

$$x_{1,t} = G_{21}^{-1}G_{22}x_{2,t} \tag{9.34}$$

That is to say that the policy function ϕ, which is the solution to the target DSGE model is:

$$\phi = G_{21}^{-1}G_{22} \tag{9.35}$$

In conclusion, now we find the solution to the macroeconomic model with dynamic planning scheme, and this solution is represented by the above policy function. This policy function tells us how control variables evolve given state variables, which are determined by the values of state variables in the previous period and the exogenous variables in the current time period. The dynamic macroeconomic system has been transformed into its Linear Time-Invariant (LTI) form, represented by the linear state-space representation and the corresponding policy rules. Such a LTI system is robust against the Lucas Critique [9].

References

1. Fernández-Villaverde, J. (2010). The econometrics of DSGE models. *Journal of the Spanish Economic Association*, *1*(2), 3–49.
2. Kydland, F. E., & Prescott, E. C. (1982). Time to build and aggregate fluctuations. *Econometrica*, *50*(6), 1345–1370.
3. King, R. G., Plosser, C. I., & Rebelo, S. T. (2002). Production, growth and business cycles: Technical appendix. *Computational Economics*, *20*(1), 87–116.
4. Christiano, L. (1990). Linear-quadratic approximation and value-function iteration: A comparison. *Journal of Business and Economic Statistics*, *8*(1), 99–113.

5. Judd, K. L., & Guu, S. M. (1993). Perturbation solution methods for economic growth models. In H. Varian (Ed.), *Economic and financial modeling with Mathematica* (pp. 80–103). New York: Springer.
6. Galí, J., & Monacelli, T. (2005). Monetary policy and exchange rate volatility in a small open economy. *The Review of Economic Studies, 72*(3), 707–734.
7. Uhlig, H. (1999). *A toolkit for analyzing nonlinear dynamic stochastic models easily* (Federal Reserve Bank of Minneapolis Working Papers), 101.
8. Blanchard, O. J., & Kahn, C. M. (1980). The solution of linear difference models under rational expectations. *Econometrica, 48*(5), 1305–1311.
9. Lucas, R. E. (1976). Econometric policy evaluation: A critique. In D. V. Pritchett (Ed.), *Carnegie-Rochester conference series on public policy* (pp. 19–46). Amsterdam: Elsevier.

PART IV

Empirical Analysis

The final stage of dynamic macroeconomics modelling exercise is to undertake empirical analysis, using data collected in corresponding economies. This part examines the empirical analysis of the FHSAM we proposed in previous chapters. It consists of three chapters. The first chapter summarizes the empirical methodologies and software tools used in the empirical analysis, with emphasis on parameter identification, including calibration and estimation methods. Data, statistics and the stylized facts in Brazil, India and China are included in the second chapter. The framework of the FHSAM, empirical methodologies and data jointly produce the empirical analysis, as shown in the third chapter.

CHAPTER 10

Empirical Methodologies and Software Tools

10.1 Empirical Methodologies

In every macroeconomic modelling exercise, the explanatory power and robustness of a DSGE model is greatly affected and determined by the quality of parameter identification. Therefore, to get better empirical analysis, an important step is to determine the values of the parameters in the model. In general, these parameters are classified into two categories: parameters that describe the characteristics of the model under steady state and the parameters that capture the dynamic features of the model. In order to assign appropriate values to these parameters, many empirical methods have been developed. These empirical methods fall into two groups: calibration and estimation.[1] In their milestone work of RBC/DSGE modelling, Kydland and Prescott [2] use the calibration method to identify the structural parameters in the DSGE model. Later, modern statistical methods have been actively introduced in DSGE modelling, as they make fuller use of information, both objective and subjective. A variety of model identification methodologies have been proposed, based on advanced statistical approaches. Christiano and Eichenbaum [3] use the Generalized Method

[1] An interesting explanation of the differences between these two methodologies is provided by Canova [1], who claims that the differences between estimation and calibration methods arise because of the different questions these two methodologies try to measure. Calibration methods try to answer the question of 'Given that the model is false, how true is it?'(p. 2) while in the case of estimation 'Given that the model is true, how false is it?'(p. 1).

D. L. Jia, *Dynamic Macroeconomic Models in Emerging Market Economies*,
https://doi.org/10.1007/978-981-15-4588-7_10

of Moments (GMM) to build the likelihood function to estimate the numerical values of model parameters. Statistical methods other than GMM have been developed as well. For example, Rotemberg and Woodford [4] try to estimate the parameters in DSGE models using a comparison between variance given by the VAR model and the targeted DSGE model. More specifically, they use the likelihood function linking the VAR model variance and the DSGE model variance and then estimate the value of DSGE model parameters by minimizing the discrepancy of impulse response functions between VAR and DSGE models. Moreover, Christiano et al. [5], Leeper and Sims [6], Kim [7] and many others adopt full-information likelihood-based estimation method in their DSGE modelling. After the late 1990s, as the accumulation of theoretical knowledge and economists' improved familiarity with the dynamic expectations system, the estimation methods based on the Bayesian techniques began to gain popularity and soon became the most widely accepted approach in DSGE parameter estimation. In the following sections, we discuss the parameterizations methodologies[2] used in this research: calibration and Bayesian estimation.

10.1.1 Calibration

Calibration[3] in macroeconomic analysis refers to a particular econometric method in which the parameters of the economic model are assumed instead of being estimated. The basic principle of calibration is to assign values to parameters based on the researcher's judgement jointly determined

[2] For more information on estimation methodologies used in DSGE modelling and their dominant position in DSGE parameterizations, see the econometrics summary conducted by Fernández-Villaverde [8].

[3] For detailed discussion on calibration, see its application in DSGE modelling exercises undertaken by Kydland and Prescott [2] and Canova and Ortega [9]. Canova [1] made a very important contribution in evaluating the calibrated models. His work also discusses the differences between estimation and calibration methods. As summarized in his work, theoretical jurisdiction of calibration could be found in the macro-level economic models, where the structural parameters are directly identified according to subjective judgements rather than statistical inference (although they admitted statistical methods might be applied to provide more accurate information than purely guessing the numerical values of the structural parameters). Early attempts to apply statistical approaches in model identification include the contribution proposed by Haavelmo [10], who systematically introduces the modern theory of probability and statistical inference as the basis of economic analysis to find the interactions among economic variables. Based on these contributions, calibration and estimation find their fruitful application in DSGE model identification exercises.

by sample data, existing information and economic intuition. Theoretically, this approach can be used in model identification for both steady-state and dynamics-related parameters. The advantage of calibration is that it works even under the condition of small sample data. This feature fits the need in the studies of the emerging market economies, as the time period of available data in these economies is typically short.

A calibration exercise typically involves the application of a parameterized structural model to address a specific question. Therefore, it is ideal for the calculation of parameters in a steady-state model. In general, the essence of the calibration technique, as indicated in the work of Canova and Ortega [9], can be demonstrated in the following 6 steps:

1. Translating the economic question into a formula system;
2. Developing or selecting an appropriate model that matches the needs of the question under analysis;
3. Choosing the primitive forms of equations to explain the endogenous variables in terms of exogenous variables and parameters;
4. Determining the parameters and the stochastic processes for the exogenous variables and then undertake simulations for these exogenous variables;
5. Comparing the results of the model to the stylized facts;
6. Further analyses.

If the model can be described as the following regression equation:

$$F(Y, X, \beta, \varepsilon) = 0 \tag{10.1}$$

where Y is the vector of endogenous variables, X is the vector of exogenous variables, β is the vector of parameters and ε represents the random error term. In a typical calibration process, we simply assume that $\varepsilon = 0$. Thus we have

$$F(Y, X, \widehat{\beta}) = 0 \tag{10.2}$$

where $\widehat{\beta}$ is the value of the parameters calculated by calibration. It is obvious that the convincing power of calibration highly depends on a strong assumption that all the factors have been well explained in the model, and thus the error term is close to zero.

In the model calibration we have demonstrated above, a wide range of available information, both objective and subjective, can be effectively utilized. For example, in a closed economy, according to the production equation described in the previous chapters, the real marginal cost of producing one unit of good is

$$mc^{ss} = \frac{1}{1 + \lambda^{p,ss}} \tag{10.3}$$

$\lambda^{p,ss}$ represents the markup in firms' price-adjusting process. In parameter calibration, $\lambda^{p,ss}$ can be calibrated as the average markup value observed in data samples. Similarly, in equations below

$$R^{k,ss} k^{ss} = \alpha * mc^{ss} * y^{ss} \tag{10.4}$$

$$w^{ss} n^{ss} = (1 - \alpha) * mc^{ss} * y^{ss} \tag{10.5}$$

where α and $1 - \alpha$ are the ratios of capital income and labour income in the total national income respectively. The calibrated values assigned to these two parameters can be calculated using data samples of GDP accounting under the income method.

In conclusion, the values of calibrated parameters are fixed during the estimation period, meaning that they are assumed to have infinitely strict priors. Economists prefer to use calibration approach for parameters that are strongly related to the steady-state condition of the model. So that the calibrated values of those parameters can be calculated according to their sample mean. As concluded by Iacoviello and Neri [11], 'We fix these parameters because they are either notoriously difficult to estimate (in the case of the markups) or because they are better identified using other information (in the case of the factor shares and the discount factors)' (p. 13).

Along with the developments of modern econometrics, estimation methods have been increasingly accepted in macroeconomics analysis, especially in research using the DSGE models. In the following section, we introduce the estimation methods with a focus on the Bayesian estimation.

10.1.2 Bayesian Estimation with Markov Chain Monte Carlo Methods and the Metropolis–Hastings Algorithm

(Bayes' Theorem) is to the theory of probability what Pythagoras theorem is to geometry.

–Jeffreys [12, p. 31].

Traditional structural models showed their limitation and weakness in the 1970s, as criticized by Lucas [13] and Sargent [14]. Critiques argue that due to the economic agent's decision-making dynamics, a structural model developed in one policy regime is unlikely to be valid under a new policy regime. Such a conclusion is drawn in the rational expectations framework, in which market participants take policy regime into account to form their economic behaviours. Therefore, modern mainstream macroeconomics framework incorporates rational expectations hypothesis into its empirical model. Early applications of DSGE models have witnessed the wide use of calibration approach in model identification, as it links observed data and model parameters; see, for example Kydland and Prescott [2] and Shoven and Whalley [15]. But the intensive reliance on researcher's subjectivity and the lack of mathematical inference limit the accuracy of the calibrated model, since it does not fully utilize information carried by data samples. Thanks to the development of mathematical techniques and the accumulation of understanding of the dynamic rational expectations system, estimation methods have been dominantly used in recent years. Scholars have proposed several estimation methodologies, such as the Maximum Likelihood Method (ML, including Quasi-Maximum Likelihood Estimator, QMLE),[4] Generalized Method of Moments (GMM),[5] Simulated Method of Moments (SMM)[6] and finally the Bayesian estimation method. The latter has become the most popular estimation methodology in DSGE modelling literature. As we have shown in the chapters of the theoretical framework, the Bayesian estimation method is currently adopted by most of the researchers using DSGE models. Therefore, we

[4] For more details of the mathematics behind ML and QMLE methods, one can find them in the work conducted by Fisher [16], who is among the pioneer advocates of the ML methods in econometrics; and White [17], who analyses the consequences and detection of model misspecification in the studies using ML and QMLE approaches.

[5] Galí and Gertler [18] make a very influential analysis using the GMM method. In this paper, they use data of the period 1960:Q1–1997:Q4 to estimate the structural parameter θ in the Phillips curve via GMM methods. Another important DSGE paper using the GMM method is the work of Galí et al. [19]. In this work, based on data of the time period from 1970 to 1998, a DSGE model with parameter values determined by GMM method is developed. It provides evidence that supports empirically a New Phillips Curve (NPC) for the Euro area.

[6] The SMM method can be viewed as an extension of the original GMM method in that it substitutes the response probabilities of the GMM method with estimators given by the Monte Carlo simulation. In McFadden's work [20], the mathematical framework of the SMM method is thoroughly discussed.

discuss it, which is also adopted in this book, in more details in this subsection. As summarized by An and Schorfheide [21], the Bayesian estimation approach outstands other estimation methods in at least three aspects. Firstly, the Bayesian method is based on the model system, which contains both steady-state and dynamic relationships, rather than merely the equilibrium relationships as in the GMM estimation method. Its fitting process is conducted in the solved DSGE model to a vector of aggregate time series. Secondly, the Bayesian estimation uses maximum likelihood function generated by the DSGE model itself rather than the discrepancy of impulse response between the DSGE and the VAR model, as in the minimum distance estimation method, which is based on the discrepancy of a traditional model and the target DSGE model. Finally, the Bayesian estimation allows us to make prior assumptions of parameter distribution, bringing in additional information on parameter estimation.

Just as we cited at the beginning of this subsection, Bayes' Theorem[7] is at the heart of probability theory. Thus, before we move further to the applications of Bayesian estimation method in the DSGE models, we need to start from the Bayes theorem, which is the fundamental of many estimation methodologies. Theoretically, all Bayesian estimation approaches are based on the Bayes' Theorem, which can be demonstrated by the equation:

$$\frac{E \bigcap H}{N} = \frac{E \bigcap H}{X} \times \frac{X}{N} = \frac{E \bigcap H}{H} \times \frac{H}{N} \tag{10.6}$$

in which N is the overall population universe, $E \bigcap H$ is the number of joint occurrences of E and H. This equation can be transformed into:

$$P(E \bigcap H) = P((E \bigcap H)|E)P(E) = P((E \bigcap H)|H)P(H) \tag{10.7}$$

Equation 10.7 is one of the standard expressions of Bayes' Theorem. It can be rewritten as:

$$P(H|E)P(E) = P((E|H)P(H) \tag{10.8}$$

If we further rearrange the equation, we can get

$$P(H|E) = \frac{P((E|H)P(H)}{P(E)} \tag{10.9}$$

[7] For more details of Bayes' Theorem and its wide applications, see the summary demonstrated by Vapnik [22].

The most fascinating feature of Bayes' Theorem as expressed in Eq. 10.9 is that it builds connections between the prior probability and the posterior probability. It indicates that the posterior probability of H, i.e. the probability of H given the fact that E occurs, $P(H|E)$ is equal to the chances of observing E if H occurs, i.e. the prior probability $P(E|H)$, times the probability of H, i.e. the prior probability $P(H)$ divided by the probability of E, i.e. the prior probability $P(E)$. This relationship provides us with the possible way to calculate the posterior possibility $P(H|E)$ by using the prior probabilities ($P(E|H)$, $P(H)$ and $P(E)$). Keeping this idea in mind, we are able to start the iteration to get the posterior probability based on an initial prior probabilities. Generally, the initial prior probabilities are assumed using the existing body of knowledge. This iteration process goes on as more data are accumulated to expand this knowledge for future research.

The application of the Bayesian estimation method in the DSGE feature models is straightforward. If the logarithm likelihood function is:

$$\ln L(\theta|Y_T^*) \tag{10.10}$$

where $L(\theta|Y_T^*)$ is the likelihood function based on the sample data. Then, we get $Y_T^* = y_t^*, t = 1, 2, \ldots, T$, with T as the sample size. All the parameters in the DSGE feature equations are assumed to be stochastic variables in the Bayesian estimation method. As a result, parameter θ is a stochastic variable with the prior probability function, $p(\theta)$. According to the Bayes' Theorem, the posterior probability function of parameter θ can be drawn as

$$p(\theta|Y_T^*) = \frac{L(\theta|Y_T^*)p(\theta)}{p(Y_T^*)} \tag{10.11}$$

The logarithm expression of Eq. 10.11 is:

$$\ln p(\theta|Y_T^*) = \ln L(\theta|Y_T^*) + \ln p(\theta) - \ln p(Y_T^*) \tag{10.12}$$

Here, $p(Y_T^*)$ is the marginal density function that is independent of parameter θ. This marginal density function can be formulated as

$$p(\theta|Y_T^*) = \int [L(\theta|Y_T^*)p(\theta)]d\theta \tag{10.13}$$

Therefore, the point estimation of parameter θ is

$$\hat{\theta} = argmin_{\hat{\theta}} \int C(\hat{\theta}, \theta)p(\theta|Y_T^*)d\theta \tag{10.14}$$

As we are going to use Dynare 4.4.3 to conduct DSGE modelling and the related analysis, the brief description of estimation in Dynare is displayed to better understand the nature of estimation in DSGE modelling. In general, Dynare estimates the unknown parameters of a model based on a linear approximation of the model, such as:

$$E_t(f(y_{t+1}, y_t, y_{t-1}, u_t; \theta)) = 0 \tag{10.15}$$

Dynare uses Kalman Filter (KF)[8] to find the likelihood. One thing that needs to be noted is that there is a very important requirement (sufficient condition) of using Kalman Filter in Dynare: the number of observed variables must be less than the number of shocks.[9] A standard Kalman Filter process can be briefly summarized in the following five equations:

$$x(t|t-1) = Ax(t-1|t-1) + Bu(t) \tag{10.16}$$

$$P(t|t-1) = AP(t-1|t-1)A' + Q \tag{10.17}$$

$$x(t|t) = x(t|t-1) + kg(t)(z(t) - Hx(t|t-1)) \tag{10.18}$$

$$kg(t) = \frac{P(t|t-1)H'}{HP(t|t-1)H' + R} \tag{10.19}$$

$$P(t|t) = (1 - kg(t)H)P(t|t-1) \tag{10.20}$$

In this process, we suppose the system is linear and its equation is:

$$x_t = Ax_{t-1} + Bu_t + w_t \tag{10.21}$$

x_t is the $n \times 1$ state vector of this system, and A represents the transition matrix, which is $n \times n$. The input of this system is captured by u (a $k \times 1$ vector), and B (a $n \times k$ matrix) depicts the transformation process from system input into system state. Finally, w is the system noise.

The observation z_t is the mapping (captured by matrix H) of system state, x_t, with the observation error, v_t:

$$z_t = Hx_t + v_t \tag{10.22}$$

[8] For more details of the Kalman Filter and its application, see the works conducted by Harvey [23], Swerling [24] and Kalman [25].

[9] For more details, see the discussion of Blanchard–Kahn condition in the previous chapter.

In Kalman Filter, we further suppose that the system noise w_t and the observation error v_t are independent multi-Gaussian distributions, thus:

$$p(w) \sim N(0, Q) \tag{10.23}$$

$$p(v) \sim N(0, R) \tag{10.24}$$

where Q and R represent the covariance matrix of system noise and observation error respectively. Therefore, the weighted average of the prior prediction and observation using Kalman weight, Kg_t, is:

$$\widehat{x_t} = \widehat{x_t}' + Kg_t(z_t - \widehat{z_t}) = \widehat{x_t}' + Kg_t(z_t - H\widehat{x_t}') \tag{10.25}$$

Based on the Kalman filtering mechanism, Dynare can deliver the Bayesian estimation of unknown parameters following the procedures as follows:

1. Computing the steady state
2. Linearizing the model
3. Solving the linearized model
4. Computing the log-likelihood via the Kalman Filter
5. Finding the maximum of the likelihood of posterior mode
6. Simulates posterior distribution with Metropolis–Hastings algorithm.

The first three steps have been discussed in the previous chapter, here we demonstrate how to develop Kalman filtering equations and the corresponding likelihood function. The solution to a DSGE model is represented in Eqs. 9.24 and 9.25, which are state transition equation and observation equation respectively. As shown in Eq. 10.11, the posterior distribution is proportional to the product of the likelihood function, $L(Y|\theta)$, and the prior probability of the parameters, $P(\theta)$: $P(\theta|Y) \propto L(Y|\theta)P(\theta)$. Then, Kalman filtering equations yield

$$\begin{aligned} &\mathbb{E}[y_t | y_{t-1}, y_{t-2}, \ldots, x_0] \\ &y_t - \mathbb{E}[y_t | y_{t-1}, y_{t-2}, \ldots, x_0] \sim N(0, I) \end{aligned} \tag{10.26}$$

That is to say, the prediction error, which is the difference between the observed data and the expected value, follows the normal distribution with zero mean. Therefore, given the prediction error and the observed data sample $(y_1, y_2, \ldots, y_t) \in Y_t$, the likelihood can be calculated. According to Bayes' Theorem, the posterior distribution of parameters θ given the observed data Y_t is

$$P(\theta|Y_t) = \frac{P(Y_t|\theta)P(\theta)}{\int P(Y_t|\theta)P(\theta)d\theta} \tag{10.27}$$

As shown above, the application of Bayesian estimation method needs to simulate the posterior distribution. To generate such simulation, we adopt Markov Chain Monte Carlo (MCMC) approach. The basic idea of MCMC is to utilize a simple heuristic process (combined with Kalman filtering functions) to generate a Markov Chain of parameters, θ, the distribution of which converges to $P(\theta|Y_t)$. The solution to a DSGE model can be represented by the law of motion, which contains the transition function and measurement function:

$$s_t = \Phi(s_{t-1}, \varepsilon_t; \theta) \tag{10.28}$$

$$y_t = \Psi(s_t, \upsilon_t; \theta) \tag{10.29}$$

Substituting Eq. 10.28 into Eq. 10.29, we get

$$y_t = \Psi(\Phi(s_{t-1}, \varepsilon_t; \theta), \upsilon_t; \theta) \tag{10.30}$$

Therefore, based on Eq. 10.28, we can calculate the probability of state s_t, $P(s_t|s_{t-1}, \theta)$, given s_{t-1} and parameters θ; using Eq. 10.29, we can calculate the probability of observation y_t, $P(y_t|y_{t-1}, \theta)$, given y_{t-1} and θ; and from Eq. 10.30, we can compute the probability of y_t, $P(y_t|s_{t-1}, \theta)$, given s_{t-1} and θ. That is to say, Bayes' Theorem, together with state-space representation of the DSGE model, gives us the ability to update our prior guess, $P(\theta)$, through data sample, Y_t, to compute the likelihood function, $P(Y_t|\theta)$, and thus the posterior distribution, $P(\theta|Y_t)$ (because $P(\theta|Y_t) \propto L(Y_t|\theta)P(\theta)$). More mathematically, $P(Y_t|\theta)$ is derived using the Markov structure as:

$$\begin{aligned} P(Y_t|\theta) &= P(y_1|\theta)\prod_{2}^{t} P(y_t|Y_{t-1}, \theta) \\ &= \int P(y_1|s_1, \theta)ds_1 \prod_{2}^{t} \int P(y_t|s_t, \theta)P(s_t|Y_{t-1}, \theta)ds_t \end{aligned} \tag{10.31}$$

To find $\int P(y_1|s_1,\theta)ds_1 \prod_2^t \int P(y_t|s_t,\theta)P(s_t|Y_{t-1},\theta)ds_t$ in Eq. 10.31 via filtering mechanism, we need Bayes' Theorem which yields

$$P(s_t|Y_t,\theta) = \frac{P(s_t|y_t,\theta)P(y_t|Y_{t-1},\theta)}{\int P(y_t|s_t,\theta)P(s_t|Y_{t-1},\theta)ds_t} \tag{10.32}$$

This is the updating rule. We also need the forecasting rule given by the Chapman–Kolmogorov equation:

$$P(s_{t+1}|Y_t,\theta) = \int P(s_{t+1}|s_t,\theta)P(s_t|Y_{t-1},\theta)ds_t \tag{10.33}$$

Equation 10.31 tells us that if we know the complete sequence of conditional probabilities at each point, $\{P(s_1|\theta), P(s_2|Y_1,\theta), P(s_3|Y_2,\theta), \ldots, P(s_t|Y_{t-1},\theta)\}$, we are able to evaluate the likelihood function $P(Y_t|\theta)$ that we are interested in. More specifically, at point t, it is possible to update the states distribution $P(s_t|Y_{t-1},\theta)$ with the new observation y_t's probability of $P(y_t|s_t,\theta)$ to get $P(s_t|Y_t,\theta)$, using Eq. 10.32. Then we can use the forecasting rule shown in Eq. 10.33 to compute the distribution of states in the next point, $t+1$. By repeating such updating and forecasting process via all the observations Y_t, we can draw the complete sequence of $\{P(s_1|\theta), P(s_2|Y_1,\theta), P(s_3|Y_2,\theta), \ldots, P(s_t|Y_{t-1},\theta)\}$.

With the result of using the Bayes' Theorem, we can compute the likelihood $P(Y_t|\theta)$ and then the posterior distribution $P(\theta|Y_t)$. This process is intuitive and straightforward as shown in Eqs. 10.31, 10.32 and 10.33. But to fulfil this process in empirical analysis is challenging since numerical integral is involved. Therefore, we need a further mathematical technique to overcome this computational problem. In this case, we use the Metropolis–Hastings algorithm[10] and the Markov Chain Monte Carlo (MCMC)[11] methods. Although the details of the application of this algorithm may be very complex and extremely mathematical, the principles of this method is straightforward: if the distribution of $P(s_t|Y_{t-1},\theta)$ is too complex to compute as in most of DSGE models, we can substitute it by

[10] Due to the limited space, we can not provide a full discussion of all the details of Metropolis–Hastings algorithm; more details can be found in the works of Roberts et al. [26] and Chib and Greenberg [27].

[11] For simplicity, some of the details of the MCMC have been omitted in this thesis; otherwise they would require hundreds of pages. Chib and Greenberg [27] and Gasparini [28] give us a wider reach in MCMC methods with greater details.

an empirical distribution of N random draws $\{s^i_{t|t-1}\}^N_{i=1}$ from a simulated sample $P(s_t|Y_{t-1}, \theta)$, which is artificially generated using the Markov Chain Monte Carlo method. Thanks to the law of large numbers, we know that as long as it is randomly drawn the distribution of $\{s^i_{t|t-1}\}^N_{i=1}$ converges to the distribution of $P(s_t|Y_{t-1}, \theta)$ as N increases. Therefore, we can write Eq. 10.31 as

$$P(Y_t|\theta) \simeq \frac{1}{N}\sum_1^N P(y_1|s^i_0, \theta)\prod_2^t \frac{1}{N}\sum_1^N P(y_t|s^i_{t|t-1}, \theta) \quad (10.34)$$

which tells us that at each point t, $P(Y_t|\theta)$ can be calculated by sampling, and then move on to the next point $t+1$ via filtering and forecasting. Going through all the observed data sample $(y_1, y_2, \ldots, y_t) \in Y_t$, we can evaluate the likelihood function $P(Y_t|\theta)$ and the posterior distribution $P(\theta|Y_t) \propto L(Y_t|\theta)P(\theta)$ such as their mean, standard deviation and other moments. This is the case when the values of the parameters are given as θ. If we change the values of these parameters (here, we assume M sets of values for parameters, $\hat{\theta}_j$, $j = 1, 2, \ldots, M$.), a series of posterior distribution of $\{P(\hat{\theta}_j|Y_t)\}^M_{j=1}$ can be identified.

Therefore, the full sequence of posterior distribution $\{P(\hat{\theta}_j|Y_t)\}^M_{j=1}$ is depicted in two dimensions: firstly, the dimension of time in observations from 1 to t; secondly, the dimension of values of θ, $\hat{\theta}_j$, $j = 1, 2, \ldots, M$. On one hand, given each $\hat{\theta}_j$, Eq. 10.34 produces the value of likelihood in t, and that in $t + 1$ using a filtering function and sampling. The result of this process is summarized in $P(\hat{\theta}_j|Y_t)$. On the other hand, the process to generate the full series of posterior distribution of $\{P(\hat{\theta}_j|Y_t)\}^M_{j=1}$ according to the prior distribution of the values of parameters, $P(\theta)$, is conducted using Metropolis–Hastings algorithm. This algorithm can be conceived as a procedure to evaluate the posterior distribution after assigning a new set of values for parameters. It goes in this way: if the new set of values enhances the posterior probability $P(\hat{\theta}_j|Y_t)$, it is accepted as one, and if it does not, a probability with positive value less than one is assigned to it. By doing so, we travel towards the direction of higher level of posterior probability instead of being trapped in local maxima. The standard procedure of Metropolis–Hastings algorithm is:

1. Initialization step: set θ_j with its initial value θ_0 and $j = 0$. Given this initial value, we compute the posterior probability, $P(\theta_0|Y_t)$, using the process we discussed previously. $j++$
2. Drawing according to the assumption of prior distribution of parameters: make a draw, $\hat{\theta}_j$, from the prior distribution of parameters $P(\theta)$ with a proposal density $den(\theta_{j-1}, \hat{\theta}_j)$.
3. Solving the model: compute the likelihood, $P(Y_t|\theta_j)$ according to 10.34, and get the posterior probability, $P(\theta_j|Y_t)$, using $P(\theta|Y_t) \propto L(Y_t|\theta)P(\theta)$.
4. Assigning a value (1 or less than 1): draw χ_j from a uniform distribution $U(0, 1)$. If $\chi_j \leq \frac{P(Y_t|\hat{\theta}_j)P\theta den(\theta_{j-1},\hat{\theta}_j)}{P(Y_t|\hat{\theta}_j)P\theta den(\hat{\theta}_j,\theta_{j-1})}$ set $\theta_j = \hat{\theta}_j$, if not set $\theta_j = \theta_{j-1}$.
5. Iteration: for all $j < M$, $j++$ and go to step 2 until $j = M$, when this process terminates with the posterior distribution of $P(\theta|Y_t)$.

In conclusion, estimation methods based on Bayes' Theorem give us a very powerful mechanism to fully utilize the information of the observed data sample,[12] regardless of the sample size, and the prior knowledge we have beyond these data sample. To practically fulfil this mechanism, we use MCMC methods and Metropolis–Hastings algorithm to evaluate the posterior distribution of $P(\theta|Y_t)$, based on sampling. Luckily, the law of large number guarantees us that if the number of draws we do in random sampling is sufficiently large, we can compute the approximate posterior distribution of $P(\theta|Y_t)$ with good accuracy, as the distribution of draws converges to the actual posterior distribution, $P(\theta|Y_t)$. Using this conclusion, we can evaluate the numerical features of objects we are interested in. For example, if the object of our interest is $g(\theta)$, and the number of draws of parameter θ is M, its expected value, $\mathbb{E}(g(\theta))$, can be computed using the following equation:

$$\mathbb{E}(g(\theta)) = \frac{\int g(\theta)P(\theta|Y_t)d\theta}{P(\theta|Y_t)d\theta} = \frac{\frac{1}{M}\sum_{j=1}^{M} g(\theta_j)P(\theta_j|Y_t)}{\frac{1}{M}\sum_{j=1}^{M} P(\theta_j|Y_t)} \tag{10.35}$$

[12] In the work of Zellner [29], Bayes' Theorem is considered as the optimal information processing rule since it makes full use of all the information embodied in the data in a very effective way, and it adds no extraneous information. For a more complete discussion of Bayesian theory, see Bernardo and Smith's contribution [30].

10.2 Software Tools

In this section, we discuss the software packages used in our empirical analysis. The basic principle of choosing appropriate software packages in our macroeconomic analysis is the strong ability of numerical and scientific calculations, especially matrix calculations, and convertibility to multiple models. Additionally, we also require advanced interface of graphic and numerical output demonstration. The programming of our model on the desired software platform should be simple and straightforward, making reading and revising more applicable. What is more, the software package we are going to use must have the ability to process large scale data samples on complicated models with multiple variables, as our FHSAM contains a variety of economic variables.

MATLAB[13] is one of the most important and popular mathematical tools in both academia and industry, as millions of researchers and engineers use it in a wide range of cases. We adopt it as the major mathematical analysis package because of its advantages in matrix calculations, which are a core part of our macroeconomic analysis. MATLAB also provides us with a powerful ability of scientific calculation and data analysis, wide range of applications with specialized functionality, multiple choices of visualized outcomes and a simplified coding process. The version we used in our analysis is MATLAB R2018a.

Along with the development of the influence and popularity of DSGE models in macroeconomic analysis, researchers need a specialized MATLAB analysis package. This need gave rise to the birth of Dynare.[14] Dynare is a MATLAB platform first developed by Michel Julilard in Paris, France, and it is now developed by the team of Dynare. Dynare has been widely adopted in modern macroeconomics analysis as it provides a software platform for a wide range of economic models. Dynare is user-friendly as well. Researchers can perform simulations with the Dynare model based on a calibration of the model parameters. Or, they can estimate these parameters using an existing dataset. The coding of Dynare is simple and straightforward. Analysts only need to input the list of model variables and the equations of the model to construct the Dynare coding file. The desired

[13] For a full description of MATLAB, see the official website of Mathworks at http://uk.mathworks.com/products/matlab/index.html?s_tid=gn_loc_drop.

[14] The full description of Dynare is available at http://www.dynare.org.

graphic and numerical outputs of the model can be instructed by analysts as well.

Based on these advantages, Dynare is now widely used in policy analysis and forecasting exercises not only by public bodies such as central banks, ministries of economy and finance, and international organizations, but also by certain private institutions. Dynare also gains its popularity in the academic world, as it is the research and teaching tool in many universities. In the previous sections, we have shown many examples of macroeconomic analyses with DSGE models, and most of these works are undertaken by using Dynare. Therefore, it is not a hard choice for us to adopt MATLAB Dynare as our major mathematical analysis software package in this thesis; the version adopted is Dynare 4.5.5.[15]

Besides MATLAB Dynare 4.5.5, we also use Origin 9.0[16] and EVIEWS 7.0[17] to undertake statistical analysis and graphing.

Appendix

A typical Dynare model contains the following parts: a list of variables, the equations, the instructions of computing, and the output control commands.

Here we demonstrate the simplest model with only two endogenous variables: y, the aggregate output gap, and c, the aggregate consumption. This simplest model can be expressed by the following equations:

$$y_t = \alpha E_t y_{t+1} + c_t \tag{10.36}$$

$$c_t = \beta c_{t-1} + \varepsilon_t,\ \varepsilon_t \sim iid(0, \sigma^2),\ |\beta| < 1 \tag{10.37}$$

It is obvious that the aggregate output gap is a forward-looking variable, determined by the expected output gap and the current level of aggregate consumption; while aggregate consumption is a backward-looking variable affected by the consumption in the last period and the random shock, which is denoted by a normalized random shock ε_t.

[15] In order to better demonstrate the application of MATLAB Dynare, we demonstrate the full Dynare code for a simple DSGE model in Appendix.

[16] Interested readers may refer to http://www.originlab.com/.

[17] Interested readers may refer to http://www.eviews.com/home.html.

By using iterated law of expectation, under transversality condition $\lim_{i\to\infty} E_t y_{t+i} = 0$, we can transfer these equations into:

$$y_t = \beta y_{t-1} + \frac{1}{1-\alpha\beta}\varepsilon_t \tag{10.38}$$

$$c_t = \beta c_{t-1} + \varepsilon_t \tag{10.39}$$

In matrix representation:

$$\begin{pmatrix} y_t \\ c_t \end{pmatrix} = \beta \begin{pmatrix} y_{t-1} \\ c_{t-1} \end{pmatrix} + \varepsilon_t \begin{pmatrix} \frac{1}{1-\alpha\beta} \\ 1 \end{pmatrix} \tag{10.40}$$

The code we need to write in a Dynare command file to construct this model is straightforward:

```
var y c;
varexo e;

parameters alpha beta;
alpha=0.5;
beta=0.5;

model(linear);
y=alpha*y(+1)+c;
c=beta*c(-1)+e;
end;

initval;
y=0;
c=5;
end;

steady;
check;
resid;

shocks;
var e; stderr 0.01;

stoch_ simul(periods=2100, order=1, irf=50, drop=400, aim_solver) y c;
```

References

1. Canova, F. (1994). Statistical inference in calibrated models. *Journal of Applied Econometrics, 9*(1), 123 141.
2. Kydland, F. E., & Prescott, E. C. (1982). Time to build and aggregate fluctuations. *Econometrica, 50*(6), 1345–1370.
3. Christiano, L. J., & Eichenbaum, M. (1992). Current real-business-cycle theories and aggregate labor-market fluctuations. *The American Economic Review, 82*(3), 430–450.
4. Rotemberg, J., & Woodford, M. (1997). An optimization-based econometric framework for the evaluation of monetary policy. *NBER Macroeconomics Annual, 12*, 297–361.
5. Christiano, L. J., Eichenbaum, M., & Evans, C. L. (2005). Nominal rigidities and the dynamic effects of a shock to monetary policy. *Journal of Political Economy, 113*(1), 1–45.
6. Leeper, E. M., & Sims, C. A. (1994). Toward a modern macroeconomic model usable for policy analysis. *NBER Macroeconomics Annual, 9*, 81–118.
7. Kim, J. (2000). Constructing and estimating a realistic optimizing model of monetary policy. *Journal of Monetary Economics, 45*(2), 329–359.
8. Fernĺndez-Villaverde, J. (2010). The econometrics of DSGE models. *Journal of the Spanish Economic Association, 1*(2), 3–49.
9. Canova, F., & Ortega, E. (2000). *Testing calibrated general equilibrium models* (Universitat Pompeu Fabra Economics Working Papers), 166.
10. Haavelmo, T. (1944). *The probability approach in econometrics.* Chicago: University of Chicago Press.
11. Iacoviello, M., & Neri, S. (2010). Housing market spillovers: Evidence from an estimated DSGE model. *American Economic Journal: Macroeconomics, 2*(2), 125–164.
12. Jeffreys, H. (1973). *Scientific inference.* Cambridge: Cambridge University Press.
13. Lucas, R. E. (1976). Econometric policy evaluation: A critique. In D. V. Pritchett (Ed.), *Carnegie-Rochester Conference Series on Public Policy* (pp. 19–46). Amsterdam: Elsevier.
14. Lucas, R. E., & Sargent, T. J. (1981). *Rational expectations and econometric practice.* Minneapolis: University of Minnesota Press.
15. Shoven, J. B. & Whalley, J. (1984). Applied general-equilibrium models of taxation and international trade: An introduction and survey. *Journal of Economic Literature, 22*(3), 1007–1051.
16. Fisher, R. A. (1992). *On the mathematical foundations of theoretical statistics.* New York: Springer.
17. White, H. (1982). Maximum likelihood estimation of misspecified models. *Econometrica, 50*(1), 1–25.

18. Galí, J., & Gertler, M. (1999). Inflation dynamics: A structural econometric analysis. *Journal of Monetary Economics, 44*(2), 195–222.
19. Galí, J., Gertler, M., & Lopez-Salido, J. D. (2001). European inflation dynamics. *European Economic Review, 45*(7), 1237–1270.
20. McFadden, D. (1989). A method of simulated moments for estimation of discrete response models without numerical integration. *Econometrica, 57*(5), 995–1026.
21. An, S., & Schorfheide, F. (2007). Bayesian analysis of DSGE models. *Econometric Reviews, 26*(2), 113–172.
22. Vapnik, V. (2013). *The nature of statistical learning theory*. New York: Springer.
23. Harvey, A. C. (1990). *Forecasting, structural time series models and the Kalman filter*. Cambridge: Cambridge University Press.
24. Swerling, P. (1958). *A proposed stagewise differential correction procedure for satellite tracking and prediciton*. Santa Monica: Rand Corporation.
25. Kalman, R. E. (1960). A new approach to linear filtering and prediction problems. *Journal of Basic Engineering and Transactions, 82*(1), 35–45.
26. Roberts, G. O., Gelman, A., & Gilks, W. (1997). Weak convergence and optimal scaling of random walk metropolis algorithms. *The Annals of Applied Probability, 7*(1), 110–120.
27. Chib, S., & Greenberg, E. (1995). Understanding the Metropolis-Hastings algorithm. *The American Statistician, 49*(4), 327–335.
28. Gasparini, M. (1995). Markov Chain Monte Carlo in practice. *Technometrics, 39*(3), 338–339.
29. Zellner, A. (1988). Optimal information processing and Bayes's theorem. *The American Statistician, 42*(4), 278–280.
30. Bernardo, J. M., & Smith, A. F. (2001). *Bayesian theory*. London: Institute of Physics Publishing.

CHAPTER 11

Data, Statistics and Stylized Facts

11.1 Data

As discussed in Chapter 2, the target economies that our research mainly analyses are 'BIC' (Brazil, India and China) out of the five 'BRICS' countries. We thereby focus on the statistics and stylized facts of the 'BIC' countries.

In the previous part, we build our macroeconomic model—FHSAM, with special emphasis on the financial market, the housing market, and household heterogeneities. In this chapter, we try to collect the corresponding time series from a variety of sources. Data collection is one of the major challenges for research in emerging market economies, where statistics are limited in terms of length and quality. In order to solve this challenge, we collect data from not only official statistics of institutes such as the National Bureau of Statistics in China,[1] India's National Data Bank of the Ministry of Statistics and Programme Implementation,[2] and the Brazilian Institute of Geography and Statistics,[3] but also international institutes like the World Bank,[4] the OECD, [5] and the IMF.[6] We also refer to commercial

[1] Available at: http://data.stats.gov.cn/english/easyquery.htm?cn=B01.

[2] Available at: http://www.mospi.nic.in/national-data-bank.

[3] Available at: https://downloads.ibge.gov.br/downloads-estatisticas.htm.

[4] http://databank.worldbank.org/data.

[5] https://stats.oecd.org/index.aspx?queryid=350.

[6] Available at: http://www.imf.org/en/data.

D. L. Jia, *Dynamic Macroeconomic Models in Emerging Market Economies*,
https://doi.org/10.1007/978-981-15-4588-7_11

Table 11.1 Time series and model variables

Model variables	*Time series*	*Description*
$gdp_t = p_{h,t} I H_t + y_t - p_{b,t} k_{b,t}$	GDP	Log deviation, Quarterly
$c_t = c_{cw,t} + c_{rw,t} + c_{bh,t} + c_{lh,t}$	Consumption	Log deviation, Quarterly
$Inv_t = Ikc_t + Ikht$	Investment	Log deviation, Quarterly
$w_t = w_{cw,t} + w_{rw,t} + w_{bh,t} + w_{lh,t}$	Wage	Log deviation, Quarterly
π_t	Inflation	%, Quarterly
$p_{h,t}$	Housing prices	Log deviation, Quarterly
r_t^l	Interest rate	%, Quarterly

statistics providers such as the Wind,[7] CEIC,[8] and Bloomberg.[9] Table 11.1 summarizes the time series collected in BIC and the corresponding model variables.

11.2 Stylized Facts

A well-designed model should be able to explain the inner workings of the economy. Such explanatory power is typically measured by the consistence between empirical results and the economic realities. Therefore, we need to set up certain benchmarks to make relevant comparisons. To achieve this aim, we make a statistical summary of those observed data samples and draw the stylized facts supported by these data samples.

Before applying the collected data samples in the DSGE model, time series should be transformed into the forms of the model variables they represent. Therefore, aggregates, such as GDP, investment, and consumption, need to be mapped into per capita form. Therefore, those aggregate variables are divided by the corresponding quantity of population to get the per capita values. Additionally, these values are further transformed into their real terms using a simultaneous inflation rate.

In Fig. 11.1, we demonstrate the real per capita expression of GDP, household consumption, fixed asset investment (FAI), investment in the housing market (FAI-RE), investment in the non-housing market

[7] Available at: http://www.wind.com.cn/en/edb.html.

[8] Available at: https://insights.ceicdata.com.

[9] Available at: https://www.bloomberg.com/professional/product/market-data.

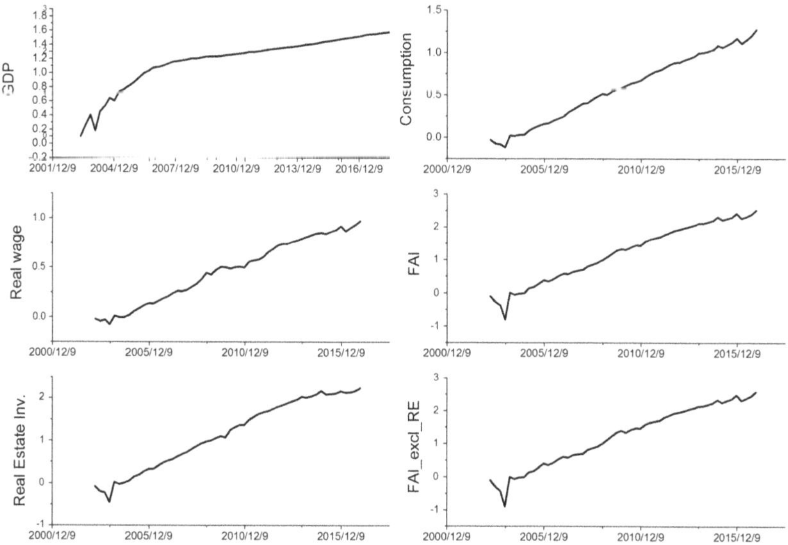

Fig. 11.1 Statistics in China: GDP, investment, consumption and working wage

(FAI-excl-RE) and working wage in China. These data are logarithm transformed and the first item is normalized to 1.

Following the same approach, we summarize the real per capita GDP, household consumption, fixed asset investment and real wage in Brazil and India, as shown in Figs. 11.2 and 11.3, respectively.

The statistics of price level including general price level, CPI and real housing price and interest rate in China, Brazil and India are also demonstrated in Figs. 11.4, 11.5, and 11.6, respectively. As in the majority of literature, these data have been demeaned using the Hodrick–Prescott Filter.[10]

To measure the consistence of our model with observed statistics, comparison between the model statistics and evidence drawn from the observed data samples. From the statistics demonstrated above, it is possible to draw certain important conclusions and stylized facts such as standard deviation of economic variables and the correlation between these variables. By

[10] For more details of Hodrick–Prescott Filter, see the works of Hodrick and Prescott [1], Cogley and Nason [2] and Ravn and Uhlig [3].

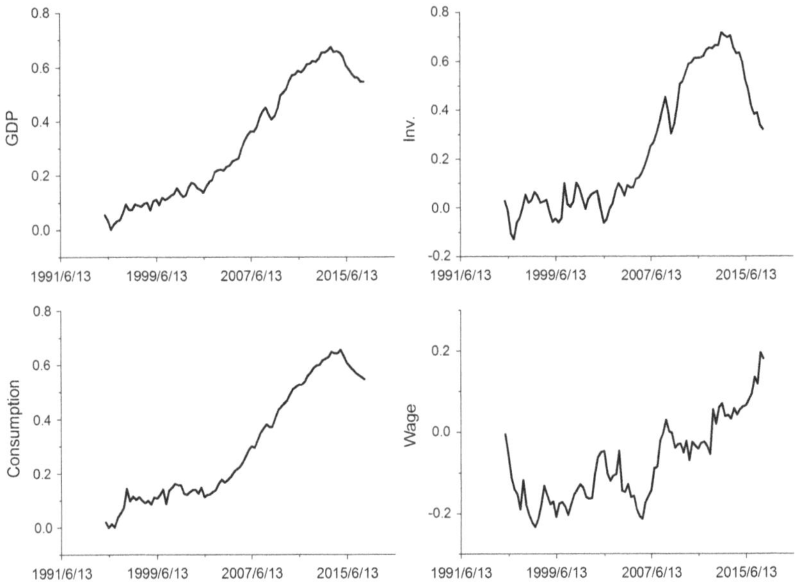

Fig. 11.2 Statistics in Brazil: GDP, investment, consumption and working wage

comparing these stylized facts with the model outputs, we can evaluate the consistency between FHSAM and reality, measuring the explanatory power. The standard deviations of real per capita GDP, real household consumption, real wages, fixed asset investment, inflation, interest rate and real housing prices in China, Brazil and India have been summarized in Table 11.2.

Similarly, we examine the correlations between economic variables drawn from the observed data samples in China, Brazil and India in Table 11.3. This table indicates a clear positive correlation between real household consumption and real GDP, 0.7389 in China, 0.6588 in India and 0.7201 in Brazil. Similarly, real fixed asset investment also moves in the same direction with real GDP. As a result, real consumption and fixed asset investment are positively correlated. These stylized facts are consistent with our theoretical hypothesis, as both real household consumption and fixed asset investment are the major components of aggregate output. Additionally, the real wage of households is also a procyclical variable with real GDP. In the theoretical part of this book, we analyse the economic correlation between real

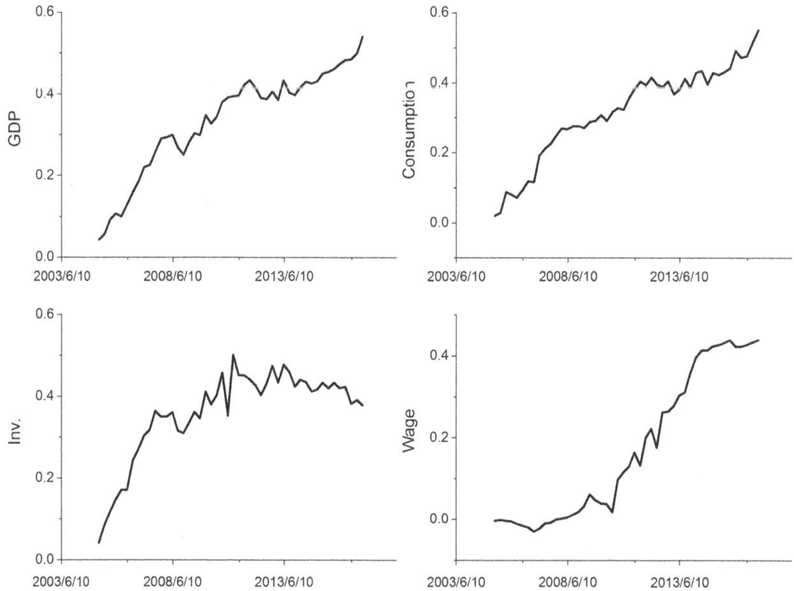

Fig. 11.3 Statistics in India: GDP, investment, consumption and working wage

housing price and aggregate output and conclude that they move in the same direction. This conclusion is supported by the empirical evidence in China, Brazil and India, as the positive correlation between real housing prices and real GDP in these three economies are 0.5624, 0.4993 and 0.5931, respectively. We also expect that larger volume of mortgage loans leads to higher level of housing demand and thus higher property prices. Moreover, the increase of real housing prices attracts more fixed asset investment. These positive correlations between real housing prices and mortgage loans[11] and between real housing prices and fixed asset investment are witnessed in China, Brazil and India. The positive correlation of

[11] In view of the limitation of the length on the exact quantity of mortgage loan in China, Brazil and India, we try to use the data of domestic credit provided by the financial sectors and aggregate banking credit as a proxy. This proximation may affect the accuracy of summarized correlation between the quantity of mortgage loans and other economic variables to a certain degree, as mortgage loans only represents part of total banking credit. But this effect is considered minor.

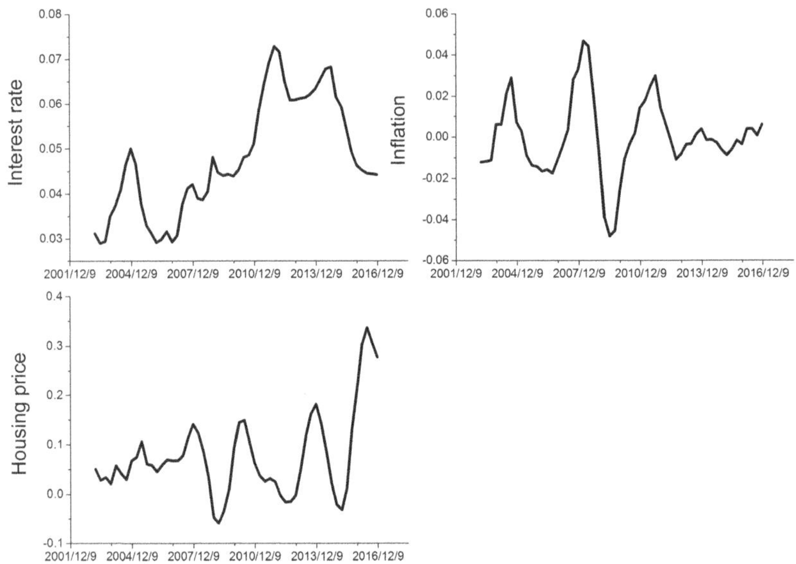

Fig. 11.4 Statistics in China: inflation, real housing price and real interest rate

inflation and real GDP is also confirmed by the stylized facts drawn from the observed data samples in these three economies. In conclusion, we find economic variables such as real household consumption, fixed asset investment, real housing prices, inflation and the volume of mortgage loans are procyclical variables to GDP.

So far, we summarize the stylized facts drawn from the observed data samples in China, India and Brazil. These stylized facts can help us to quantitatively evaluate the explanatory power of our model: the better agreement between the model outputs and the stylized facts, the higher explanatory power our model possesses. In the following chapter, we compare these statistical summaries of observed samples with the statistical features of model outputs to quantify the consistence of our model with the real-world economies.

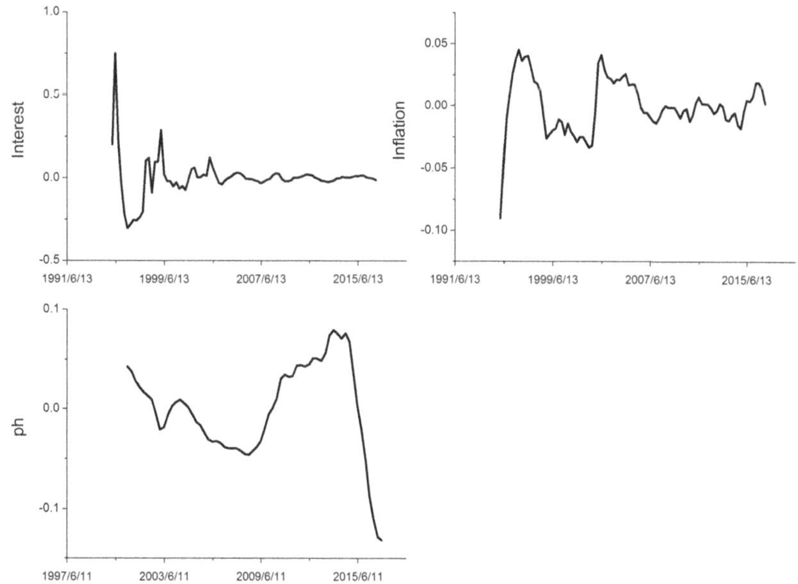

Fig. 11.5 Statistics in Brazil: inflation, real housing price and real interest rate

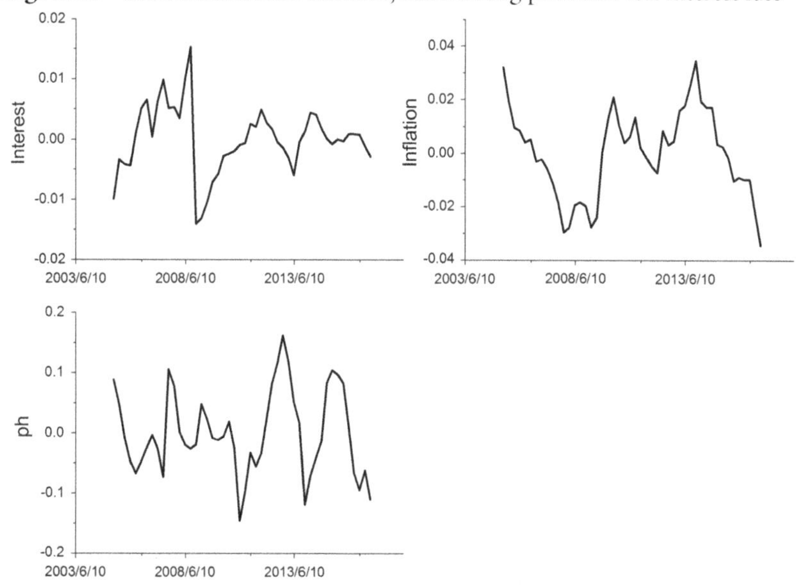

Fig. 11.6 Statistics in India: inflation, real housing price and real interest rate

Table 11.2 Stylized facts: standard deviations

Variables	*China*	*India*	*Brazil*
Consumption	0.017293	0.023951	0.021869
Inv.	0.045452	0.032922	0.051168
p_h	0.093910	0.066017	0.047502
π	0.018656	0.016518	0.013638
r	0.012772	0.015619	0.012246
GDP	0.030811	0.029240	0.029302
wage	0.033235	0.037720	0.040966

Table 11.3 Stylized facts: correlations

Variables	*China*	*India*	*Brazil*
c, GDP	0.7389	0.6588	0.7201
Inv., GDP	0.7234	0.7332	0.7474
p_h, GDP	0.5624	0.4993	0.5931
wage, GDP	0.6460	0.6263	0.6953
π, GDP	0.6413	0.6321	0.6682
p_h, c	0.4132	0.3964	0.4064
p_h, Llh	0.6263	0.5574	0.6012
c, Inv.	0.5994	0.5460	0.5377
p_h, Inv.	0.6332	0.5574	0.6012
Llh, GDP	0.7145	0.7193	0.7481

References

1. Hodrick, R. J., & Prescott, E. C. (1997). Postwar US business cycles: An empirical investigation. *Journal of Money, Credit, and Banking*, *29*, 1–16.
2. Cogley, T., & Nason, J. M. (1995). Effects of the Hodrick–Prescott filter on trend and difference stationary time series implications for business cycle research. *Journal of Economic Dynamics and Control*, *19*(1), 253–278.
3. Ravn, M. O., & Uhlig, H. (2002). On adjusting the Hodrick–Prescott filter for the frequency of observations. *The Review of Economics and Statistics*, *84*(2), 371–376.

CHAPTER 12

Empirical Analysis

12.1 Empirical Analysis of the Basic Model

In this section, we examine the empirical analysis of the basic model in the BIC countries, using the analytical methodologies and data sets, which we have discussed in the previous chapters. The major concern of this basic model is to install social stratification in the household sector in the model economy. In the household sector, households are grouped into two social classes, each with distinct economic features. Thus, the differences in economic conditions of these two groups of households and their diverse economic behavioural patterns give us a direct image of how social structure may contribute to the distinct welfare conditions and economic performance.

12.1.1 The Empirical Results

As we have discussed previously, in the model specification exercise, two methodologies have been developed to determine the values of model parameters. Because both of them have their own advantages and limitations,[1] modern DSGE modelling uses the combination of them to find

[1] Iacoviello and Neri [1] conclude that calibration methods are adopted when the values of parameters are 'either notoriously difficult to estimate or better identified using other information' (p. 13).

D. L. Jia, *Dynamic Macroeconomic Models in Emerging Market Economies*,
https://doi.org/10.1007/978-981-15-4588-7_12

Table 12.1 The calibration of parameters in the basic model

Parameter	*China*	*Brazil*	*India*
β_u	0.9925	0.9925	0.9925
β_r	0.9700	0.9700	0.9700
α	0.35	0.35	0.35
σ_u	1	1	1
σ_r	1	1	1
ξ_u	1	1	1
ξ_r	1	1	1
ν_u	0	0	0
ν_r	0	0	0
δ	0.025	0.025	0.025
f	0.65	0.65	0.65
Ψ_u	2.58	2.58	2.58
Ψ_r	2.00	2.00	2.00

the most convincing values for model parameters.[2] Following this principle, we fix certain parameters using calibration methods and estimate others using the Bayesian estimation method. Because our basic model contains two groups of households with different economic features, we try to identify the related parameters using a variety source of information. More specifically, the existing body of literature in DSGE modelling in emerging market economies only focuses on the standard households, which fall into the category of urban households in the basic model. Therefore, the parameters related to these households can be identified through calibration using useful information provided by the existing literature.[3] We use the Bayesian estimation method to determine the values of parameters such as household labour factors, Ψ_u and Ψ_u, and household's real money balance factors, γ_u and γ_r. The summary of the calibrated parameters and the estimated parameters can be seen in Tables 12.1 and 12.2, respectively.

We set urban household's discounting factor $\beta_u = 0.9925$. Based on Eq. 6.32, this implies that the steady-state annual real interest rate is 3%, which is the typical value of long-run average of the real interest rate in

[2] For example, factor shares and discount factors are typically calibrated using evidence suggested by the existing literature, while the household labour factors and preference factors are usually estimated using observed sample.

[3] For detailed information of how these parameters are determined, see the contributions of Bin [2, 3], Chen and Xu [4], Xi and He [5] and Luo and Wu [6].

Table 12.2 The estimation of parameters in the basic model: China

		Prior distribution		*Posterior distribution*		
Parameter	*Distr.*	*Mean*	*Std. Dev.*	*Mean*	5%	95%
ρ_z	Beta	0.95	0.10	0.9911	0.9845	0.9974
d	Beta	0.05	0.10	0.0016	0.0000	0.0035

emerging market economies. As discussed in the theoretical analysis, rural households evaluate the future utility using discounting factor, β_r, which is smaller than β_u, reflecting the fact that they do not possess physical capital assets. In our basic model, we thereby set $\beta_u > \beta_r = 0.9700$ for China, Brazil and India. This assumption is adopted in both advanced and full models.

The depreciation rate of physical capital is calibrated $\delta = 0.025$, indicating an annual rate of 10%, a typical general value economists summarize from historical economic statistics. This calibration is supported by the mainstream DSGE modelling exercises we discussed in the previous chapters. Since there is one type of physical capital in the basic model, only one capital depreciation rate is included. Moreover, the factor share of physical capital α in the Cobb–Douglas production function 6.10 is assumed to be 0.35, as suggested and justified by the majority of DSGE modelling literature.[4] Parameters Ψ_u and Ψ_r capture the degree of negative utility caused by sacrificing leisure time to work of urban and rural households. As we have discussed in the theoretical framework, rural households tend to work longer time per day as they have minor economic resources compared to their urban counterparts. Therefore, rural households show more willingness to sacrifice their leisure time to work (or put it in another way, show less aversion to work) than urban households do, implying a smaller

[4] More specifically, developed economies tend to have capital factor share in the range of 0.36–0.38, as shown in Bernanke et al. [7], Smets and Wouters [8], Christiano et al. [9], Iacoviello and Neri [1] and many others. Typically, these developed economies possess higher levels of physical capital and thus depend more on fixed assets than most of the emerging market economies do. Therefore, it is natural for DSGE economists to adopt a lower physical capital factor share in their models when analysing emerging market economies. For example, in Peiris et al. [10], Gabriel et al. [11], Bin [3] and many others, the capital factor share in production is within the region of 0.33–0.36. Therefore, we calibrate this physical capital factor share in our basic model as $\alpha = 0.35$.

value of $\Psi_r < \Psi_u$. In our model, we set $\Psi_r = 2.00$ and $\Psi_u = 2.58$ in that according to Eqs. 6.31 and 6.33, the steady- state rural and urban household working hours per day are 12 hours and 8 hours, respectively. This is consistent with the labour market analysis of emerging market economies including Brazil, India and China.[5]

We set $\sigma_u = 1$ and $\sigma_r = 1$, so that the first terms in Eqs. 6.1 and 6.2 are turned into their logarithm expression. Similarly, we assume $\xi_u = 1$, $\xi_r = 1$, $\nu_u = 0$ and $\nu_r = 0$. These specifications have been widely used in mainstream DSGE modelling literatures. In this basic model, the f parameter captures the urban household share in production. To better specify its value, it is required to find the long-term average value of the corresponding economic variable. In Iacoviello and Neri's work [1], the observed wage share has been used in their calibration exercise. Following this idea, we try to find statistical evidence to specify the value of f. Based on long-run economic statistics of wage share in different household groups and social classes, we set $f = 0.65$. This ratio well accords with the actual condition in China, as shown in Fig. 12.1.[6]

Besides these calibrated parameters, we also use the Bayesian estimation methods to specify the appropriate values for the basic model parameters in Brazil, India and China.[7] The prior mean of ρ_z is assumed to be 0.95, and the prior distribution is assumed to be beta distribution. We also estimate the persistence parameter d. As previously discussed, Bayesian estimation approaches give us more freedom in parameter identification, in that they allow us to make certain assumptions of the prior mean and prior distribution of the estimated parameters. Therefore, such model identification

[5] According to the statistics suggested by Messenger et al. [12], Clark [13], Spector et al. [14], Hu and Khan [15], Wong et al. [16] and many others, empirical evidence indicates that a large portion of workers, especially in construction and labour-concentrated manufacture industries, in emerging market economies like Brazil, India and China, work 10–14 hours per day. As a result, it is reasonable for us to assume $\Psi_r = 2.00$, implying that on average rural household work 12 hours per day.

[6] According to the statistics from OECD, World Bank and IMF, similar results can be witnessed in Brazil and India. Therefore, it is reasonable for us to set the urban household income share $f = 0.65$ in Brazil, India, and China accordingly, implying that urban households possess roughly two-thirds of total household income.

[7] More specifically, we use data samples of GDP to estimate the values of the parameters. For China, the data samples cover the time period of 2003Q1–2018Q4; for Brazil, the data samples cover the time period of 1995Q1–2018Q4; For India, the data sample cover the time period of 2005Q1–2018Q4.

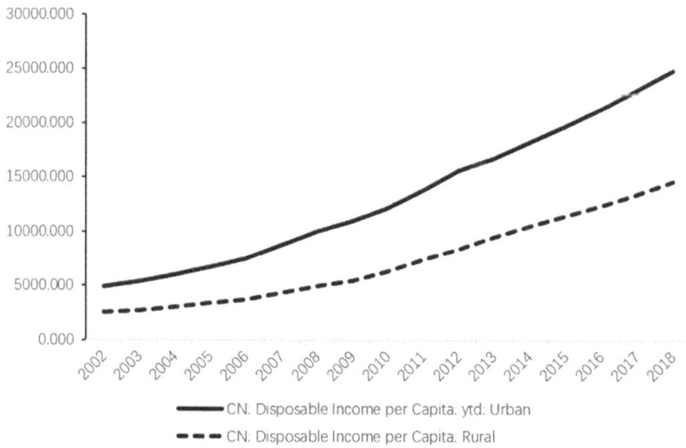

Fig. 12.1 Diverse income levels of urban and rural households in China

Table 12.3 The estimation of parameters in the basic model: Brazil

	Prior distribution			*Posterior distribution*		
Parameter	*Distr.*	*Mean*	*Std. Dev.*	*Mean*	5%	95%
ρ_z	Beta	0.95	0.10	0.9894	0.9842	0.9962
d	Beta	0.05	0.10	0.0007	0.0000	0.0023

exercise requires a combination of subjective and objective efforts. Previous literature and findings can give us much useful information of subjective prior assumption. In general, the prior distribution of persistence factors such as d and ρ_z in this basic model is assumed to be beta distribution, and the prior distribution of standard deviation of exogenous shocks is assumed to be inverse gamma distribution. In conclusion, we summarize the results of Bayesian estimation for ρ_z and d in China, Brazil and India in Tables 12.2, 12.3, and 12.4, respectively.

After model identification, we can further move on to analyse the dynamics of this basic model and to find out its dynamic properties and statistical features. Generally, these statistical features are mainly fitted into two categories: the standard deviations of model outputs and the correlations between major economic variables in the model economy. A good and robust economic model must possess statistical and dynamic properties

Table 12.4 The estimation of parameters in the basic model: India

	Prior distribution			Posterior distribution		
Parameter	*Distr.*	*Mean*	*Std. Dev.*	*Mean*	5%	95%
ρ_z	Beta	0.95	0.10	0.9941	0.9892	0.9980
d	Beta	0.05	0.10	0.0011	0.0000	0.0022

Table 12.5 The basic model statistical features: standard deviations

Stdev.	*Model output (data)*		
	China	*Brazil*	*India*
Consumption	0.007610 (0.017293)	0.006798 (0.023951)	0.006753 (0.021869)
Investment	0.014848 (0.045452)	0.013840 (0.032922)	0.011976 (0.051168)
Inflation	0.010786 (0.018656)	0.010732 (0.016518)	0.010742 (0.013638)
GDP	0.02200 (0.030811)	0.020399 (0.029240)	0.018365 (0.029302)
Real interest	0.000491 (0.012772)	0.000488 (0.015619)	0.000439 (0.012245)
Real wages	0.01762 (0.033231)	0.016233 (0.037720)	0.015676 (0.040966)

Table 12.6 The basic model statistical features: correlations

Correlations	*Model output (data)*		
	China	*Brazil*	*India*
Consum., GDP	0.9598 (0.7389)	0.9565 (0.7201)	0.9654 (0.6588)
Inv., GDP	0.9676 (0.7234)	0.9890 (0.7474)	0.9891 (0.7332)
Wage, GDP	0.9576 (0.6460)	0.9542 (0.6953)	0.9636 (0.6263)
Consum., Inv.	0.9078 (0.5994)	0.9265 (0.5377)	0.9166 (0.5460)

well consistent with those of the observations. To better demonstrate these statistical properties of the basic model, we summarize the standard deviations of model economy in Table 12.5 and the correlations in Table 12.6. In order to make clearer comparison of statistical features between model economy and the stylized facts, we put the corresponding standard deviations of observed samples in brackets in Tables 12.5 and 12.6. Although this basic two-layered model only contains several preliminary elements of our full model, it shows good performance in simulating economic fluctuations in China, Brazil and India. In the first table, it is shown that this basic two-layered model yields very promising results, compared with the observations in the corresponding economies summarized in Table 11.2. When applying this basic model in China, Brazil and India, we get good consistence between the model output standard deviation of GDP with the observed data samples in these countries. The standard deviations of inflation generated by applications of the basic model in China, Brazil and India are very close to those summarized in the stylized facts as well. The standard deviations of other economic variables in the model economy including consumption, wage, investment and interest rate are smaller than their observed values. Such limitations are consistent with our expectation in that the basic model only possesses a small part of economic features of the full model. This can be materially improved by adding more economic properties including household and production heterogeneities, short-term nominal rigidities, collateral effects and the financial market, as we are going to do in the advanced and the full models.

In Table 12.6, the correlations suggested by the basic model have been summarized. Both investment and consumption show strong correlations with the aggregate output (GDP). Additionally, consumption and investment are also highly correlated. Empirical analysis indicates that this basic model successfully depicts the positive correlations between consumption, investment and GDP. These model suggested correlations are higher than those we witnessed in data samples. This is so in that the basic model simplifies certain economic assumptions, and the accuracy of its performance can be improved by refining the structure of the model economy.

12.1.2 The Impulse Responses

In order to analyse the dynamics of the basic model, we carefully investigate the impulse responses of important economic variables to productivity shocks in China, Brazil and India. The theoretical framework hypothesizes that a positive productivity shock yields higher aggregate output, investment and consumption, pushing up the real wage of households. Increased income further contributes to the growth of household demand, stimulating investment in physical assets to meet such increased aggregate demand. Moreover, a higher level of investment pushes up the real interest rate. This feedback circle can persist for certain periods of time until the economy reaches its new equilibrium. During this process, it is expected that real aggregate output, investment and interest rates, after immediate rise in response to the positive productivity shock, gradually return to their equilibrium levels. In response to a positive productivity shock, households' real

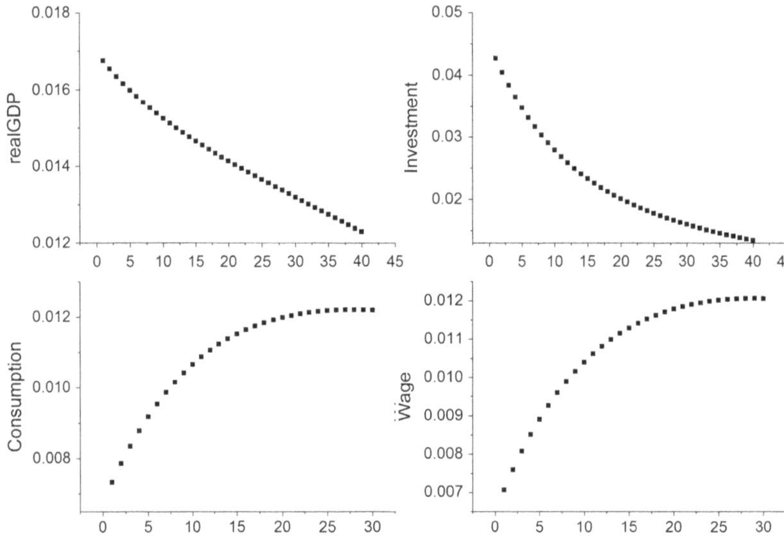

Fig. 12.2 Basic model impulse responses in China: real GDP, investment, consumption and wages

wages and their consumption are expected to increase over time to reach their new equilibrium level that is higher than their original values. Based on similar mechanisms, inflation drops when a positive productivity shock emerges, as more products are produced at lower costs, and goes back to zero in the following periods. Figures 12.2, 12.3, 12.4, 12.5, 12.6 and 12.7 illustrate the corresponding impulse responses generated by models specified for China, Brazil and India. From these figures, we can clearly see the good coherence of dynamic properties with our economic intuition and theoretical hypothesis.

In conclusion, this basic two-layered model, although only contains very few components of the full model, shows a good performance in terms of plausible consistence of statistical features, such as standard deviations and correlations, between the model economy and the observed samples in China, Brazil and India. Impulse responses of economic variables including real GDP, wage, consumption, investment, interest rate and inflation are coherent with our theoretical hypotheses and economic intuition. Therefore, this basic model can be a very good starting point and prototype

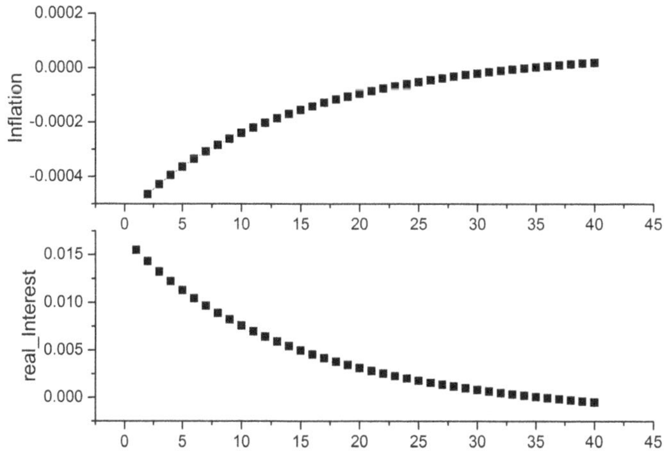

Fig. 12.3 Basic model impulse responses in China: inflation and real interest rate

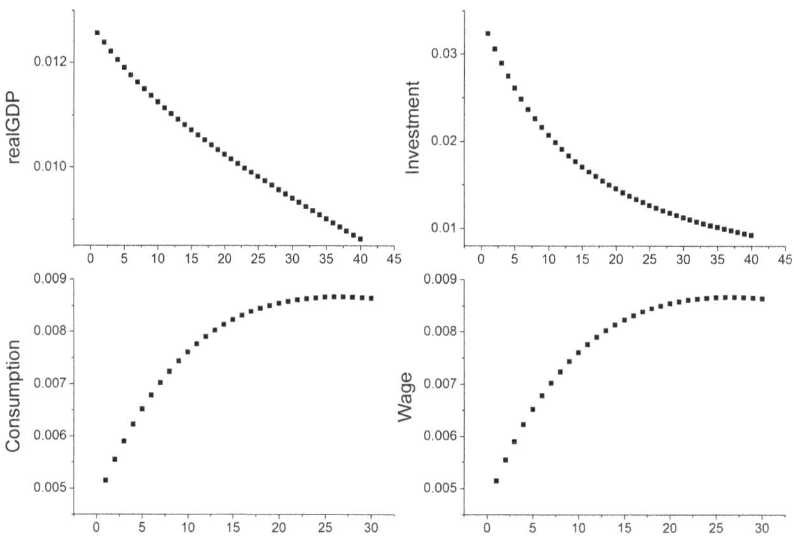

Fig. 12.4 Basic model impulse responses in Brazil: real GDP, investment, consumption and wages

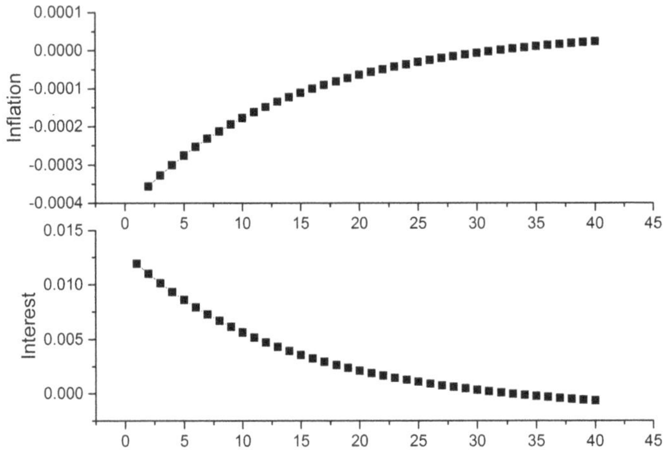

Fig. 12.5 Basic model impulse responses in Brazil: inflation and real interest rate

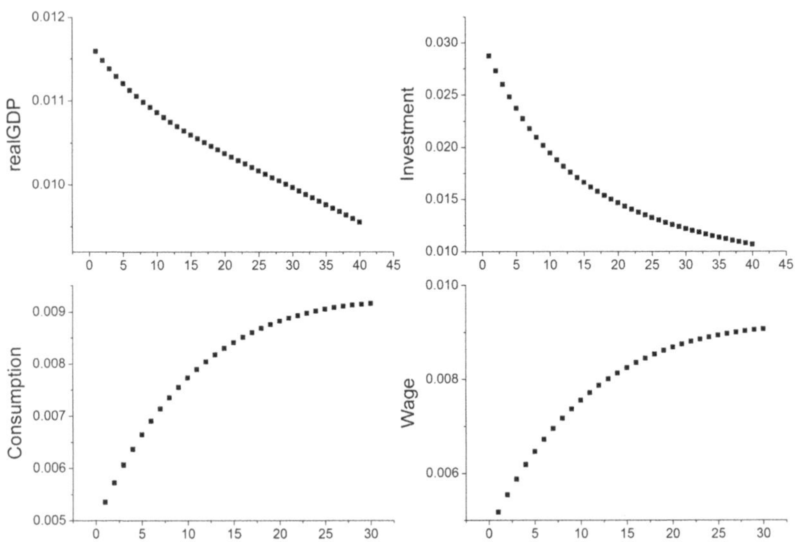

Fig. 12.6 Basic model impulse responses in India: real GDP, investment, consumption and wages

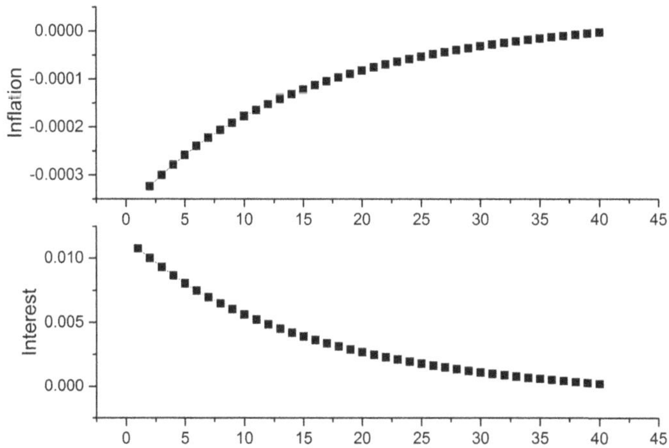

Fig. 12.7 Basic model impulse responses in India: inflation and real interest rate

to develop the advanced and full models by adding more detailed economic features like short-run nominal rigidities, the housing market, heterogeneities in households and the financial market. By doing so, we expect to develop dynamic expectation systems that can better depict the actual economic performance in emerging market economies like China, Brazil and India. In the following two sections, we demonstrate the improved performance of the advanced and full models.

12.1.3 Social Stratification

One of the major improvements of FHSAM framework is to model social stratification in the household sector. In this basic two-layer model, the parameter denotes the structure of social classes is f in Eq. 6.10. There are varieties of alternatives to calibrate this parameter: the wage share of urban and rural households, the population share of working people of urban and rural households, economic importance of urban and rural households, working hour share of urban and rural households and some complex indices of urban and rural households by weighting average of several ratios. Based on the parameters calibrated and estimated above, we can analyse the different model output to distinct value of f to depict the

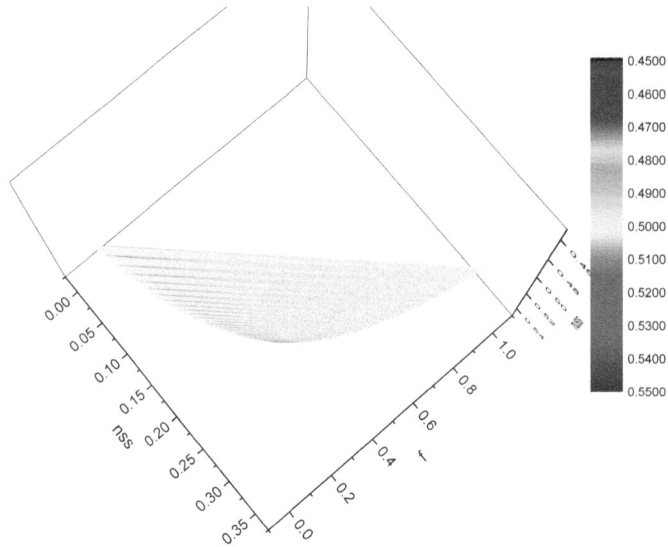

Fig. 12.8 Steady-state labour provided by urban and rural households at different level of f

economic change brought by different urban–rural households structure in the steady state.

According to the labour of urban and rural households described in Eqs. 6.36 and 6.37. The steady-state labour of rural household n_r^{ss} is simple and only determined by parameter Ψ_r, which represents the disutility of labour to rural households. The larger the Ψ_r, the more willingly the rural households enjoy leisure. Theoretical framework suggests that $\Psi_u \geq \Psi_r$, meaning that compared with urban households, rural households are more willing to provide labour to earn wages. This is consistent with their junior wealth and economic condition in the economy (they do not possess any physical capital asset). As shown in Fig. 12.8, different level of f leads to different labour provided by urban households (nss), while the labour of rural households are constant as 0.5 $(= \frac{1}{\Psi_r})$. The labour provided by urban households increases as f becomes larger. But the second-order feature shows that it is increasing at a decreasing speed, reflecting the increasing willingness to have leisure.

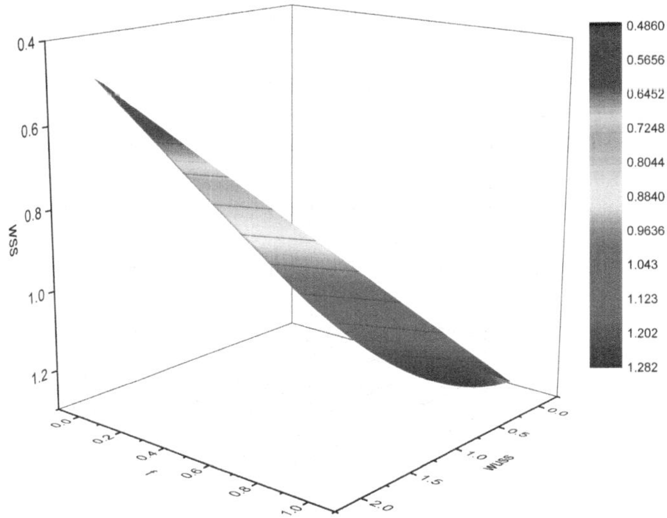

Fig. 12.9 Steady-state wage of urban and rural households at different level of f

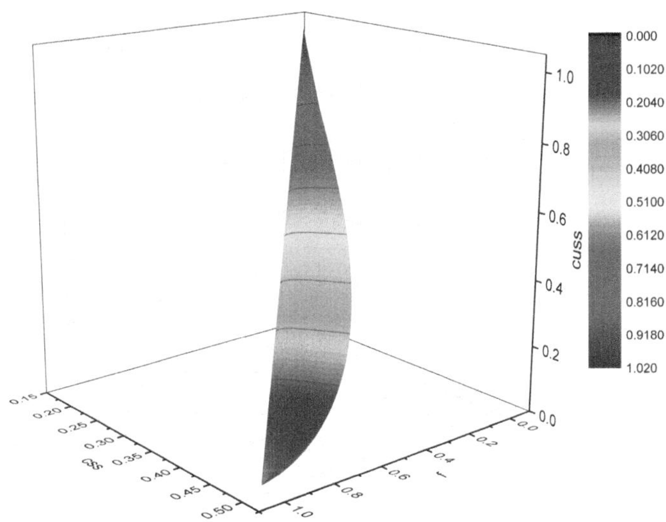

Fig. 12.10 Steady-state consumption of urban (cuss) and rural (css) households at different level of f

The corresponding urban and rural household wages distribution to f can be shown in Fig. 12.9. This figure shows the positive correlation between wage and f: w_u^{ss} increases as f grows (for rural households, w_r^{ss} increases as $(1-f)$ becomes larger). This relationship is consistent with our theoretical model and economic commonsense: as the economy becomes more and more reliant on a certain household group, the corresponding wage to that group should be increased to attract more households to provide sufficient labour.

In Fig. 12.10, we display the correlation of steady-state consumption of urban and rural households with respect to different levels of f. The dynamics are similar here as it is in the labour market we have just discussed. As one group of households becomes more important to the economy (for urban households, f increases; for rural households, $(1-f)$ increases), they get higher level of income, which determines the budget constraint for consumption. Thus, if f increases, the consumption of urban households, c_u^{ss}, becomes larger; Similarly, if $(1-f)$ becomes larger, the consumption of rural households, c_r^{ss}, increases. As discussed in the theoretical framework,

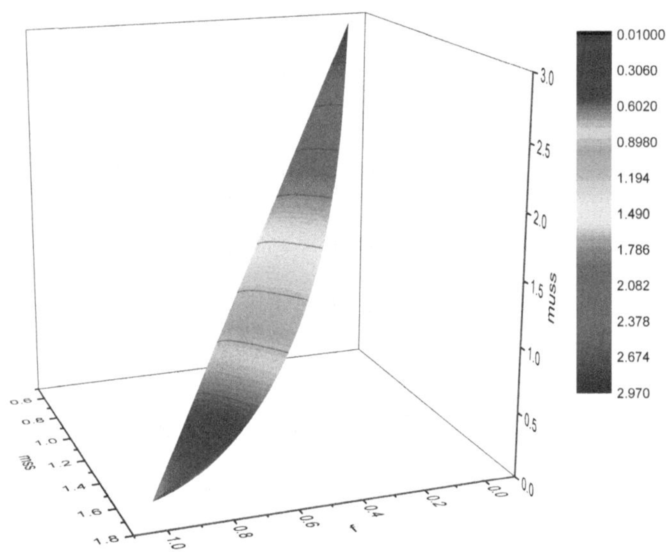

Fig. 12.11 Steady-state real money balance of urban (muss) and rural (mss) households at different levels of f

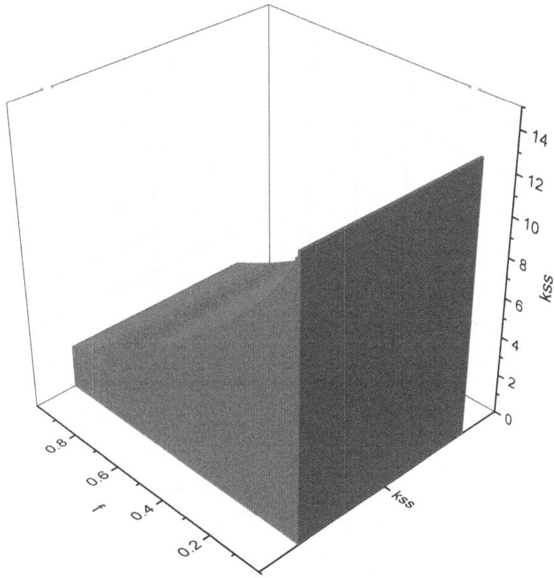

Fig. 12.12 Steady-state physical capital asset (kss) at different level of *f*

rural households tends to have higher propensity of consumption than urban households do. This can be witnessed in Fig. 12.10 as well.

Similar to the situation in the labour and consumption markets, the real money balance of a group of households moves together with the share of that group in the economy. This relationship can be seen in Fig. 12.11.

In Fig. 12.12, the steady-state capital, k^{ss}, moves as f changes: the higher f is, the lesser k^{ss} will be. That is to say, as urban households become more dominant in the economy, the need of capital in the steady state decreases. The theoretical logic behind this phenomenon is that as f decreases, the share of urban households' contribution to production becomes lower; they, thus, get less real wages and rely more on capital rental income. As a result, the demand for capital increases. This phenomenon can be explained by the lower spending propensity and higher level of work aversion of urban households.

Same phenomenon occurs in the relationship between f and the steady-state investment, in^{ss}, as illustrated in Fig. 12.13. While f decreases, meaning that rural households are more and more important in the

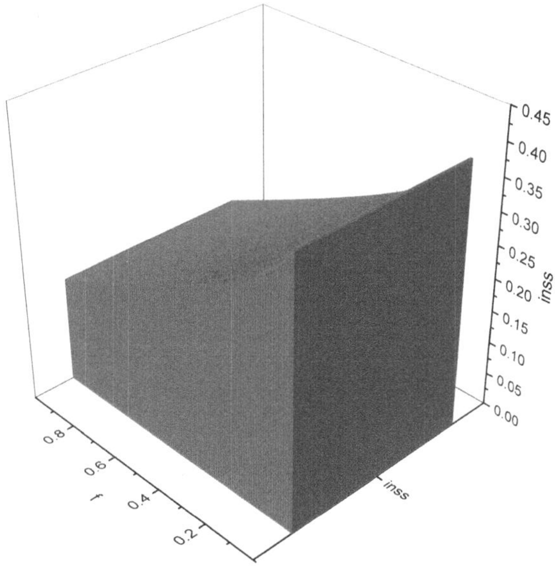

Fig. 12.13 Steady-state real money balance of urban and rural households at different level of f

economy, the necessary investment to keep the system in the steady state, in^{ss}, increases.

12.2 Empirical Analysis of the Advanced Model

The advanced model is developed based on the basic two-layered model via refining the model economy, such as adding short-term rigidities in the non-housing market, introducing an explicit housing market and considering more details of heterogeneities in the households sector. Accordingly, as economic features become more comprehensive, more exogenous shocks are investigated in this advanced model as well. These shocks include productivity shocks in both housing and non-housing markets, a monetary policy shock (interest-rate shock in the Taylor rule) and the housing preference shock. As more economic features have been added into the model, the number of parameters that need to be identified increases accordingly. This section examines the empirical analysis of the advanced model, including parameter calibration and estimation, empirical study of the model economy and the impulse responses.

12.2.1 Parameter Identification

Similar to the procedure in the empirical analysis of the basic model, the empirical analysis of the advanced model starts from parameter identification, using information and observed data samples collected in China, Brazil and India. As we have done in the previous section, the parameters that are calibrated are summarized in Table 12.7. Because more groups of households have been introduced into this advanced model, more parameters need to be identified. For example, we set the discount factors for each group of households: $\beta_{rw} = 0.9650$, $\beta_{cw} = 0.9650$, $\beta_{bh} = 0.9700$ and $\beta_{lh} = 0.9925$. The latter two values are similar to those in the basic model, leading to the fact that the equilibrium annual real interest rate is around 3%. Such identification also accords with the assumption that the discount factor of household borrowers are lower than that of household lenders, so that household borrowers have the motivation to borrow from household lenders close to the borrowing limit (shown in Eq. 7.12). Construction workers and rural migrant workers are not explicitly identified in the basic model. These workers share one thing in common: they do not possess physical capital and marketable real estate assets. Their access to

Table 12.7 The calibration of parameters in the advanced model

Parameter	*Value*	*Parameter*	*Value*
β_{cw}	0.9650	$\mu 1$	0.45
β_{rw}	0.9650	$\mu 2$	0.10
β_{lh}	0.9925	$\mu 3$	0.25
β_{bh}	0.9700	$\mu 4$	0.20
α	0.35	θ_{π}	0.75
δ_h	0.015	β_1	0.40
δ_{kc}	0.025	β_2	0.25
δ_{kh}	0.020	β_3	0.35
X_{ss}	1.15	m	0.70
b_{cw}	0.65	b_{bh}	0.40
b_{rw}	0.60	b_{lh}	0.35
η_{cw}	0.50	η_{bh}	0.50
η_{rw}	0.50	η_{lh}	0.50

the financial and the housing markets is so limited that the only resource of income is their working wages. The major difference between these two types of households is that they work in different sectors. Therefore, the discount factors of these two groups of households are identical and smaller than those of household borrowers and lenders. In our model, we set $\beta_{cw} = 0.9650$ and $\beta_{rw} = 0.9650$.

The household's utility of consumption in this advanced model considers habit formation as shown in Eqs. 7.1, 7.3, 7.7 and 7.8. The degree of household's habit formation is captured by parameters b_{cw}, b_{rw}, b_{bh} and b_{lh}. As suggested by Bouakez et al. [17] and Iacoviello and Neri [1], wealthier households exhibit higher level of flexibility in consumption and thus lower degree of habit formation than those with less wealth resource do. In literature, such as works of Bouakez and Kano [18], Smets and Wouters [19] and Iacoviello and Neri [1], the ranges of the value of habit formation parameters of household lenders and borrowers are 0.30–0.45. Additionally, these findings also suggest the value of habit formation parameters of households without ownership of physical capital and financial assets are higher, ranging from 0.57 to 0.68. Therefore, we set $b_{lh} = 0.35$, $b_{bh} = 0.40$, $b_{rw} = 0.60$ and $b_{cw} = 0.65$. The value of habit formation parameter of rural migrant workers are slightly lower than that of construction workers ($b_{rw} = 0.60 < b_{cw} = 0.65$) is to reflect the difference between the sectors where they work.[8]

There are two sectors included on the supply side of the advanced model economy: the housing sector and the non-housing sector. Accordingly, two types of physical capital assets are adopted in these two sectors: the one used in the housing market, k_h, and the one in the non-housing market, k_h. The depreciation rates of these two types of physical capital assets, δ_{kh} and δ_{kc}, are different. Additionally, housing assets are explicitly included in this advanced model. Like physical capitals, real estate depreciates, at the rate of δ_h. By the nature of housing, its depreciation rate is lower than that of physical capital assets, which are explicitly used in the production of either housing services or other goods and services. In most of the traditional DSGE modelling efforts, the quarterly depreciation rate of physical

[8] Construction workers typically work on construction sites. In these locations, the consumption market is normally less inclusive than that in cities, in which rural migrant workers work. Therefore, we expect that the degree of habit formation in consumption is higher for construction workers than for rural migrant workers. We thereby set $b_{rw} = 0.60 < b_{cw} = 0.65$.

capital assets in the non-housing market is assumed to be 2.5%, implying an annual depreciation rate of 10%. Therefore, we set $\delta_{kc} = 0.025$ in our advanced and full models. As we have discussed in the theoretical framework, the production of housing is more based on traditional technology than the production of non-housing goods and services. For example, the development of information technology and biochemistry in the modern era have far less influence on housing production than on the production of non-housing goods and services. It is reasonable for us to assume that physical capital assets used in housing production are subject to technology progress at a lower growth rate than in the non-housing production, and that the capital depreciation rate is lower in the housing sector than in the non-housing sector. To reflect this fact, we set the quarterly depreciation rate of physical capital assets used in housing production $\delta_{kh} = 0.02$, slightly lower than that in the non-housing sector. The depreciation rate of housing asset is $\delta_h = 0.015$, lower than the depreciation rates of physical capital assets, implying an annual depreciation rate of 6%.

We make a similar assumption here in the advanced model as in the basic model that the factor share of physical capital in the production in the non-housing sector is $\alpha = 0.35$. This calibration is consistent with the identification in most of the DSGE modelling literature, especially those with a focus on emerging market economies. Additionally, it needs to identify the values of factor shares, β_1, β_2 and β_3, of labour in the production function 7.22, as three types of households, n_{rw}, n_{bh} and n_{lh}, are assumed to work in this sector. In the basic two-layered model, the factor share of urban households in production is $f = 0.65$, which has been supported by long-run statistical evidence. In this advanced model, two types of households are categorized as urban households: household borrowers and household lenders. As household lenders are physical capital owners and are at the status of surplus, they account for a larger portion of labour factor share in production. Therefore, we set the factor share of household lenders' labour in production $\beta_1 = 0.40$ and the factor share of household borrowers' labour $\beta_2 = 0.25$, the sum of these two factor shares is 0.65, equal to the value in the basic model. Finally, the factor share of rural migrant workers' labour is $1 - 0.65 = 0.35$.

Similar to the parameter identification in the non-housing sector, statistical information and findings in previous studies are utilized to identify the values of parameters in housing production 7.23. In general, four elements are involved in the production of housing: labour provided by construction workers, $n_{cw,t}$, land, l_t, intermediate goods, $k_{b,t}$, and physical capital,

$k_{h,t}$. We utilize some of the calibrations in the existing works to set the factor share of intermediate goods in the housing production $\mu_2 = 0.10$. According to theoretical framework, land plays a very important role in housing production. Based on the survey of related literature, the factor share of land in housing production in our advance and full models has been calibrated as $\mu_3 = 0.25$. We set the factor share of labour in housing production $\mu_1 = 0.45$, higher than that in the non-housing production. This is so in that the production of housing relies heavier on traditional technology and requires more labour input than non-housing production. Finally, the physical capital, $k_{h,t}$, factor share in housing production is $\mu_4 = 0.25$.

A valuable quality of the advanced models is that it allows household borrowers to get mortgage loans from household lenders, using their real estate assets as collateral. The standard procedure of a mortgage loan is: the borrowers accumulate money up to the amount of down payment and borrow the rest from lenders, using their property as collateral. In the model economy, there is a more general assumption that mortgage loans can be used not only in the purchase of housing assets but also in expenditure on consumption.[9] This assumption is consistent with the real-world situation in that people get mortgage loans and use them to invest in the housing market and to spend in consumption. Under such mechanism, the maximum volume of mortgage loan a borrower can obtain is determined by the expected value of the collateralized real estate assets and the Loan-to-Value (LTV) ratio, m, as shown in Eq. 7.12. Higher level of m (or put it in another way, lower level of down payment) leads to larger borrowing limit of mortgage loans, given other factors unchanged. In the real world business, this Loan-to-Value ratio varies from time to time and country to country. Generally, the value of the LTV ratio is higher in developed economies with more sophisticated legal systems, financial markets and credit systems and lower in developing economies including Brazil, China and India. According to the data from Federal Housing Finance Board,[10] the average LTV ratio in the United States between 1973 and 2006 was 0.76. Before the subprime crisis, more than 25% of new homebuyers used LTV ratios higher

[9] As shown in Eq. 7.11 the budget constraint of household borrower, mortgage loans can be a general resource to support their investment in housing assets and their expenditure on consumption.

[10] See Table 19 at https://www.fhfa.gov/DataTools/Downloads/Pages/Monthly-Interest-Rate-Data.aspx.

than 80%. In developing economies, the value of LTV tend to be lower. Therefore, it is reasonable to set $m = 0.70$ in Brazil, China and India.

As demonstrated in the theoretical framework, the advanced and the full models contain the feature of short-term nominal rigidities in the consumption market. This feature is achieved via the Calvo pricing mechanism, in which retailers have the ability to adjust their price to maximize their profits. They buy wholesale goods, y_t, produced by the wholesale producers, at the price of $p_t^{wholesale}$ in a fully competitive wholesale market. After that, they pack these purchased wholesale products costlessly, and then sell them at the price of $p_{y,t} = X_{y,t} p_{y,t}^{wholesale}$, in which $X_{y,t}$ represents the markup of retailer price above the wholesale price. The average markup of retailers is assumed to be $X_{ss} = 1.15$ in the advance and full models. This assumption implies that the steady-state markup in the monopoly non-housing market is 15%. It is consistent with most of the DSGE literature with short-run nominal rigidities. Under such Calvo pricing mechanism, another important parameter related to nominal rigidity is θ_π. In each period of time, only a fraction $(1 - \theta_\pi)$ of retailers are randomly selected to adjust their price to maximize their profits. While the remaining fraction, (θ_π), of retailers can only index their price to the inflation in the previous period. As a result, the average life of the price of final goods is $\frac{1}{1-\theta_\pi}$. In the advance and full models, we set $\theta_\pi = 0.75$, which is a standard value in most of DSGE modelling and implies that the average length of price is 4 quarters. We set the structural parameters in households' utility functions, $\eta_{cw} = 0.50$, $\eta_{rw} = 0.50$, $\eta_{bh} = 0.50$ and $\eta_{lh} = 0.50$, in accordance with the findings in previous DSGE modelling contributions.

After calibration, we estimate the remaining parameters using Bayesian estimation approach previously discussed. We estimate these parameters using data samples of Brazil, China and India to get the accurate model for each of these economies.[11] The standard procedure of the Bayesian

[11] More specifically, we use data samples of GDP, investment and consumption to estimate the values of the parameters. For China, the data sample covers the time period 2003Q1–2018Q4; for Brazil, the data sample covers the time period 1995Q1–2018Q4; and for India, the data sample covers the time period 2005Q1–2018Q4. We adopt same data sets in the empirical analysis of the advanced model and the full model. The length of the data sample is not as long as in the case of developed economies, in which data samples with the length of more than 50 years can be collected. But, thanks to the important feature of the Bayesian estimation methods, information carried in small samples can be fully utilized to generate convincing results. Therefore, the Bayesian estimation methods are suitable for the empirical analysis in the emerging market economies.

Table 12.8 The estimation of parameters in the advanced model: China

	Prior distribution			*Posterior distribution*		
Parameter	*Distr.*	*Mean*	*Std. Dev.*	*Mean*	5%	95%
ρ_{GDP}	Beta	0.50	0.10	0.4719	0.4437	0.5021
ρ_{Ac}	Beta	0.80	0.10	0.9974	0.9950	0.9994
ρ_{Ah}	Beta	0.80	0.10	0.6998	0.5676	0.7271
ρ_r	Beta	0.50	0.10	0.5557	0.5446	0.5656
ρ_π	Beta	0.80	0.10	0.8471	0.8302	0.8655
$\rho_{\pi,r}$	Beta	0.50	0.10	0.3393	0.3030	0.3765
ρ_j	Beta	0.50	0.10	0.6281	0.6138	0.6415
e_r	Inv. Gamma	0.01	inf.	0.0308	0.0287	0.0366
e_π	Inv. Gamma	0.01	inf.	0.0079	0.0037	0.0077
e_j	Inv. Gamma	0.01	inf.	0.0860	0.0792	0.0935
e_{Ac}	Inv. Gamma	0.01	inf.	0.0140	0.0097	0.0165
e_{Ah}	Inv. Gamma	0.01	inf.	0.0095	0.0071	0.0107

estimation methods starts from making assumptions of the prior distributions of the corresponding parameters. The summary of these assumptions of the priors are shown in the left part of Tables 12.8 (China), 12.9 (Brazil) and 12.10 (India). Generally, these assumptions are well consistent with previous DSGE literature. We use beta distributed priors to estimate the values of the persistence parameters including those in the interest rate Eq. 7.40, ρ_{GDP}, ρ_r and $\rho_{\pi,r}$, those in the technology and housing preference evolution Eq. 7.58, ρ_{Ac}, ρ_{Ah} and ρ_j and the one in the inflation Eq. 7.39, ρ_π. In accordance with previous findings in DSGE modelling, we set the prior means of ρ_{GDP}, ρ_r and ρ_j as 0.50 and those of ρ_{Ac}, ρ_{Ah} and ρ_π as 0.80. In order to get a convincing estimation, we set the prior standard deviation of these estimations 0.10. For the estimation of the standard errors of the shocks, we use inverse gamma distribution as prior with infinite range and a mean of 0.01.

The estimation results of China, Brazil and India have been displayed in the right part of the Tables 12.8 (China), 12.9 (Brazil) and 12.10 (India).

12.2.2 Empirical Study of the Model Economy

Given the calibration and estimation of parameters, we complete the advanced models for China, Brazil and India. Based on these DSGE models, quantitative analysis of consistence between statistical features of the

Table 12.9 The estimation of parameters in the advanced model: Brazil

	Prior distribution			*Posterior distribution*		
Parameter	*Distr.*	*Mean*	*Std. Dev.*	*Mean*	5%	95%
ρ_{GDP}	Beta	0.50	0.10	0.4813	0.3949	0.5597
ρ_{Ac}	Beta	0.80	0.10	0.9922	0.9835	0.9988
ρ_{Ah}	Beta	0.80	0.10	0.7535	0.6318	0.8717
ρ_r	Beta	0.50	0.10	0.4475	0.3611	0.5156
ρ_π	Beta	0.80	0.10	0.8108	0.7546	0.8803
$\rho_{\pi,r}$	Beta	0.50	0.10	0.3177	0.2704	0.3840
ρ_j	Beta	0.50	0.10	0.4915	0.4110	0.5904
e_r	Inv. Gamma	0.01	inf.	0.0132	0.0098	0.0160
e_π	Inv. Gamma	0.01	inf.	0.0100	0.0027	0.0166
e_j	Inv. Gamma	0.01	inf.	0.0829	0.0762	0.0924
e_{Ac}	Inv. Gamma	0.01	inf.	0.0134	0.0075	0.0249
e_{Ah}	Inv. Gamma	0.01	inf.	0.0112	0.0030	0.0224

Table 12.10 The estimation of parameters in the advanced model: India

	Prior distribution			*Posterior distribution*		
Parameter	*Distr.*	*Mean*	*Std. Dev.*	*Mean*	5%	95%
ρ_{GDP}	Beta	0.50	0.10	0.5026	0.4817	0.5312
ρ_{Ac}	Beta	0.80	0.10	0.9877	0.9803	0.9971
ρ_{Ah}	Beta	0.80	0.10	0.8415	0.7988	0.8669
ρ_r	Beta	0.50	0.10	0.4949	0.4710	0.5265
ρ_π	Beta	0.80	0.10	0.7741	0.7420	0.8160
$\rho_{\pi,r}$	Beta	0.50	0.10	0.2739	0.2417	0.2998
ρ_j	Beta	0.50	0.10	0.5075	0.4913	0.5270
e_r	Inv. Gamma	0.01	inf.	0.0197	0.0142	0.0239
e_π	Inv. Gamma	0.01	inf.	0.0074	0.0030	0.0035
e_j	Inv. Gamma	0.01	inf.	0.0809	0.0673	0.0959
e_{Ac}	Inv. Gamma	0.01	inf.	0.0140	0.0087	0.0176
e_{Ah}	Inv. Gamma	0.01	inf.	0.0082	0.0040	0.0138

model economy and the stylized facts, summarized from the observed data samples, can be conducted. As in the empirical analysis of the basic model, we first compare the standard deviations of important economic variables including aggregate output, household consumption, real wage, investment and inflation. In view of the advanced model containing the housing market, we can also calculate the degrees of fluctuation of the housing prices in the model economy. We summarize the model-generated standard

Table 12.11 The advanced model statistical features: standard deviations

Stdev.	*Model output (data)*		
	China	*Brazil*	*India*
Consumption	0.015114 (0.017293)	0.016102 (0.021869)	0.014683 (0.023951)
Investment	0.041103 (0.045452)	0.036459 (0.051168)	0.035372 (0.032922)
Inflation	0.013757 (0.018656)	0.013625 (0.013638)	0.013629 (0.016518)
GDP	0.026874 (0.030811)	0.027505 (0.029302)	0.027139 (0.029240)
Real interest	0.015481 (0.012772)	0.015077 (0.012245)	0.015233(0.015619)
Real wages	0.046083 (0.033231)	0.035604 (0.040966)	0.039629 (0.037720)
Housing prices	0.099408 (0.093910)	0.068958 (0.047502)	0.052063 (0.066017)

deviations of China, Brazil and India in Table 12.11. In order to make a clearer comparison of model-generated outputs and the stylized facts, we put the corresponding standard deviations of the observed data sample in brackets in Table 12.11. From this table, we clearly see the good coherence between model outputs and the stylized facts in all three economies we analyse. The results show that after adding important economic features to the basic model, the advanced model indicates better coherence with the observed data than the basic model. The degree of the aggregate output (GDP) is increased from around 2% to the value higher than 2.9% and is very similar to those in the real data (3.08% in China, 2.924% in Brazil and 3.930% in India). The standard deviation of real consumption in the advanced model is also enhanced from less than 1% to the value around 1.5%, which is very close to the value drawn from the data sample. Additionally, the advance model shows a strong consistence with observed data in the standard deviation of housing prices. As shown in Table 12.11, the standard deviations of real housing prices in the model economy of China, Brazil and India are close to the values summarized in the observed data in these economies, indicating the robustness of our advanced model. Similar improvement of the advanced model can be witnessed in the standard deviations of real wage and real interest rate, as model-generated data shows strong consistence with the observations in China, Brazil and India. These empirical evidence validate the assumptions of the advanced model and our efforts to refine the structure of the model economy.

As in the empirical analysis of the basic model, correlations between major economic variables described by the model economy are summarized to evaluate the consistence of model output and the stylized facts.

Table 12.12 The advanced model statistical features: correlations

Correlations	*Model output (data)*		
	China	*Brazil*	*India*
Consum., GDP	0.7852 (0.7389)	0.7759 (0.7201)	0.7399 (0.6588)
Inv., GDP	0.7210 (0.7234)	0.7290 (0.7474)	0.7729 (0.7331)
Wage, GDP	0.5842 (0.6460)	0.5855 (0.6953)	0.6101 (0.6263)
Inflation, GDP	0.6646 (0.64134)	0.6240 (0.6321)	0.6503 (0.6682)
Consum., Inv.	0.4981 (0.5994)	0.4806 (0.5377)	0.5153 (0.5460)
p_h, GDP	0.8255 (0.5624)	0.7925 (0.5931)	0.7903 (0.4993)
p_h, Consum.	0.5096 (0.4132)	0.4340 (0.4064)	0.4370 (0.3964)
p_h, Inv.	0.7887 (0.6332)	0.7906 (0.6013)	0.7897 (0.5574)
p_h, Llh	0.7386 (0.6263)	0.7173 (0.6309)	0.7400 (0.6050)
Llh, GDP	0.7578 (0.7145)	0.7539 (0.7481)	0.7559 (0.7193)

This is all shown in Table 12.12. In general, the advanced model has very good consistence with the stylized facts in terms of correlations between these important variables. The correlation between consumption and GDP in China is 0.7852, which is very close to the value observed in data from 2003Q1 to 2018Q4, 0.7389. Such good consistence between model performance and actual data can be witnessed in Brazil (model: 0.7759, data: 0.7201) and India (model: 0.7399, data: 0.6588) as well. Economists believe that both real household consumption and fixed asset investment are procyclical variables. Additionally, there is a positive correlation between these two variables. From statistics of China, Brazil and India, we get empirical evidence showing that the degrees of such positive correlations in these three economies are 0.5994, 0.5377 and 0.5460, respectively. The advanced model shows its ability to accurately reproduce similar results with very similar correlation in the corresponding economies. As shown in Table 12.12, the model-generated results are close to the stylized facts in China (0.4981), Brazil (0.4806) and India (0.5153). Compared to the basic model, the advanced model gives a much better coherence of correlations between investment and GDP in all three economies: China (model: 0.7210, data: 0.7234), Brazil (model: 0.7290, data: 0.7474) and India (model: 0.7729, data: 0.7331). This result firmly supports our theoretical construction of the advanced model, especially the structure of production in both housing and non-housing sectors. We expect a positive correlation between the real wages of households and the overall economic output (GDP) in that real wage is a procyclical variable moving in the same direction with GDP. In the basic model, the value of such positive correlation has been overestimated because of the simplification of the model structure. The average value of correlations between real wage and GDP in China, Brazil and India is higher than 0.90, which is far from the value calculated from the observed data (around 0.65). Based on the refined structure of the model economy, the consistence between statistic qualities of the advanced model and the facts drawn from the observed data has been highly improved. In China, statistics show that this positive correlation is 0.6460. The corresponding value implied by the advanced model is 0.5842. In Brazil, the correlation between real wage and GDP is 0.6953 and the value given by the advanced model is 0.5855. In India, such values are 0.6101 and 0.6263, respectively, indicating a better consistence between model performance and the stylized facts. Inflation, as most of the economists believe, is positively correlated with GDP as well. Statistics tell us that the correlations between inflation rate and GDP in China, Brazil and India are 0.64134, 0.6321 and 0.6682, respectively. The values of such correlations in China, Brazil and India given by the basic model are all higher than 0.90, far away from the values calculated from the data sample, which is around 0.65. The advanced model improves the consistence of such correlation with respect to the stylized facts in all three economies: In China, the values given by the advanced model and drawn from data sample are 0.6646 and 0.64134, respectively; In Brazil, 0.6240 and 0.6321; In India, 0.6503 and 0.6682. Since the housing market has been explicitly installed in the advanced model, we expect this model to give results of good coherence with the stylized facts in terms of correlations between housing prices and other economic variables such as GDP, investment and consumption. In the discussion of the theoretical analysis, we conclude that real housing prices, investment and consumption are all procyclical variables and that there are positive correlations among these variables. Statistics of China, Brazil and India support our theoretical anticipation as shown in Table 12.12. Data sample of China suggests that the correlation between real housing price and GDP is 0.5624. In Brazil, the degree of this correlation is 0.5931 and in India 0.4993. The corresponding values given by the advanced model in these countries are 0.8255, 0.7925, and 0.7903. At first glance, the advanced model successfully captures the positive correlation between the real housing prices and the real GDP, while the amplitude of such correlation suggested by the advanced model is about 30% higher than that calculated from the observed data. This can be explained by two facts. In the first place, our advanced model, as any other models, has its limitation in that it cannot inclusively include every aspect of the real economy. In this advanced model, only two sectors are included—the housing market and the non-housing market. This simplification benefits us with the feasibility of model construction and programming, but, at the same time, may lead to the overvaluation of the correlation between housing prices and the aggregate output. This is so since, firstly, the real housing prices are more directly linked with other economic variables. Secondly, the degree of correlation between real housing prices and real GDP calculated from the observed data may be misleading, underestimating the true intensity of such correlation. The statistics that we use to calculate correlations are housing price indices in the target economies, in which housing prices data is quite limited in terms of quality and length of time. Therefore, the information contained in these statistics may underestimate the long-run correlation between real housing prices and real GDP. In the chapter of theoretical analysis, we conclude that the real housing prices move in the same direction with real household consumption, since they are procyclical variables driven by similar fundamental economic forces. The rise of the real housing prices tends to be correlated with an increase in real household consumption and vice versa. In the data sample of China, Brazil, and India, we do see such positive correlations between real housing prices and real household consumption. The degree of such correlation is 0.41326 in China, 0.4064 in Brazil and 0.3964 in India. Similar to the correlation between real housing prices and real GDP, model economy shows strong coherence with reality in term of the positive correlation between real housing prices and real household consumption in all targeted economies, while exhibiting a slightly higher level of intensity of such correlation than the stylized facts (0.5096 in China, 0.4340 in Brazil and 0.4370 in India). Similar results can be seen in the case of the correlation between real housing price and real fixed asset investment, in which the model-generated degree of correlation (0.7887 in China, 0.7906 in Brazil and 0.7897 in India) is consistent with stylized facts (0.6332 in China, 0.6013 in Brazil and 0.5574 in India) in the direction of correlation but higher amplitude. These phenomena can be explained by the similar reasons used in the case of the correlation between real housing price and real household consumption.

In the advanced and full models, the mortgage loans between household borrowers and household lenders play a very important role not only in the housing market but also in the overall economy. In the theoretical framework, we conclude that the mortgage loan is a procyclical variable and moves in the same direction with real housing prices. This theoretical hypothesis is supported by the data samples observed in China, Brazil and India. The advanced model also provides results of good consistence with stylized facts in all these three economies. In China, the observed data shows that the degree of correlation between mortgage loans, Llh, and real GDP is 0.7145, and the corresponding value implied by the advanced model is 0.7578, demonstrating a good coherence between model performance and the stylized facts. Similar consistence can be observed in Brazil (model: 0.7539, data: 0.7481) and India (model: 0.7559, data: 0.7193) as well. The positive correlation between real housing prices and mortgage loans is confirmed by both data samples and model outputs. In China, the degree of such correlation suggested by data sample is 0.6263 and the corresponding value of model performance is 0.7386. In Brazil, data and model yield 0.6309 and 0.7173, respectively. In India, such values are 0.6050 and 0.7400.

In conclusion, the advanced model, after equipping certain important economic features including short-run nominal rigidity in the consumption market, a housing market with mortgage loan mechanism and more detailed structure in the household sector, shows stronger ability to accurately reproduce economic performance of high consistence with historical data in China, Brazil and India, in terms of volatilities of and correlations between major economic variables. The high level of consistence between model results and the stylized facts support our hypotheses and assumptions of the theoretical framework.

12.2.3 The Impulse Response

After summarizing the structural results of the advanced model, the next step of the empirical analysis is to quantitatively analyse the dynamics of the advanced model. To study the dynamic features of the advanced model, we need to investigate whether the responses of the model economy to exogenous innovations are consistent with our theoretical hypotheses summarized in Tables 7.2, 7.3, and 7.4. As in the standard dynamic modelling exercise, this step is mainly focused on the impulse responses of major economic variables to shocks involved in the advanced model. In general, impulse responses of economic variables to productivity shocks in the housing and non-housing markets, monetary policy shocks (interest-rate shocks) and housing preference shocks in China, Brazil and India are illustrated and discussed.

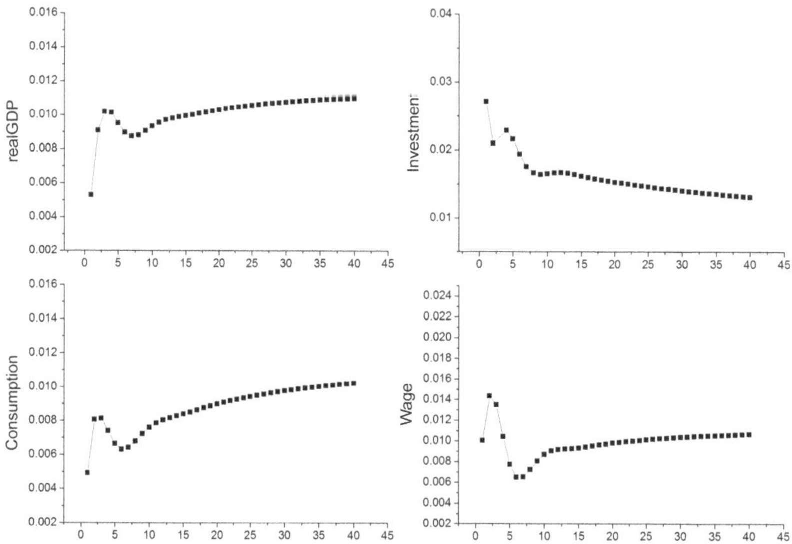

Fig. 12.14 Impulse responses to productivity shocks in the non-housing market of the advanced model in China: real GDP, investment, consumption and wages

In the first place, the responses of real sector variables, such as real GDP, fixed asset investment, household consumption and wages, to the productivity shock in the non-housing market are investigated. As shown in Fig. 12.14, we summarize the impulse responses of real GDP, fixed asset investment, household consumption, and wage to an i.i.d. positive productivity shock in the non-housing market. It indicates that such productivity shocks give rise to the increase of real GDP by 0.53% in the first quarter. There are fluctuations between the 2nd quarter and the 10th quarter. In the 3rd quarter, the growth of real GDP reaches its maximum value of 1.16% and then begins to descend. From the 3rd quarter to the 8th quarter, the deviation of real GDP from its steady-state value decreases from 1.16 to 0.065%. Then, the real GDP continues to increase to the new equilibrium value of 1% after the 10th quarter. Similar profile of impulse responses can be witnessed in the case of household consumption and wages, as shown in the bottom part of Fig. 12.14. The initial response of real household consumption is 0.51%, very close to that of real GDP. The maximum deviation is also in the 3rd quarter with the value of 0.84%. After about 10 quarters,

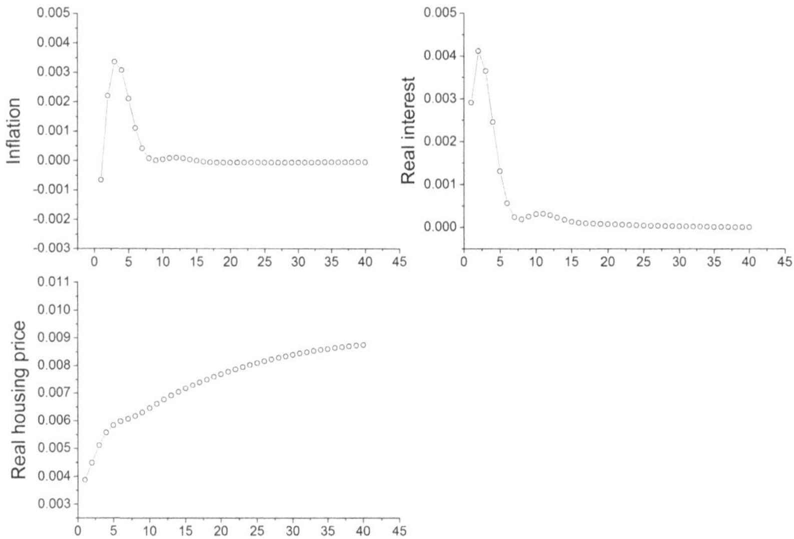

Fig. 12.15 Impulse responses to productivity shocks in the non-housing market of the advanced model in China: inflation, real interest rate and housing prices

the effect of productivity shocks gradually fades away, as household consumption arrives at its new steady-state value, which is 1%. The similarity of impulse responses of real GDP, household consumption and wage is consistent with the conclusion of strong positive correlation hypothesized in the theoretical framework and witnessed in the stylized facts. The movement of real GDP after the productivity shocks in the non-housing market is similar to that of inflation as shown in Fig. 12.15. This figure shows that the inflation rate is almost unchanged in the first quarter and increases to 0.90% in the following two quarters. Like real GDP, inflation returns to its steady-state value, which is zero, after the 10th quarter. A positive productivity shock in the non-housing market brings positive effects on fixed asset investment and the real interest rate. Fixed asset investment, as most of modern macroeconomic theories and models suggest, reacts more actively than aggregate output. As shown in Fig. 12.14, the productivity shock leads to an initial increase of nearly 3% in fixed asset investment in the first quarter, gradually descending to the new equilibrium value of 1% in the following periods. The increase of investment in physical capital is accompanied by the increase of the real interest rate, whose initial response is 0.3% and quickly grows to 0.43% in the 2nd quarter. Like investment in physical assets, the real interest rate returns to its new equilibrium value after about 10 quarters. Because the advanced model contains a housing market, we can quantitatively analyse the impulse response of real housing prices to such productivity shock. In the theoretical framework, we expect the real housing prices to increase when productivity is enhanced in the non-housing market. This is so because such an increase in productivity raises the aggregate real output and real wages of households, supporting a higher level of housing demand. Such a process of growth in real housing prices is captured in the advanced model as shown in the third figure in Fig. 12.15, demonstrating that real housing prices gradually increase after the positive productivity shock in the non-housing market. This continuous growth of real housing prices after a non-housing productivity shock is in good consistence with our economic intuition and theoretical hypothesis, which maintains that positive productivity shocks in the non-housing market raise aggregate output and real wages, stimulating households to invest more in housing assets.

In general, it can be drawn that the initial responses of economic variables including real aggregate output, household consumption, wages, interest rate, and inflation to a standard positive productivity shock in the non-housing market are positive. Among these variables, fixed asset investment has the strongest response. These variables tend to continue increasing for about 4 quarters and then begin to drop, but still at a positive value. The effects of the non-housing productivity shock for these economic variables last about 10 quarters, when they reach their new equilibrium value of around 1%. All of these results produced by the advanced model show good coherence with similar results of the existing literature and our theoretical hypotheses.

We summarize the impulse responses to a positive non-housing productivity shock in the advanced model specified for Brazil, as shown in Figs. 12.16 and 12.17. These figures demonstrate that impulse responses are similar to those in the case of China.

Similarly, the impulse responses of variables such as real GDP, fixed asset investment, household consumption and wages to a standard positive productivity shock in the non-housing market in the model specified for India are illustrated in Fig. 12.18. The impulse responses of variables like inflation, real interest rate and housing prices are shown in Fig. 12.19.

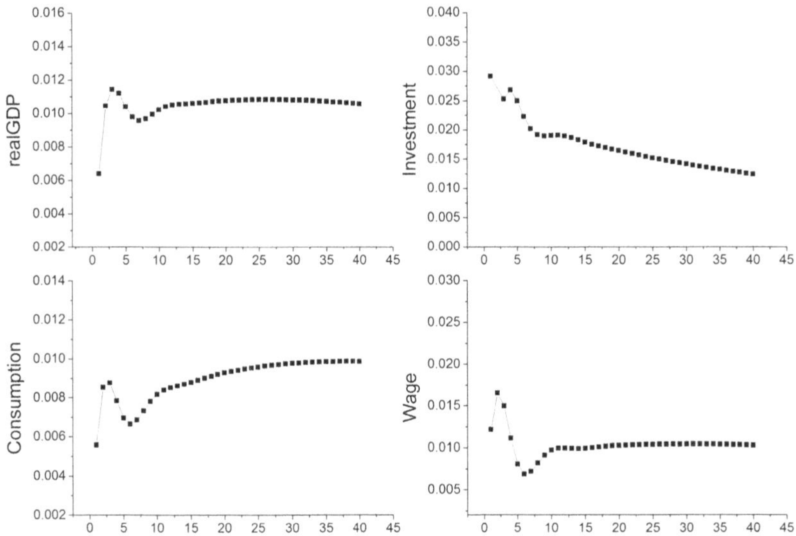

Fig. 12.16 Impulse responses to productivity shocks in the non-housing market of the advanced model in Brazil: real GDP, investment, consumption and wages

After demonstrating the impulse responses to the non-housing market productivity shock in the models specified for China, Brazil and India, we can conclude that a positive non-housing productivity shock produces the positive responses of real economic variables such as real GDP, investment, household consumption and wages. Inflation, real interest rate and housing price also increase after the positive productivity shock in the non-housing market. On average, it takes about 8–10 quarters for the economy to reach its new equilibrium condition, where real GDP, fixed asset investment, household consumption and wages are about 1% higher than their original levels, and inflation and real interest rate return to their original levels. Within this reacting process, the deviations of aggregate output, wage and consumption go up for the first 3 quarters, when the maximum deviation (the first turning point) occurs, and then begin to drop for the following 3–4 quarters, when the second turning point emerges. After the second turning point, these deviations return to its new steady-state level, which is around 1%. This is consistent with the theoretical framework, concluding that the 1% increase in productivity in the non-housing market raises

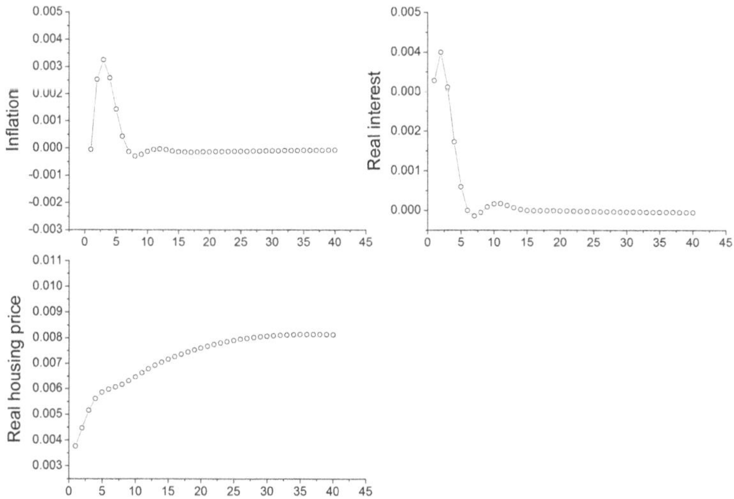

Fig. 12.17 Impulse responses to productivity shocks in the non-housing market of the advanced model in Brazil: inflation, real interest rate and real housing price

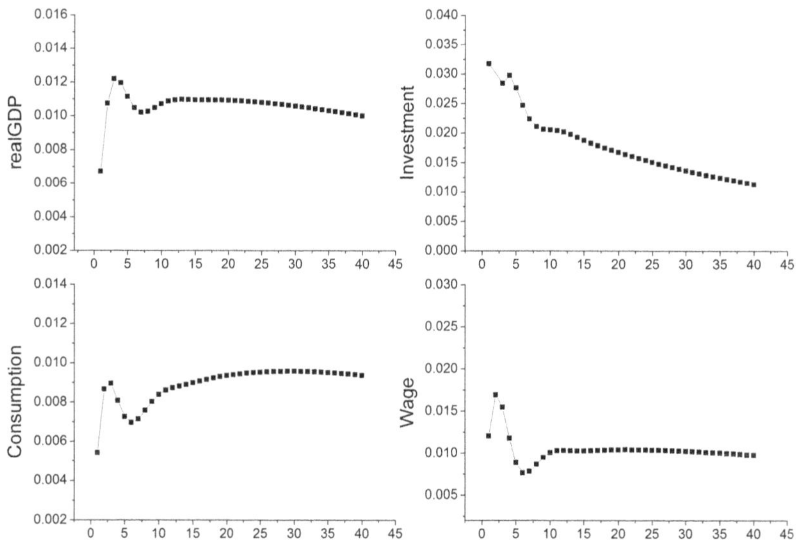

Fig. 12.18 Impulse responses to productivity shock in the non-housing market of the advanced model in India: real GDP, investment, consumption and wages

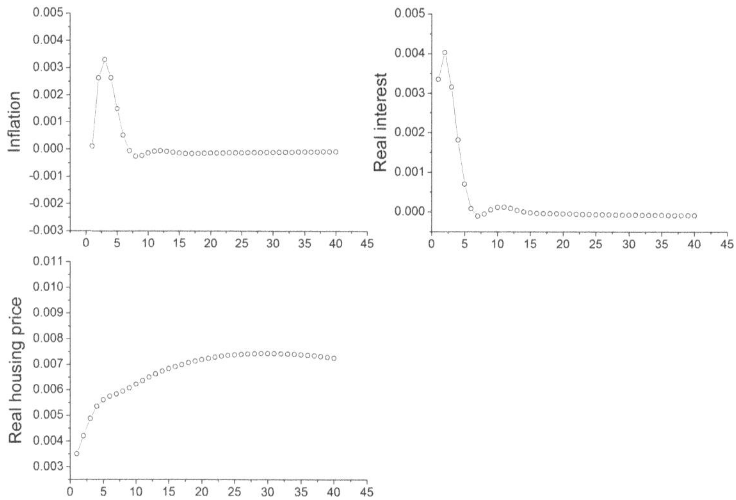

Fig. 12.19 Impulse responses to productivity shock in the non-housing market of the advanced model in India: inflation, real interest rate and housing prices

real aggregate output, investment, household consumption and wage by a similar ratio. The overshooting effects, the double turning points in the impulse response figures, can be mainly explained by the short-term nominal rigidities in the non-housing market.

The theoretical framework of the advanced model tells that a positive productivity shock in the non-housing market is expected to push up inflation in the consumption market and the real interest rate at the beginning, since the investment in fixed physical asset increases. These positive deviations of inflation and real interest rate tend to return to zero after several quarters. The advanced model economy yields such impulse responses in good coherence with our theoretical hypotheses. The model-generated impulse responses, as shown earlier in the figures, indicate that inflation goes up for three quarters after the positive non-housing productivity shock, reaching the maximum level around 0.35%. After about 3 quarters, inflation begins to descend, returning to its original level at about 8 quarters. The effect of positive non-housing productivity shock to real interest rate is similar. The average length of impulse response is about 8 quarters, after when the deviation of real interest rate returns to zero. The

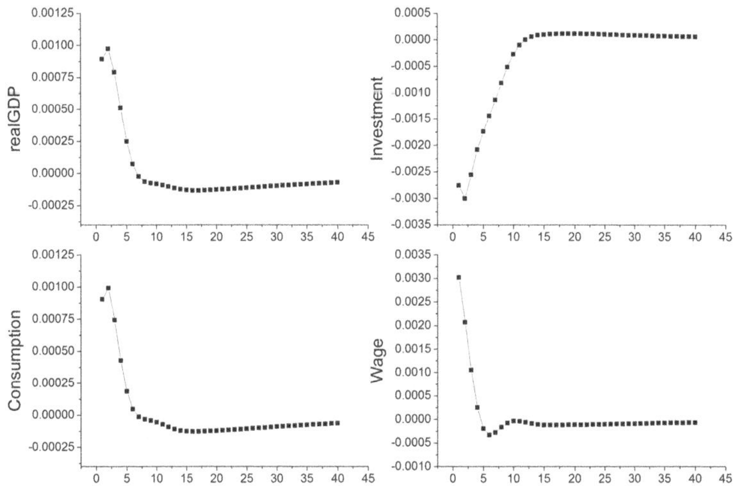

Fig. 12.20 Impulse responses to productivity shocks in the housing market of the advanced model in China: real GDP, investment, consumption and wages

maximum effect, around 0.4%, arrives one quarter earlier in the case of the real interest rate than inflation.

The advanced model also successfully delivers plausible impulse responses of real housing prices to the shock of non-housing productivity. In the theoretical framework, we conclude that such a positive shock gives rise to a gradual increase of real housing prices based on the economic mechanism included in the advanced model. In the first place, the advancement of productivity in the non-housing market pushes up real wages for households working in this market, raising both consumption and real estate investment. The increase of real wages upholds the ability to purchase real estate assets. Because housing is explicitly introduced into the utility function of household borrowers and lenders, households' stronger capability to buy real estate assets leads to a higher level of housing demand. Due to this increase in housing demand, real housing prices begin to grow. This process continues for several periods, gradually pushing up real housing prices to their new equilibrium level, which is higher than its original value by the amount around the value of the productivity shock. As shown in Figs. 12.15, 12.17 and 12.19, the impulse responses of real housing prices

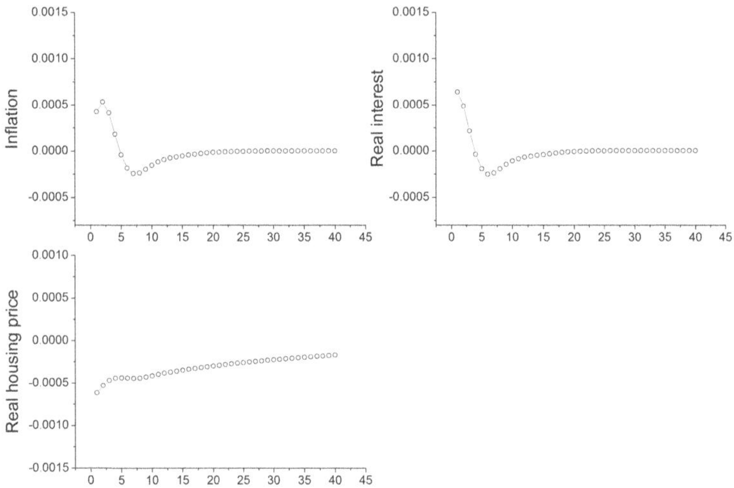

Fig. 12.21 Impulse responses to productivity shocks in the housing market of the advanced model in China: inflation, real interest rate and real housing prices

suggested by our advanced model is consistent with the process discussed above. After a 1% positive non-housing productivity shock, real housing prices begin to rise from the first quarter. The initial increase of real housing prices is around 0.35% in China, Brazil and India. In the following periods, real housing prices increase at a decreasing rate. Real housing prices increase gradually for a longer period of time than in the case of inflation and the real interest rate, reaching the new equilibrium level around 0.8–0.9% after about 20 quarters.

Besides productivity shocks in the non-housing market, the advanced model is able to generate impulse responses to the productivity shocks in the housing market, which has been explicitly introduced into the advanced model. In our theoretical analysis, we conclude that a positive housing productivity shock initially gives rise to the increase of housing supply, pulling down the real housing prices and thus investment in fixed assets. Because productivity plays a minor role in housing production, such effects are considered to be small, compared to those in the case of productivity shock in the non-housing market. The positive housing productivity shock increases the real wages of workers working in this market and thus stimulates their consumption in the non-housing market. Therefore, the overall effect of

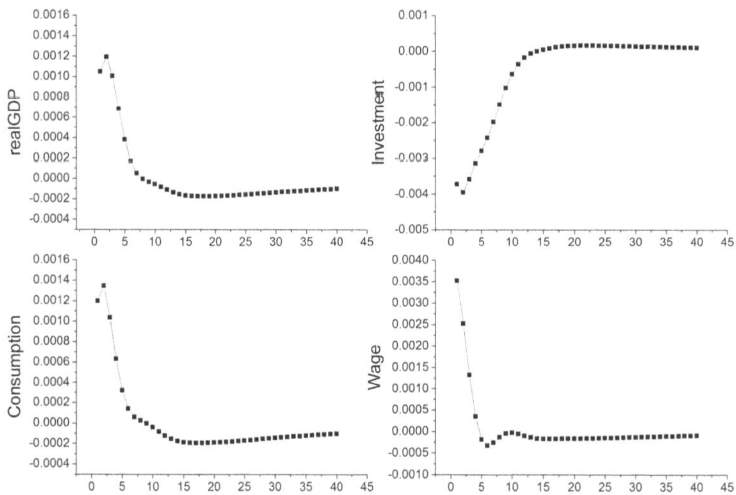

Fig. 12.22 Impulse responses to productivity shocks in the housing market of the advanced model in Brazil: real GDP, investment, consumption and wages

real GDP, household consumption and wages is positive after the positive housing productivity shock. The impulse responses implied by the advanced model are well consistent with these theoretical hypotheses. Figure 12.20 summarizes the impulse responses of real GDP, household consumption, fixed asset investment and wages in the advanced model specified for China. Real GDP, household consumption and wages respond positively to the positive housing productivity shocks. A 1% positive productivity shock in the housing market leads to an initial increase of 0.08% in overall real GDP and household consumption for the first quarter. The maximum deviation of real GDP and household consumption emerges in the second quarter with the value around 0.1%. After the second quarter, the responses begin to descend and gradually return to the value near the original level after 8 quarters. As in the theoretical hypothesis, the initial response of investment in fixed physical asset is minus, with the value around 0.4%. After the second quarter, investment in fixed physical asset begins to rise and reaches the value near its original level after 10–15 quarters. Figure 12.21 demonstrates the responses of inflation, the real interest rate and housing prices to the positive housing productivity shocks. Coherent with our theoretical hypotheses, the initial reaction of real housing prices to such shock

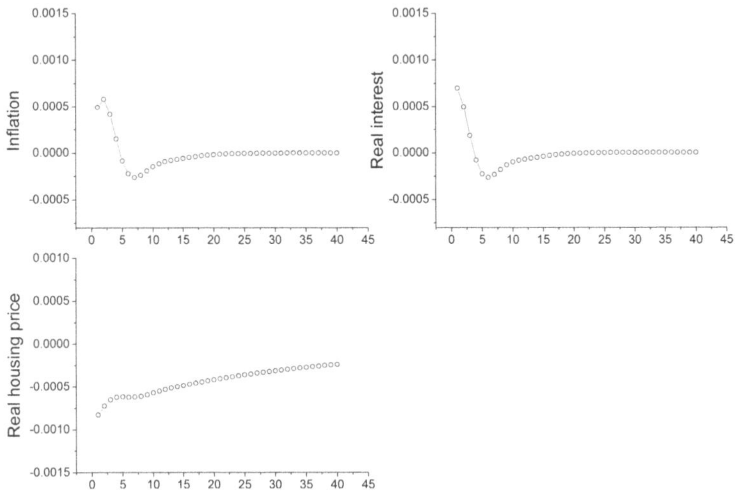

Fig. 12.23 Impulse responses to productivity shocks in the housing market of the advanced model in Brazil: inflation, real interest rate and real housing prices

is negative, with the value around 0.085% in the first quarter. Afterwards, real housing prices begin to rise and gradually rise to its original level after 20–25 quarters (Figs. 12.22 and 12.23).

Similar impulse responses to the positive housing productivity shock can be witnessed in the results implied by the advanced models specified for Brazil and India as well, as shown in Figs. 12.24 and 12.25. In conclusion, the impulse responses to the productivity shock in the housing market are much less active than the productivity shock in the non-housing market. This is so because the housing market, compared to the non-housing market, is more dependent on traditional technology, labour and land, especially the latter, the supply of which is fixed in the advanced model. In conclusion, the impulse responses of the advanced model are well consistent with our theoretical hypotheses.

One of the major aims of the advanced model is to quantitatively analyse the economic impact of changes in households' attitude towards housing asset. Theoretically, a positive shock of households' housing preference encourages the increase of housing demand, pushing up real housing prices and investment in fixed physical assets in the housing market. This process can be found in the impulse responses generated by the advanced model

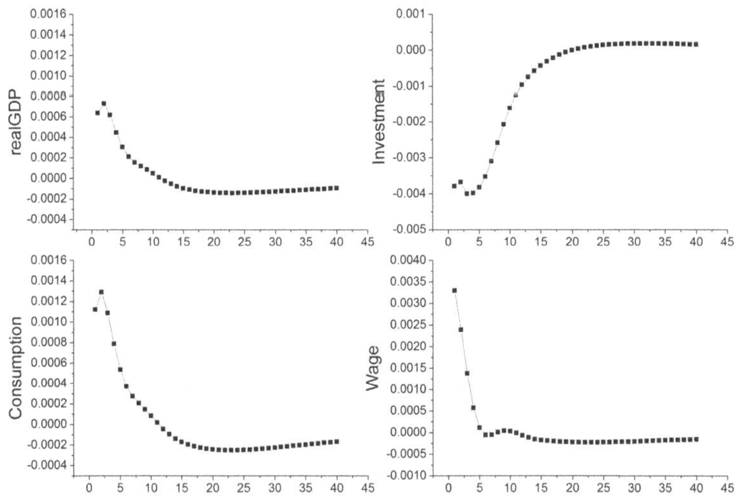

Fig. 12.24 Impulse responses to productivity shocks in the housing market of the advanced model in India: real GDP, investment, consumption and wages

of China, as shown in Fig. 12.26. The impulse response figure demonstrates that a 1% positive housing preference shock (housing demand shock) causes real GDP to rise in the first three quarters, with the maximum value of 0.15% occurred in the third quarter. After three quarters, the deviation of real GDP begins to return to zero. The effect of this housing preference shock on real GDP lasts about 8–10 quarters, after which real GDP returns to its original value. The responses of real wages and household consumption are positive in the first two quarters. The 1% positive housing preference shock causes real wages to rise by 0.2% and household consumption by 0.15% in the second quarter. From the third quarter, both real household consumption and wages begin to descend. Before they return to their original level, they drop to negative values from 5th to 10th quarter. Such overshooting effect can be explained by short-run nominal rigidity in the non-housing market. As we have discussed in the theoretical framework, real investment in fixed physical asset contains two parts: the investment in the housing market and the one in the non-housing market. A positive housing demand shock increases the investment in the housing market, because more real estate needs to be produced. On the other hand, the increase of investment in the housing market generates crowding-out

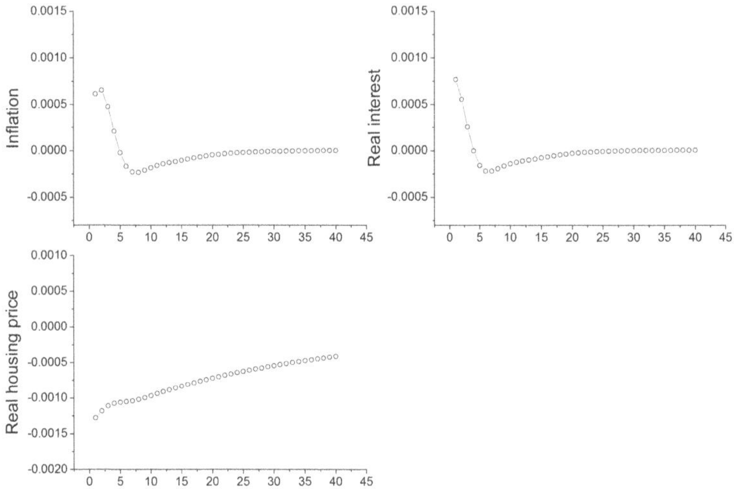

Fig. 12.25 Impulse responses to productivity shocks in the housing market of the advanced model in India: inflation, real interest rate and real housing prices

effects on investment in the non-housing market under the budget constraint condition. This is because production in the non-housing market is more sensitive to capital input than that in the housing market.[12] The overall effect of real investment in fixed physical assets is expected to be negative at the beginning. In the following periods, the increase of real wages cause household consumption to rise, thus pushing up investment in the non-housing market as well. Therefore, the overall investment in physical asset starts to increase after the positive housing demand shock. This process can be seen in Fig. 12.26, indicating that the initial reaction of real investment in fixed physical asset is around −0.2%. Afterwards, real investment begins to rise in the following three quarters, with the maximum value of 0.29% occurred in the 4th quarter after the housing demand shock. The effect of housing demand shock on real investment lasts about 10–15 quarters, when real investment returns to its original level.

Theoretically, the positive housing demand shocks give rise to the increase of real housing prices. Such relationship is well-documented in

[12]As described in the production functions 7.22 and 7.23, the factor share of physical capital is $\mu_4 = 0.20$ in the housing market and $\alpha = 0.35$ in the non-housing market.

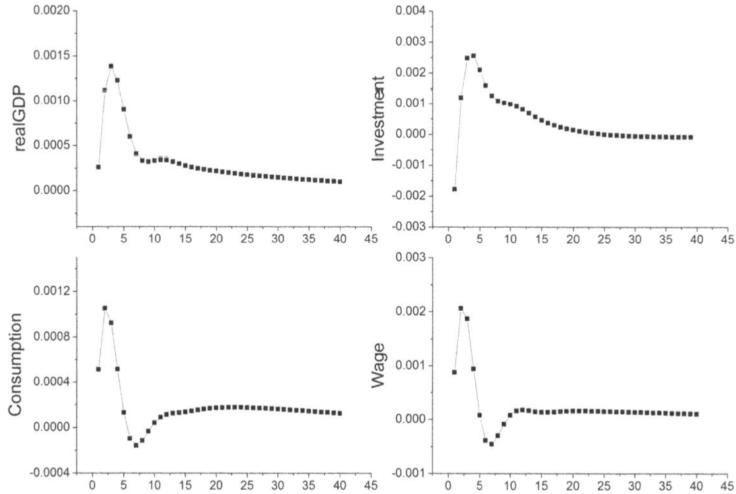

Fig. 12.26 Impulse responses to housing preference shocks of the advanced model in China: real GDP, investment, consumption and wages

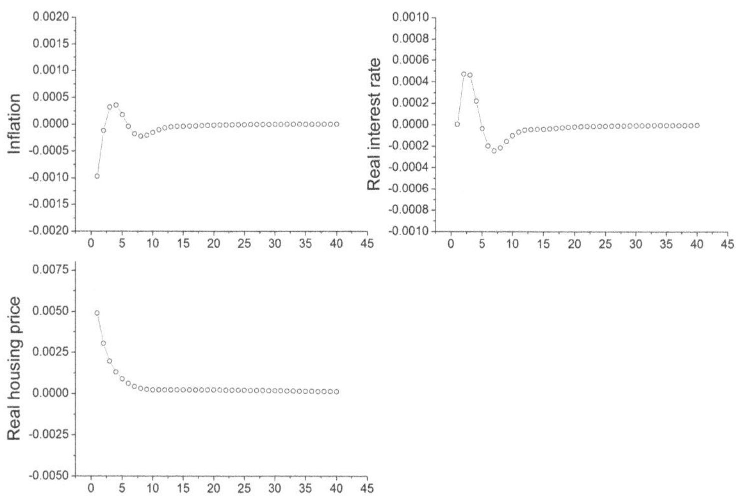

Fig. 12.27 Impulse responses to housing preference shocks of the advanced model in China: inflation, real interest rate and real housing prices

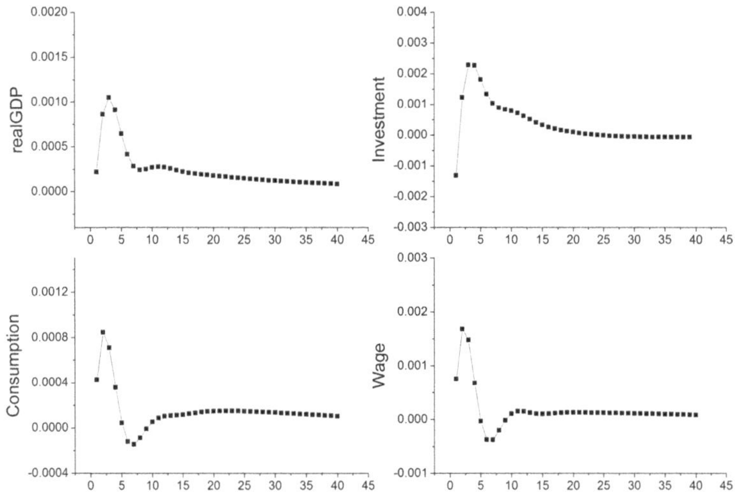

Fig. 12.28 Impulse responses to housing preference shocks of the advanced model in Brazil: real GDP, investment, consumption and wages

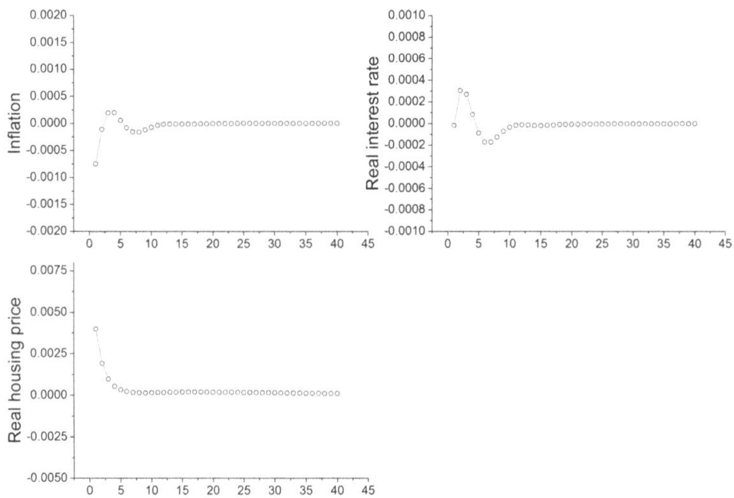

Fig. 12.29 Impulse responses to housing preference shocks of the advanced model in Brazil: inflation, real interest rate and real housing prices

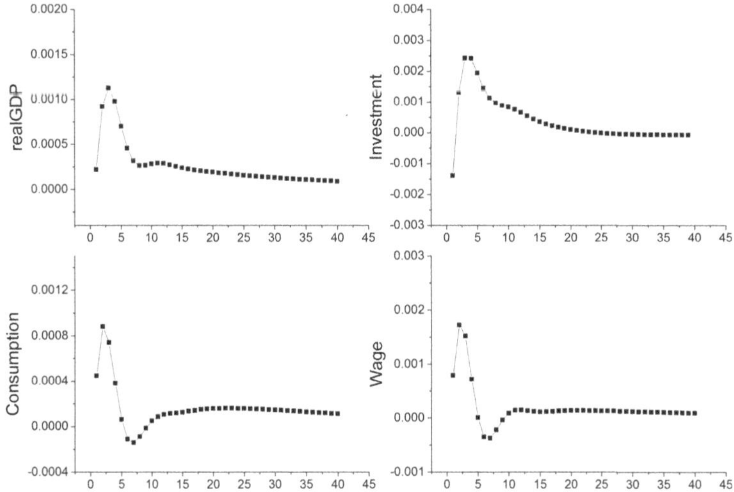

Fig. 12.30 Impulse responses to housing preference shock of the advanced model in India: real GDP, investment, consumption and wages

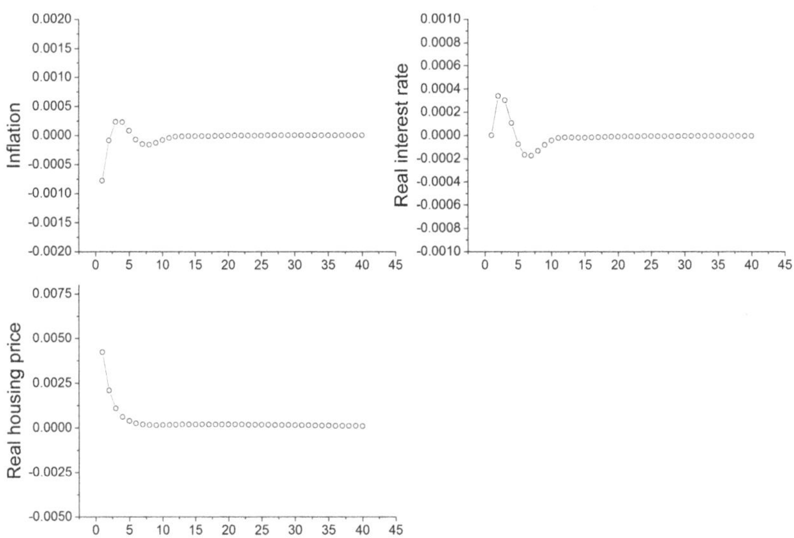

Fig. 12.31 Impulse responses to housing preference shock of the advanced model in India: inflation, real interest rate and real housing prices

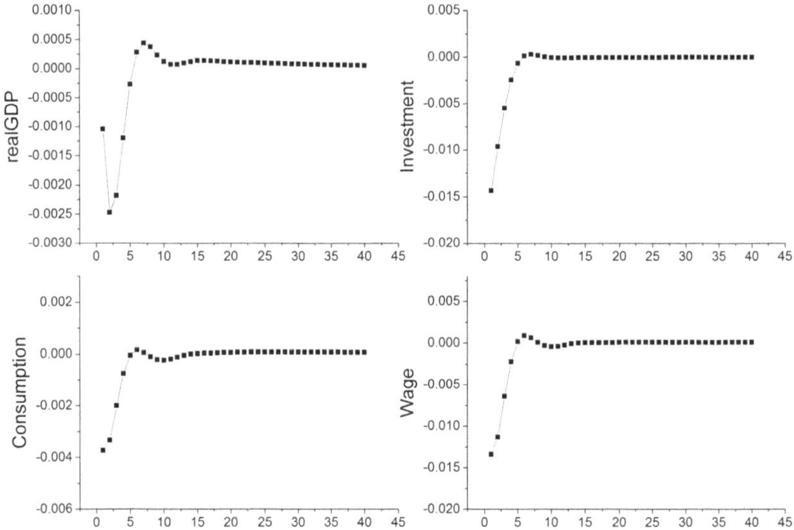

Fig. 12.32 Impulse responses to interest-rate shocks of the advanced model in China: real GDP, investment, consumption and wages

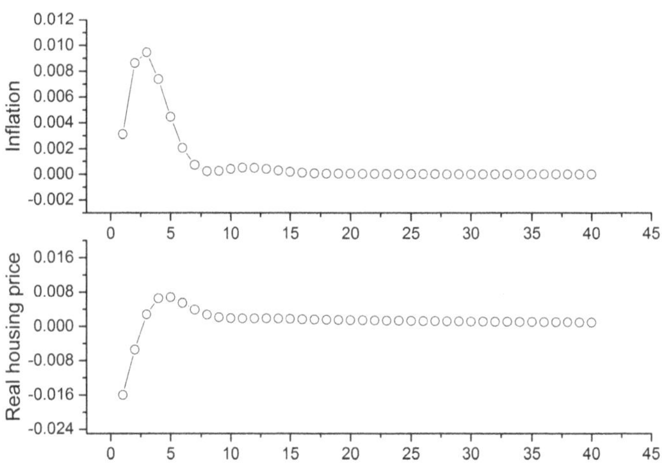

Fig. 12.33 Impulse responses to interest-rate shocks of the advanced model in China: inflation, real interest rate and real housing prices

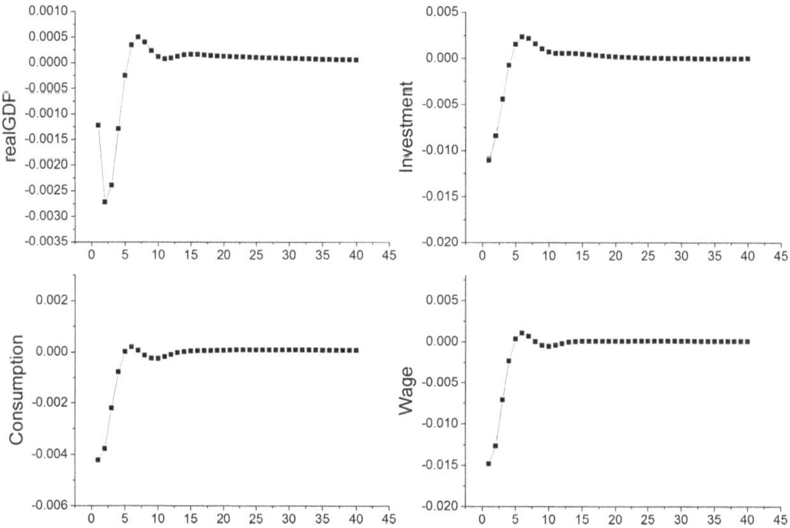

Fig. 12.34 Impulse responses to interest-rate shocks of the advanced model in Brazil: real GDP, investment, consumption and wages

the existing literature including the works of Iacoviello and Neri [1], in which the positive 1% housing demand shock causes real housing prices to rise by about 0.6–0.8% initially, gradually returning to the original level in the following periods. We summarize the advanced model's responses of real housing prices, interest rate and inflation to the positive 1% housing demand shock in Figs. 12.27 (China), 12.29 (Brazil) and 12.31 (India). In these figures, we can see that the advanced model yields similar impulse responses of real housing prices to the housing demand shocks. A 1% positive housing preference shock increases real housing prices in the first quarter by about 0.5%. The effect of housing demand shock on real housing prices lasts about 8–10 quarters, until the deviation of real housing prices returns to zero. This figure also indicates that a positive housing preference shock causes real interest rate to rise by around 0.05% in the second and third quarter. After 10–12 quarters, real interest rate returns to its original level. This is consistent with the length of response of real investment in fixed physical asset. The initial response of inflation to the positive shock of housing demand is negative. This is to reflect the fact that the increase of housing demand pushes up household's investment in housing asset, decreasing their ability to undertake consumption expenditures. Along with the growth of real wage and consumption, inflation in consumption market begins to rise in the following periods, reaching maximum level of 0.05% at the fourth quarter. Similarly, the housing demand shock effect on inflation lasts 10–12 quarters, after when inflation returns to its original value (Figs. 12.28 and 12.30).

In conclusion, the advanced model successfully yields the quantitative results of impulse responses to the housing demand shock for important economic variables such as real GDP, investment in fixed physical asset, wages, consumption, inflation, real interest rate, and real housing prices. Based on the economy maintained by the advanced model, we can quantify the effect of housing demand shocks on real housing prices: A 1% positive housing preference shock causes real housing price to increase by 0.5% at maximum in the beginning. The average length of such effect is around 8–10 quarters. This finding is consistent with documented findings. By using this advanced model, we are able to precisely analyse the dynamic relationship between the housing demand shock and economic variables.

The advanced model needs to answer the question how economic variables respond to the changes of monetary policy. In this advanced model, monetary policy is achieved via the Taylor rule mechanism shown in Eq. 7.40. Theoretically, a positive shock of real interest rate casts downward pressure on real investment in fixed physical asset and thus causes the aggregate output to decrease. As a result, both real wage and household consumption drop in response to such positive real interest-rate shock. Inflation rises at the beginning, as the increase in the real interest rate pushes up the cost of production and therefore the level of inflation. Afterwards, inflation returns to its original level. As most economists believe, an increase in the real interest rate deteriorates households' ability to afford housing investment, decreasing the effective housing demand. Therefore, real housing prices tend to drop after the rise of real interest rate. As real housing prices decrease, housing demand rebounds in the following periods, returning to its original level prior to the shock.

Figure 12.32 demonstrates the response of real GDP to a positive 1% monetary policy shock suggested by the advanced model specified for China. This interest rate innovation causes real GDP to drop by 0.1% in the first quarter after the shock. The drop of real GDP reaches its largest value of −0.25% in the second quarter after the positive interest-rate shock. From the 3rd quarter, real GDP begins to rebound for the next 4 quarters and reaches the value of 0.05% in the 8th quarter. Afterwards, the deviation of

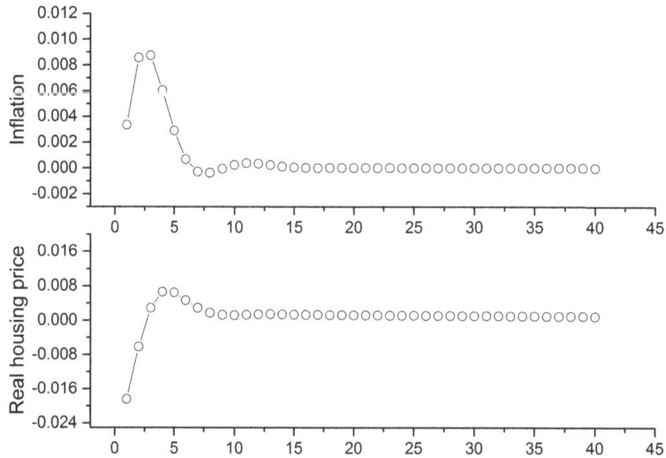

Fig. 12.35 Impulse responses to interest-rate shocks of the advanced model in Brazil: inflation, real interest rate and real housing prices

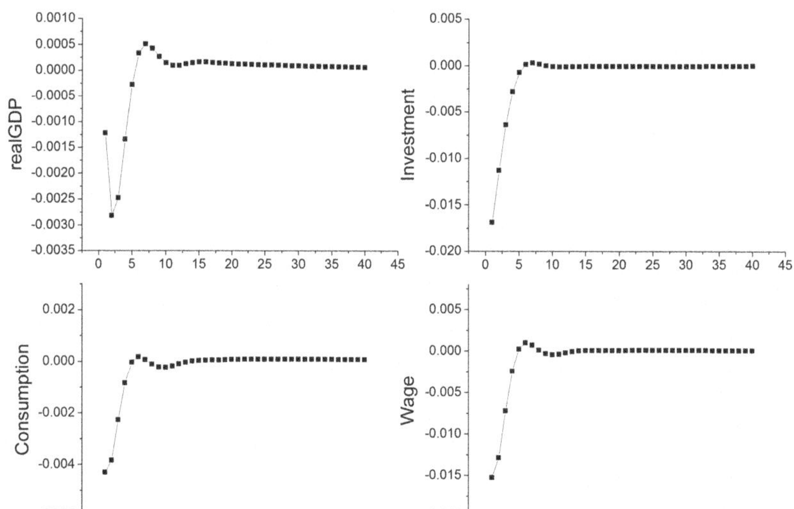

Fig. 12.36 Impulse responses to interest-rate shocks of the advanced model in India: real GDP, investment, consumption and wages

real GDP returns to its original level. The average length of the real interest rate effect on real GDP is about 10–12 quarters. The negative effect of the increase in real interest rate on investment is also captured by the advanced model. Figure 12.32 indicates that a unit increase of the real interest rate causes real investment in fixed physical assets to drop by around 1.5% in the first quarter. Real investment gradually rebounds to its original value in the following periods. After 10 quarters, the deviation of real investment becomes zero. Similar responses can be seen in real wages and household consumption. The initial impact of 1% positive interest rate shock on real wage is about −1.30% and on household consumption −0.40%. The effect of this interest-rate shock lasts about 10–12 quarters as in the case of real investment in fixed physical assets.

Figure 12.33 illustrates the responses of inflation and real housing prices to the positive interest-rate shock implied by the advanced model specified for China. The results are well consistent with our theoretical analysis and documented findings. A positive 1% real interest-rate shock causes real housing prices to decrease by around 1.60% and inflation to increase by 0.30% in the first quarter. It takes 10–15 quarters for inflation and real housing prices to return to their original level.

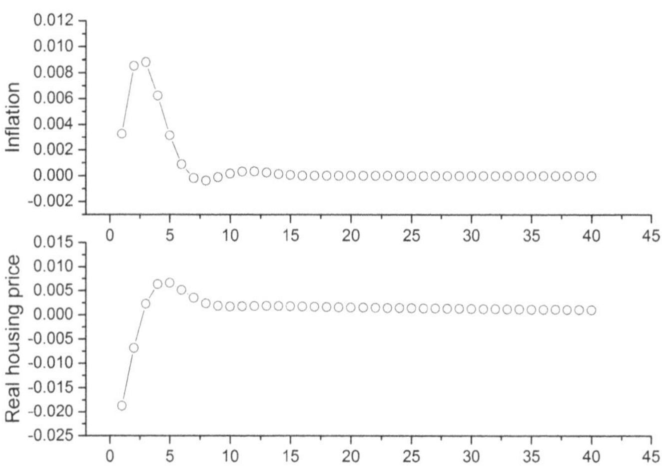

Fig. 12.37 Impulse responses to interest-rate shocks of the advanced model in India: inflation, real interest rate and real housing prices

We demonstrate the impulse responses of economic variables to the positive real interest-rate shock suggested by the advanced model specified for Brazil and India in Figs. 12.34, 12.35, 12.36, and 12.37, respectively. In conclusion, the economic system implied by the advanced model exhibits good consistency of dynamics with stylized facts and theoretical hypotheses.

12.3 Empirical Analysis of the Full Model

The full model moves one step further than the advanced model in that it contains the financial frictions in the financial market, where financial intermediaries absorb deposits from households and make loans to entrepreneurs who are looking for credit to pay their working capital expenditure. By introducing a financial market into the advanced model, we successfully build up the full model with complete features including financial frictions, housing market, household heterogeneities and short-term nominal rigidity in non-housing market.

12.3.1 Parameter Identification

The procedure of empirical analysis of the full model is similar to that of the advanced model. The first task is to properly specify all the parameters included in this full model. As we have discussed before, to get accurate values of model parameters, both calibration and estimation methods are adopted. We summarize the parameter calibration for the full model in Table 12.13. The majority of the full model is identical to that of the advanced model, thereby we keep most of the parameter calibration results as in the advanced model. For simplicity, we skip the details of parameter calibration that have discussed in the previous section. The only difference here is the parameters related to financial friction—κ and ι. As we have discussed in the theoretical framework, financial intermediaries take in deposits from households, paying out the risk-free rate and make loans to entrepreneurs at a rate higher than the risk-free rate. Financial friction emerges in this process. In the first place, to overcome 'information asymmetry', financial intermediaries need to pay certain costs to get accurate and complete information about the potential borrower. Secondly, the investment of entrepreneurs is no longer risk free. Financial intermediaries who grant loans to the borrowers face the risk that borrowers fail to make full loan repayment on time. If it happens, the borrower goes bankrupt and the financial intermediary gets the remaining value of the borrower. As a result,

Table 12.13 The calibration of parameters in the full model

Parameter	*Value*	*Parameter*	*Value*
β_{cw}	0.9650	$\mu 1$	0.45
β_{rw}	0.9650	$\mu 2$	0.10
β_{lh}	0.9925	$\mu 3$	0.25
β_{bh}	0.9700	$\mu 4$	0.20
α	0.35	θ_{π}	0.75
δ_h	0.015	β_1	0.40
δ_{kc}	0.025	β_2	0.25
δ_{kh}	0.020	β_3	0.35
X_{ss}	1.15	m	0.70
b_{cw}	0.65	b_{bh}	0.40
b_{rw}	0.60	b_{lh}	0.35
η_{cw}	0.50	η_{bh}	0.50
η_{rw}	0.50	η_{lh}	0.50
κ	0.05	$\Psi(R^d)$	0.50

under optimal loan contract, the equilibrium of financial markets is realized when the loan premium fully reflects the monitoring cost, captured by κ as shown in Eq. 8.36, and the bankruptcy risk, captured by ι as shown in Eq. 8.35. In our analysis, we fix $\kappa = 0.05$, meaning that the monitoring cost is equal to 5% of the total loan value. We also set $\Psi(R^d) = 0.50$. This calibration is supported by empirical research and findings in both developed and emerging market economies such as the works conducted by Chowdhury et al. [20] focusing developed economies, Cabezon [21] focusing on emerging market economies.

Using the same data sets observed in China, Brazil and India, we estimate the values of the rest of the parameters in the full model. The estimation results are shown in Tables 12.14 (China), 12.15 (Brazil) and 12.16 (India). As in the empirical analysis of the advanced model, we demonstrate both prior and posterior distribution with posterior mean and 5 and 95% confidence intervals. The estimation process is identical to that in the advanced model, here we use beta distribution as priors to estimate the value of parameters of persistence including those in the interest rate Eq. 8.16, ρ_{GDP}, ρ_r and $\rho_{\pi,r}$, those in the technology and housing preference evolution Eqs. 7.58, ρ_{Ac}, ρ_{Ah} and ρ_j the one in the inflation Eq. 8.15, ρ_{π}. For the estimation of the standard errors of the shocks, we use inverse gamma distribution as prior with infinite range and a mean of 0.01.

Table 12.14 The estimation of parameters in the full model: China

	Prior distribution			*Posterior distribution*		
Parameter	*Distr.*	*Mean*	*Std. Dev.*	*Mean*	5%	95%
ρ_{GDP}	Beta	0.50	0.10	0.4637	0.4305	0.4919
ρ_{Ac}	Beta	0.80	0.10	0.9947	0.9899	0.9981
ρ_{Ah}	Beta	0.80	0.10	0.8035	0.7750	0.8496
ρ_r	Beta	0.50	0.10	0.5772	0.5763	0.5779
ρ_π	Beta	0.80	0.10	0.7378	0.7375	0.7381
$\rho_{\pi,r}$	Beta	0.50	0.10	0.2789	0.2785	0.2793
ρ_j	Beta	0.50	0.10	0.5495	0.5487	0.5504
e_{rd}	Inv. Gamma	0.01	inf.	0.0317	0.0262	0.0367
e_π	Inv. Gamma	0.01	inf.	0.0049	0.0024	0.0081
e_j	Inv. Gamma	0.01	inf.	0.0910	0.0786	0.0949
e_{Ac}	Inv. Gamma	0.01	inf.	0.0126	0.0097	0.0155
e_{Ah}	Inv. Gamma	0.01	inf.	0.0089	0.0068	0.0109

Table 12.15 The estimation of parameters in the full model: Brazil

	Prior distribution			*Posterior distribution*		
Parameter	*Distr.*	*Mean*	*Std. Dev.*	*Mean*	5%	95%
ρ_{GDP}	Beta	0.50	0.10	0.4761	0.4130	0.5372
ρ_{Ac}	Beta	0.80	0.10	0.9957	0.9923	0.9989
ρ_{Ah}	Beta	0.80	0.10	0.8528	0.7623	0.9385
ρ_r	Beta	0.50	0.10	0.4952	0.4518	0.5361
ρ_π	Beta	0.80	0.10	0.7578	0.7347	0.7804
$\rho_{\pi,r}$	Beta	0.50	0.10	0.2951	0.2301	0.3714
ρ_j	Beta	0.50	0.10	0.5009	0.4606	0.5447
e_r	Inv. Gamma	0.01	inf.	0.0145	0.0119	0.0179
e_π	Inv. Gamma	0.01	inf.	0.0075	0.0026	0.0139
e_j	Inv. Gamma	0.01	inf.	0.0801	0.0736	0.1012
e_{Ac}	Inv. Gamma	0.01	inf.	0.0112	0.0077	0.0119
e_{Ah}	Inv. Gamma	0.01	inf.	0.0089	0.0030	0.0146

12.3.2 *Empirical Study of the Model Economy*

Based on the values calculated by calibration and estimation, we specify the full models for China, Brazil and India. Using these models, we can make empirical analysis of economic mechanism and dynamics of the economic system implied by the full model. The results show promising consistence between model performance and stylized facts. As in the empirical analysis of the advanced model, we compare the standard deviation of major

Table 12.16 The estimation of parameters in the full model: India

Parameter	*Prior distribution* Distr.	Mean	Std. Dev.	*Posterior distribution* Mean	5%	95%
ρ_{GDP}	Beta	0.50	0.10	0.4845	0.4784	0.4945
ρ_{Ac}	Beta	0.80	0.10	0.9953	0.9908	0.9994
ρ_{Ah}	Beta	0.80	0.10	0.8086	0.8001	0.8219
ρ_r	Beta	0.50	0.10	0.4954	0.4889	0.4995
ρ_π	Beta	0.80	0.10	0.7587	0.7505	0.7669
$\rho_{\pi,r}$	Beta	0.50	0.10	0.2913	0.2825	0.3027
ρ_j	Beta	0.50	0.10	0.5262	0.5229	0.5312
e_r	Inv. Gamma	0.01	inf.	0.0191	0.0151	0.0251
e_π	Inv. Gamma	0.01	inf.	0.0068	0.0025	0.0134
e_j	Inv. Gamma	0.01	inf.	0.0828	0.0712	0.0923
e_{Ac}	Inv. Gamma	0.01	inf.	0.0126	0.0068	0.0181
e_{Ah}	Inv. Gamma	0.01	inf.	0.0074	0.0021	0.0122

economic variables such as aggregate output, consumption, investment, inflation and housing prices produced by the full model with stylized facts based on the observed samples. This comparison is shown in Table 12.17, demonstrating a good consistence between model results and stylized facts in China, Brazil and India. We also summarize the comparison between model implied correlations between economic variables and those drawn on stylized facts. All these results indicate the good coherence between model performance and the observed samples. For example, the standard deviation of GDP implied by our full model is 2.9844% (China), 2.9949% (Brazil) 2.9819%, very close to those calculated from observed samples:

Table 12.17 The statistical features of the full model: standard deviations

(Stdev.	*Model output (data)* China	*Brazil*	*India*
Consumption	0.016044 (0.017293)	0.016250 (0.021869)	0.015278 (0.023951)
Investment	0.041322 (0.045452)	0.043749 (0.051168)	0.041974 (0.032922)
Inflation	0.013923 (0.018656)	0.013687 (0.013638)	0.013741 (0.016518)
GDP	0.029844 (0.030811)	0.029949 (0.029302)	0.029819 (0.029240)
Real interest	0.015245 (0.012772)	0.015389 (0.012245)	0.015409 (0.015619)
Real wage	0.053277 (0.033231)	0.055053 (0.040966)	0.051887 (0.037720)
Housing price	0.098147 (0.093910)	0.069565 (0.047502)	0.088658 (0.066017)

3.0811% (China), 2.9302% (Brazil) and 2.9240% (India). Additionally, the full model also generates correlations between major economic variables, consistent with stylized facts. For instance, the correlation between consumption and GDP captured by the full model is 0.7315 (China), 0.7144 (Brazil) and 0.7114 (India), all of which lie closely to their counterparts drawn from the stylized facts: 0.7389 (China), 0.7201 (Brazil) and 0.6588 (India).

12.3.3 The Impulse Responses

After demonstrating the good coherence between model results and the stylized facts in terms of the standard deviations of economic variables and of the correlations between major economic variables, the dynamic features of the model economy is summarized in the impulse responses. Impulse responses tell us how economic variables in the full model react to the innovations such as productivity shocks, interest-rate shocks and housing demand shocks. In this subsection, to better demonstrate the effect of collateral mortgages in the housing market and of financial frictions, both of which are the major contributions of this full model, figures of impulse responses figures with comparison between results drawn from the full model and the model without collateral mortgage and financial frictions (the baseline model) are displayed.[13] In the following figures we draw impulse responses generated by the full model (Full) in solid black line and the ones yielded by the model without collateral mortgage (Baseline) and financial friction in dashed red line (Table 12.18).

As in the previous section, we first demonstrate the reactions of economic variables to the productivity shock in the non-housing market, $A_{c,t}$. In the theoretical perspective, a positive non-housing productivity shock leads to the increase of aggregate output and thereby pushes up the household income. Such increase in household income supports a higher level of consumption expenditure and real estate investment. As a result, both inflation and real housing prices tend to rise. On the supply side, investment in fixed physical assets, both in housing and non-housing markets, positively responds to this increase in demand, leading to a higher level

[13]It is easy to get this baseline model from the full model, by simply shutting down the function of mortgage loan and financial frictions. To remove the collateral mortgage and financial frictions in the full model, we set $\beta_2 = 0$ and $\beta_1 = 0.65$ in 8.9 and $\iota = \kappa = 0$ in 8.35 and 8.36.

Table 12.18 The statistical features of the full model: correlations

Correlations	*Model output (data)*		
	China	*Brazil*	*India*
Consum., GDP	0.7315 (0.7389)	0.7144 (0.7201)	0.7114 (0.6588)
Inv., GDP	0.7296 (0.7234)	0.7682 (0.7474)	0.7768 (0.7331)
Wage, GDP	0.6119 (0.6460)	0.6117 (0.6953)	0.6230 (0.6263)
Inflation, GDP	0.6523 (0.6413)	0.6311 (0.6321)	0.6658 (0.6682)
Consum., Inv.	0.5418 (0.5994)	0.5036 (0.5377)	0.5233 (0.5460)
p_h, GDP	0.7971 (0.5624)	0.7120 (0.5931)	0.6697 (0.4993)
p_h, Consum.	0.4460 (0.4132)	0.4231 (0.4064)	0.3932 (0.3964)
p_h, Inv.	0.6840 (0.6332)	0.6467 (0.6013)	0.6241 (0.5574)
p_h, Llh	0.7245 (0.6263)	0.7304 (0.6309)	0.7166 (0.6050)
Llh, GDP	0.7551 (0.7145)	0.7455 (0.7481)	0.7201 (0.7193)

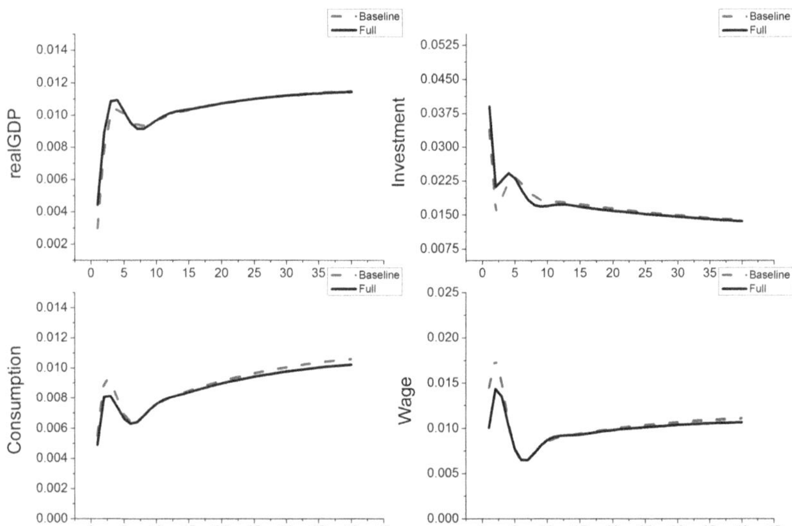

Fig. 12.38 Impulse responses to productivity shocks in the non-housing market of the full model in China: real GDP, investment, consumption and wages

of real interest rate. Such feedback cycle keeps on processing for certain length of time until new equilibrium is achieved when all markets clear. In the new equilibrium, GDP, real investment, consumption, wages, and real housing prices become higher than their pre-shock level.

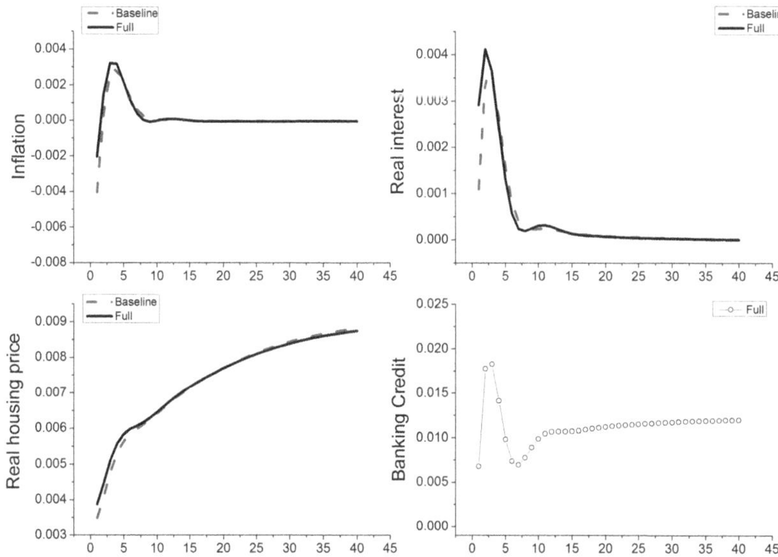

Fig. 12.39 Impulse responses to productivity shocks in the non-housing market of the full model in China: inflation, real interest rate, real housing prices and bank credit

As shown in Fig. 12.40, the full model specified for China responds to positive non-housing productivity shocks than the model without collateral mortgage and financial frictions. In the full model, a 1% positive productivity shock in the non-housing market causes real GDP to rise by 0.5% in the first quarter, quickly reaching 1.1% in the third quarter. While in the baseline model without collateral and financial frictions, such increase is 0.3% in the first quarter and 1.05% in the third quarter. The average length of the i.i.d. non-housing productivity shock effect on real GDP is about 10–15 quarters, after when real GDP arrives at its new level, about 1% higher than its original level. Similarly, real investment in fixed physical asset reacts to the shock more actively in the full model than in the baseline model: the initial increase is 4.25% in the full model and 3.50% in the baseline model. This finding shows that the collateral and financial frictions amplify the impulse responses of real GDP to the non-housing productivity shocks, consistent with the findings of many literature especially the works of Bernanke et al. [7] and Iacoviello and Neri [1] (Fig. 12.38).

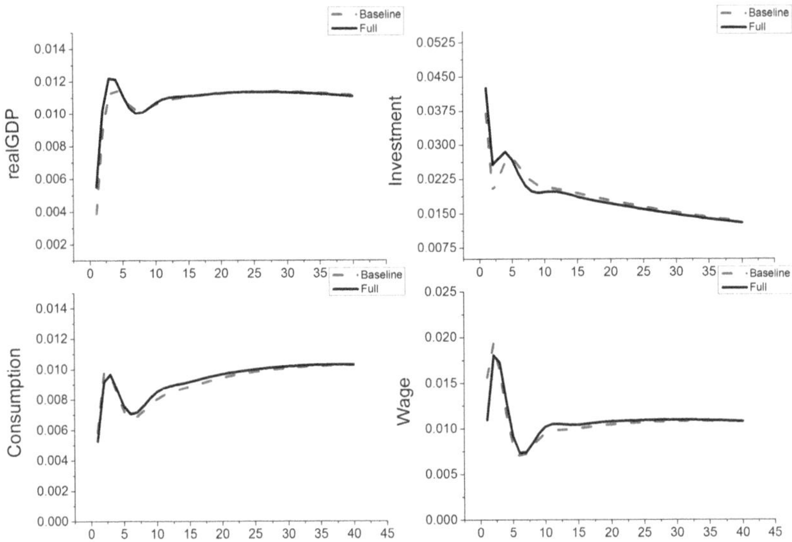

Fig. 12.40 Impulse responses to productivity shocks in the non-housing market of the full model in Brazil: real GDP, investment, consumption and wages

Figure 12.39 demonstrates how inflation, real interest rate and real housing prices respond to the positive non-housing productivity shocks. The amplification effect of collateral mortgage and financial frictions can be witnessed in these impulse responses as well. In the full model, there is a variable that is not included in the previous models—bank credit. As we have discussed in the theoretical framework, entrepreneurs seek for loan from financial intermediaries to meet their working capital expenditure, which is primarily composed of wage payments (as shown in Eq. 8.33). In the theoretical perspective, bank credit should respond positively to the positive non-housing productivity shock, which pushes up both labour demand and real wages. What is more, because of the definition of working capital, the impulse response of bank credit should be similar to that of real wages in Fig. 12.39. The impulse response of banking credit is illustrated in Fig. 12.39. Since only the full model contains this feature, there is no comparison between the full model and the baseline model in this case. This figure shows that a positive non-housing productivity shock causes bank credit to increase by 0.73% initially in the first quarter. In the following two quarters, bank credit keeps on increasing until it reaches around 1.90% in

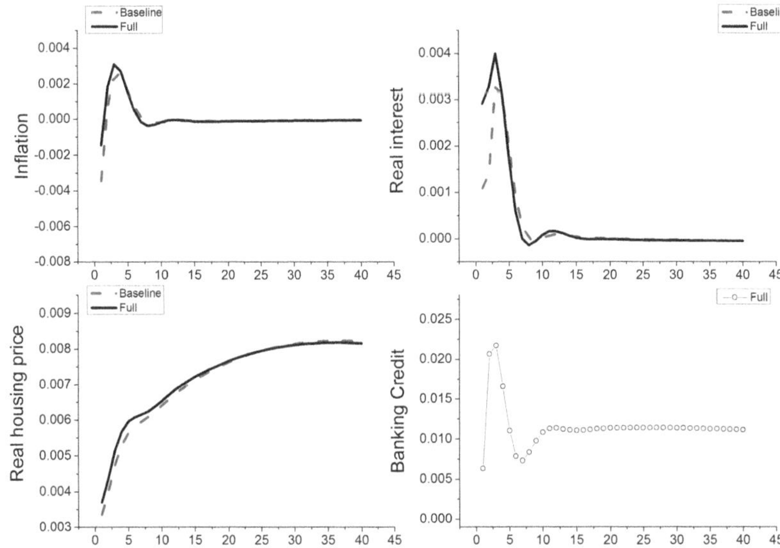

Fig. 12.41 Impulse responses to productivity shocks in the non-housing market of the full model in Brazil: inflation, real interest rate, real housing prices and bank credit

the third quarter after the shock, nearly twice as much as the original 1% productivity shock. The effect of non-housing productivity shock on bank credit lasts about 10–15 quarters, as in the case of real GDP and wages.

We summarize the impulse responses to a positive non-housing productivity shock in the full models specified for Brazil, as shown in Figs. 12.40 and 12.41.

Similarly, the impulse responses of variables such as real GDP, fixed asset investment, household consumption and wages to a standard positive productivity shock in the non-housing market are demonstrated in Fig. 12.42. The impulse responses of variables like inflation, real interest rate, housing price and bank credit are shown in Fig. 12.43.

In conclusion, we can see the clear amplification effects of collateral mortgage and financial frictions in impulse responses of economic variables such as real GDP, investment in fixed physical assets, inflation, real interest rate and housing prices to the productivity shock in the non-housing market.

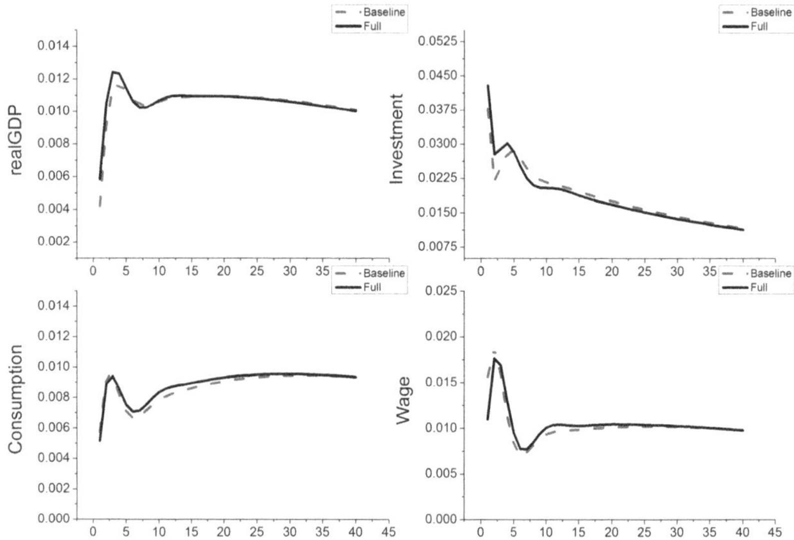

Fig. 12.42 Impulse responses to productivity shocks in the non-housing market of the full model in India: real GDP, investment, consumption and wages

The theoretical framework of the full model concludes that a positive productivity shock in the housing market, enhances the housing supply, pushing down real housing prices. The growth of productivity in the housing market increases the real wages and thus the income of households working in this market. Due to such increase in income, households undertake more consumption expenditure, increasing the demand in the non-housing market. Therefore, real GDP increases after the positive shock in housing productivity, and investment in fixed physical assets increases in the following periods. Because households working in the housing market only account for a minor part of total households, we expect the positive effect of this productivity shock in the housing market to be less intensive than the effect of the shock in the non-housing market.

In Figs. 12.44, 12.45, 12.46, 12.47, 12.48 and 12.49, we demonstrate the impulse responses of economic variables to an i.i.d. positive housing productivity shock in models specified for China, Brazil and India. These figures show that model implied impulse responses are in good coherence with our theoretical expectations. Real GDP positively reacts to such

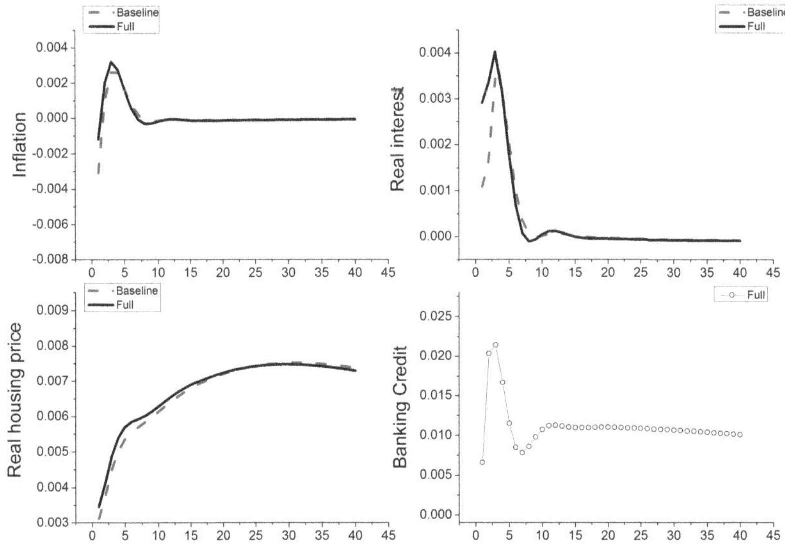

Fig. 12.43 Impulse responses to productivity shocks in the non-housing market of the full model in India: inflation, real interest rate, real housing prices and bank credit

productivity shocks, with an increase of about 0.085% in the first quarter and the maximum growth of about 0.10% occurred in the second quarter. Afterwards, real GDP returns to a new equilibrium level. Real housing prices drop by 0.07% in the first quarter after the positive housing productivity shock and gradually return to a new equilibrium level as we concluded in the theoretical framework.

Theoretical framework and empirical evidence suggest that the housing market plays an important role in modern economic systems, asking for dynamic macroeconomic models with fuller consideration of this market. Both the empirical analyses and the theoretical approaches have demonstrated that housing demand shocks (i.e. housing preference shocks in our advanced and full model) is able to cause volatile responses of other economic variables such as aggregate output, consumption, investment, real housing price, interest rate, inflation and so on. A positive housing demand shock leads to a higher level of real housing prices and investment in fixed physical assets in the housing market. It also induces real wages of

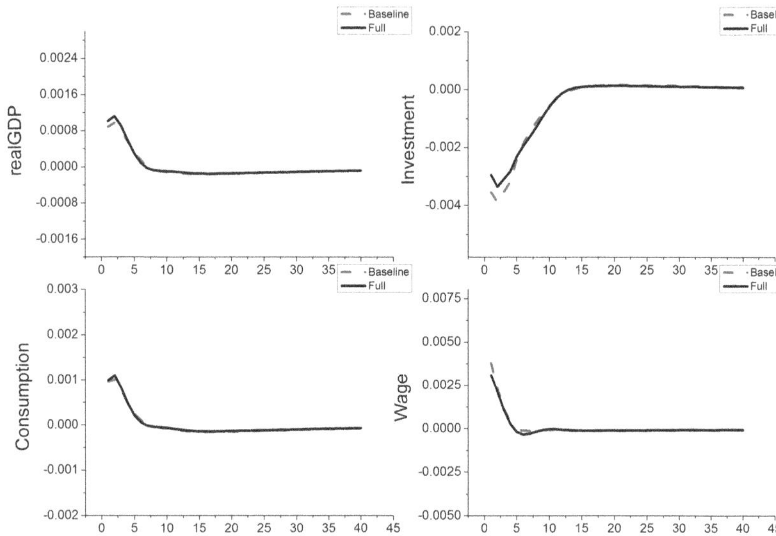

Fig. 12.44 Impulse responses to productivity shocks in the housing market of the full model in China: real GDP, investment, consumption and wages

workers in this market to rise. Therefore, consumption and investment in fixed physical assets in the non-housing market began to rise. Because this housing preference shock does not increase the productivity, the new equilibrium value of economic variables including real GDP, investment, wages, consumption, real interest rate, inflation, real housing prices and so on are equal to their pre-shock values. Figures 12.50, 12.51, 12.52, 12.53, 12.54 and 12.55 are the impulse responses of economic variables to the positive housing demand shock in the full models specified for China, Brazil and India.

These figures indicate that the effect of collateral mortgages and financial frictions on the impulse responses to housing demand shock is very obvious. As shown in Fig. 12.50, the maximum increase of real GDP after a 1% positive housing demand shock is about 0.05% in the baseline model without collateral and financial frictions, much less than 0.12% in the full model. Collateral mortgage and financial frictions make more difference in impulse responses of real investment to housing demand shock. The altitude of impulse responses of real investment in the full model has almost

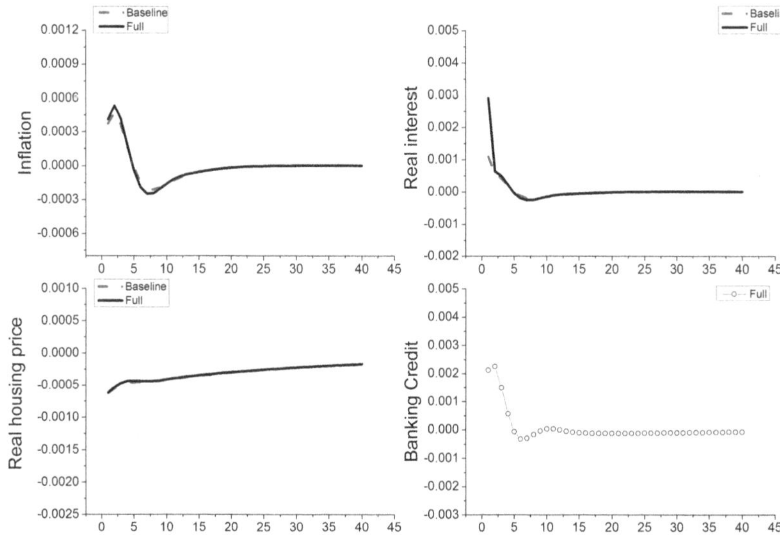

Fig. 12.45 Impulse responses to productivity shocks in the housing market of the full model in China: inflation, real interest rate and real housing prices

tripled that in the baseline model, in which collateral mortgages and financial frictions are removed from the model economy.

In conclusion, the economic system implied by the full model successfully captures the dynamics of the actual economy, in that impulse responses of important economic variables such as real GDP, investment in fixed physical asset, wages, consumption, inflation, real interest rate and real housing prices to housing demand shock are in good consistence with stylized facts and theoretical hypotheses. Based on these quantitative results, we can more accurately investigate the effect of a housing demand shock on aggregate output (real GDP), investment on fixed physical assets and real housing prices: a 1% positive housing preference shock causes real GDP to increase by 0.12% at a maximum and causes real housing prices to increase by 0.5%. The average length of such effect is around 8–10 quarters. This finding is consistent with the findings of other contributors. Using this model, we are able to precisely analyse the dynamic relationships between housing demand shock and economic variables.

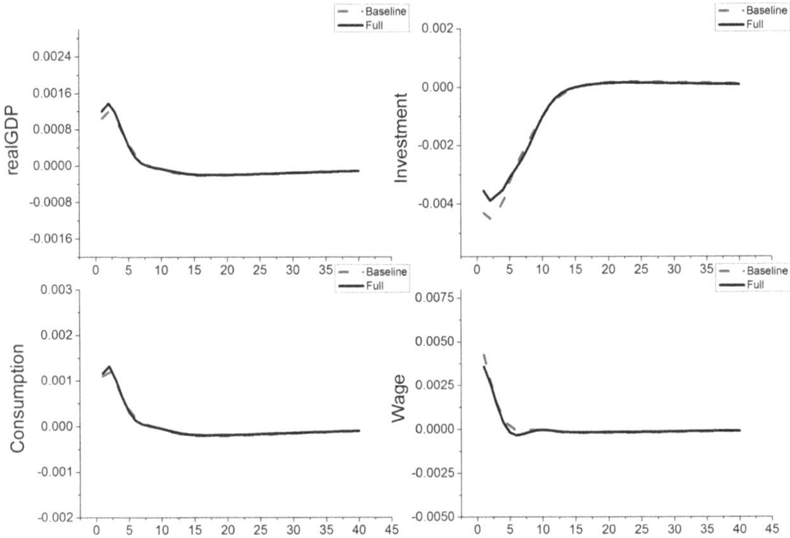

Fig. 12.46 Impulse responses to productivity shocks in the housing market of the full model in Brazil: real GDP, investment, consumption and wages

According to the theoretical analysis, we believe that economic variables such as real GDP, investment in fixed physical assets, household consumption and wages decrease after a hike of the interest rate. This has been well-documented in previous studies, with strong theoretical support and empirical evidence. What is more, a higher level of interest rate deteriorates the household's ability to make consumption expenditure and housing purchase, pushing down housing demand and the demand in the non-housing market. Therefore, both real housing prices and inflation are expected to decrease after the positive interest-rate shock. It is also natural for us to expect that the full model with collateral mortgages and financial frictions are more sensitive to the changes of interest rate than the baseline model. This is consistent with the 'financial accelerator' effect and collateral effect supported by a large amount of theoretical analysis and empirical evidence. Figures 12.56, 12.57, 12.58, 12.59, 12.60 and 12.61 illustrate how economic variables respond to an adverse monetary policy shock in the full models and the baseline models specified for China, Brazil and India. We can see that the impulse responses produced by the full model are coherent

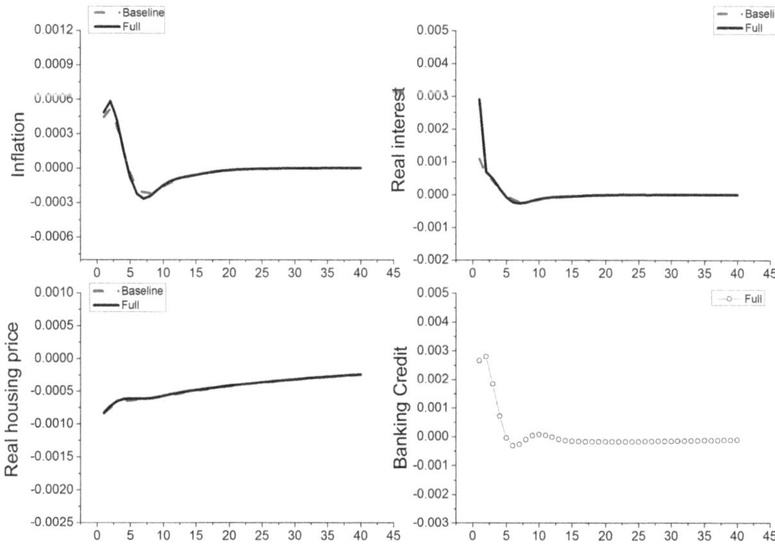

Fig. 12.47 Impulse responses to productivity shocks in the housing market of the full model in Brazil: inflation, real interest rate and real housing prices

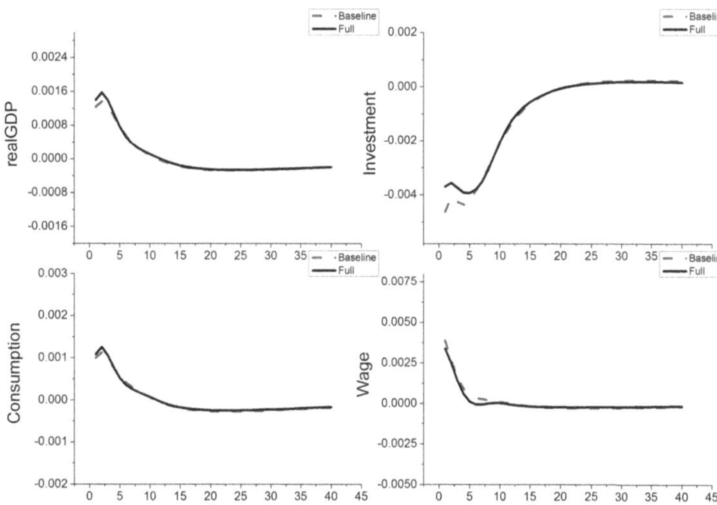

Fig. 12.48 Impulse responses to productivity shocks in the housing market of the full model in India: real GDP, investment, consumption and wages

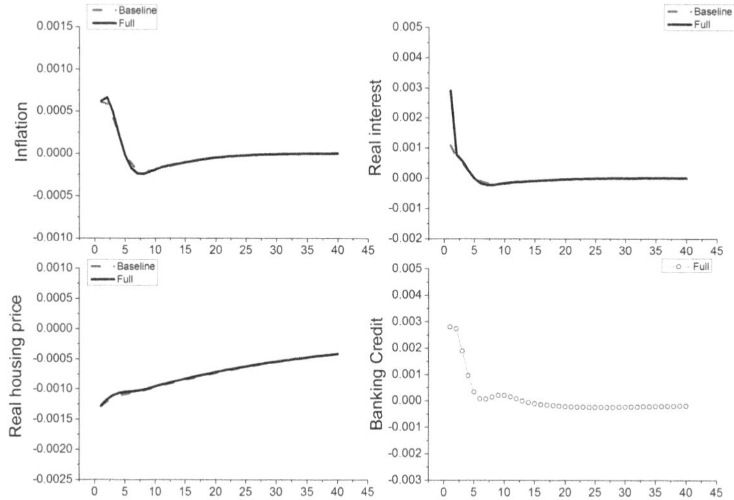

Fig. 12.49 Impulse responses to productivity shocks in the housing market of the full model in India: inflation, real interest rate and real housing prices

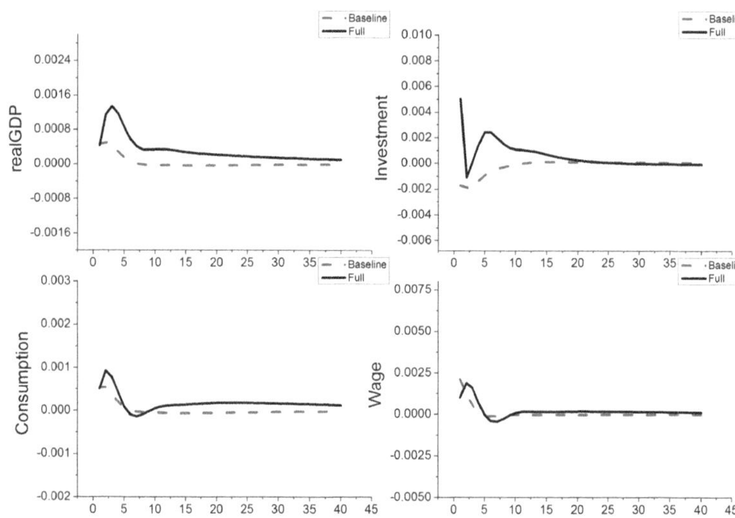

Fig. 12.50 Impulse responses to housing preference shocks of the full model in China: real GDP, investment, consumption and wages

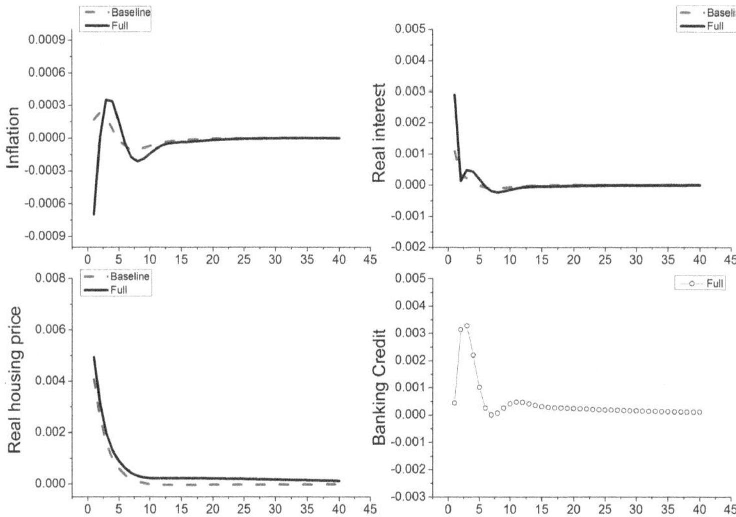

Fig. 12.51 Impulse responses to housing preference shocks of the full model in China: inflation, real interest rate and real housing prices

with our theoretical expectations. This is so in two folds. In the first place, we do witness that impulse responses produced by the full model are more intensive than that generated by the baseline model that is without collateral and financial friction effects. Taking real GDP for example, the maximum altitude of impulse response to an i.i.d. positive interest-rate increase in the full model has almost doubled the value in the baseline model. Similar situation happens in the case of real investment's impulse response. Without collateral mortgages and financial frictions, a 1% increase of interest rate is followed by a 0.8% drop of real investment. While the value of the decrease in investment to a same interest-rate change is around 1.5%, it almost doubles the number in the baseline model. Collateral mortgages and financial friction effects amplify the real housing prices' impulse response to the monetary policy change as well. As shown in Fig. 12.57, 1% increase of interest rate causes real housing prices to drop by 1%, without collateral mortgage and financial friction effects, and by 1.70%, with collateral mortgages and financial friction effects.

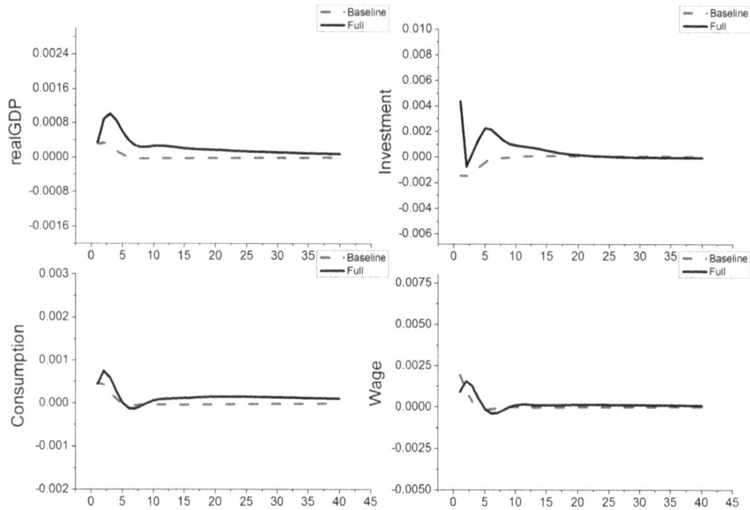

Fig. 12.52 Impulse responses to housing preference shocks of the full model in Brazil: real GDP, investment, consumption and wages

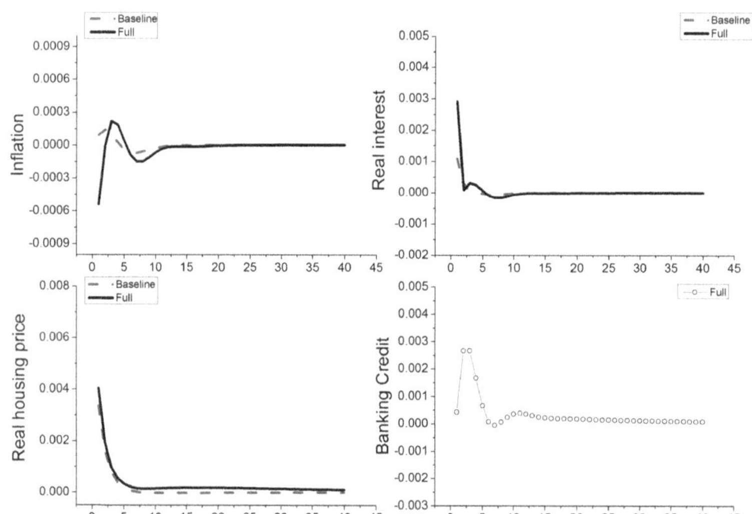

Fig. 12.53 Impulse responses to housing preference shocks of the full model in Brazil: inflation, real interest rate and real housing prices

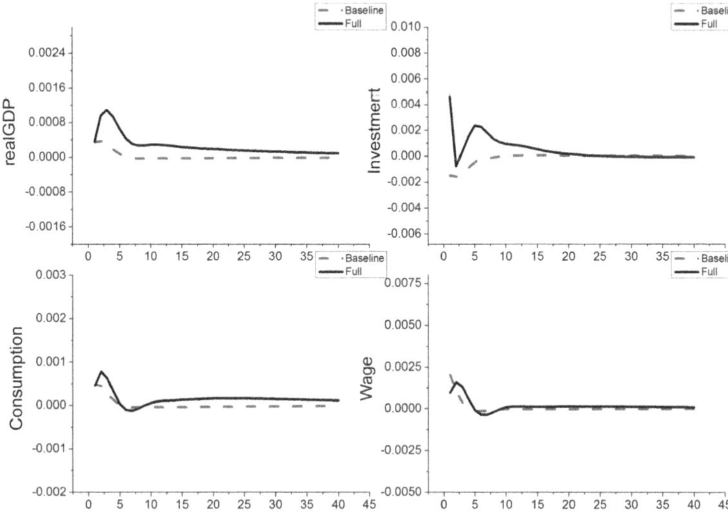

Fig. 12.54 Impulse responses to housing preference shocks of the full model in India: real GDP, investment, consumption and wages

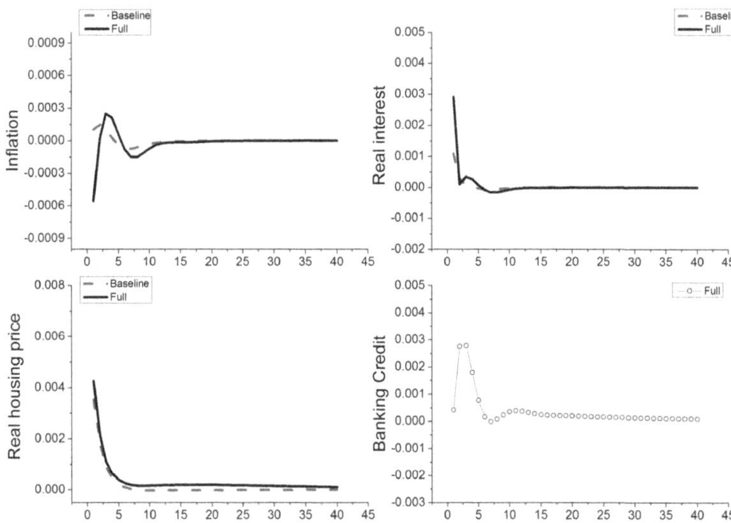

Fig. 12.55 Impulse responses to housing preference shocks of the full model in India: inflation, real interest rate and real housing prices

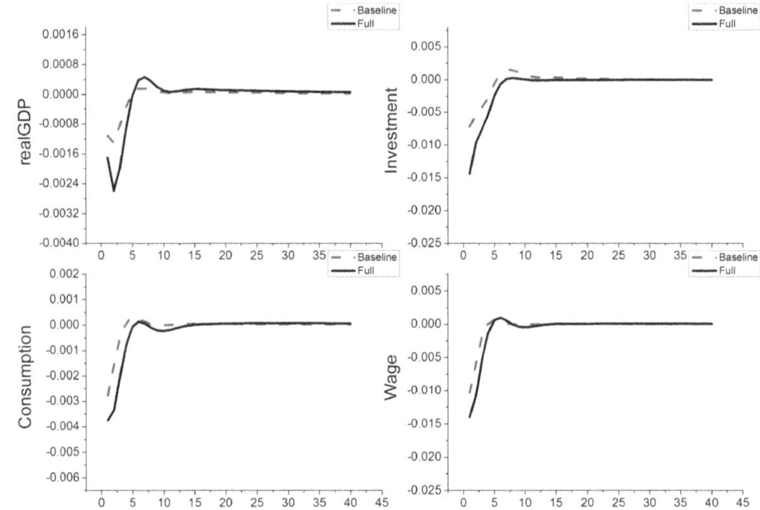

Fig. 12.56 Impulse responses to interest-rate shocks of the full model in China: real GDP, investment, consumption and wage

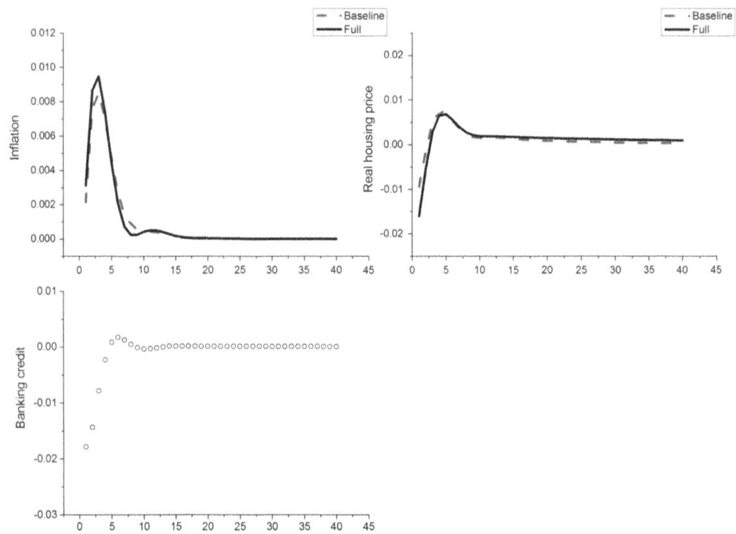

Fig. 12.57 Impulse responses to interest-rate shocks of the full model in China: Inflation, real interest rate and real housing price

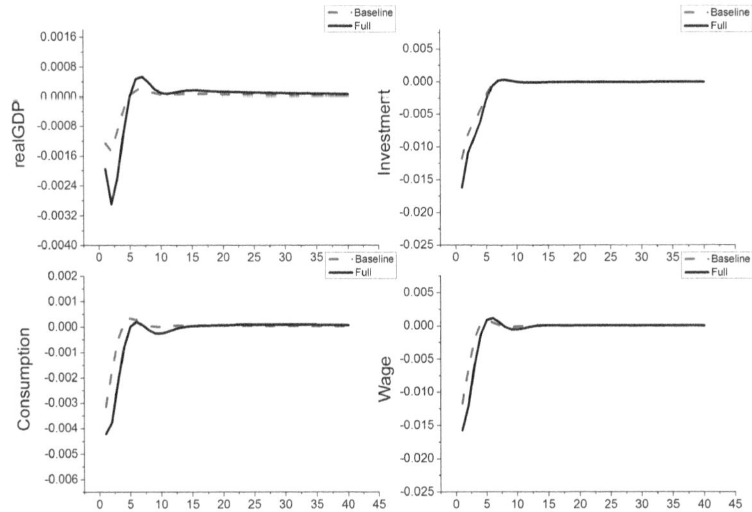

Fig. 12.58 Impulse responses to interest-rate shocks of the full model in Brazil: real GDP, investment, consumption and wage

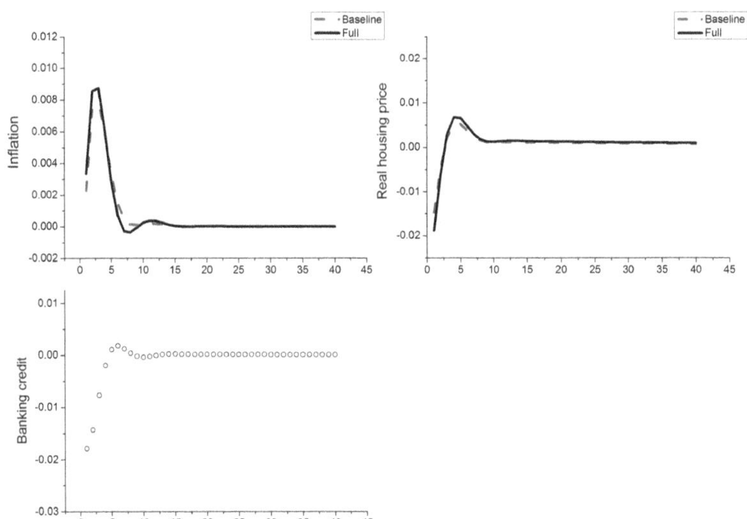

Fig. 12.59 Impulse responses to interest-rate shocks of the full model in Brazil: Inflation, real interest rate and real housing price

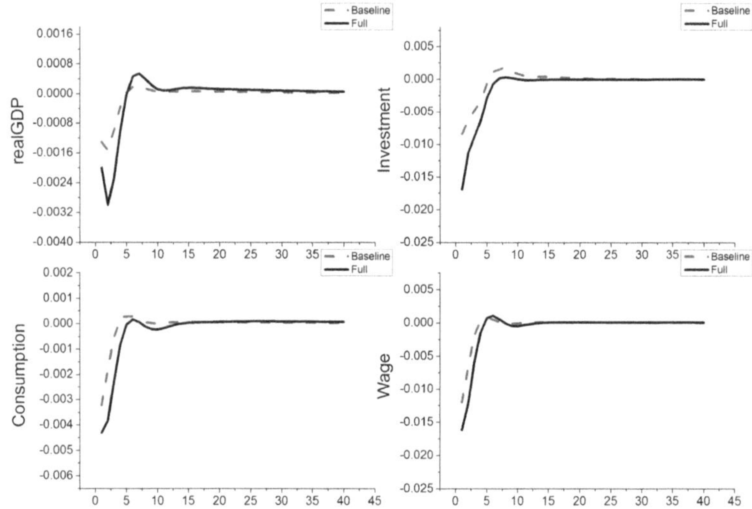

Fig. 12.60 Impulse responses to interest-rate shocks of the full model in India: real GDP, investment, consumption and wage

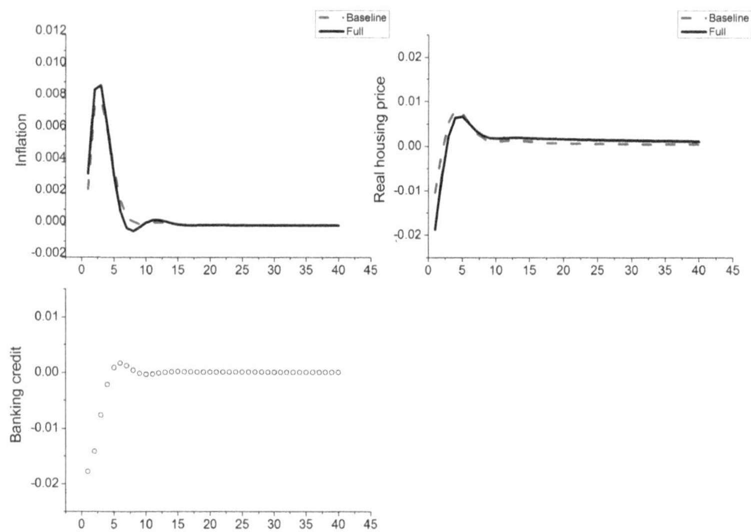

Fig. 12.61 Impulse responses to interest-rate shocks of the full model in India: inflation, real interest rate and real housing price

After summarizing the performance of the full model in terms of statistical features including standard deviations and correlations and impulse responses, we can conclude that the full model successfully yields results with good coherence with respect to our theoretical hypotheses and the stylized facts. This model is able to give us the accurate information of macroeconomic mechanism and of the movements of economic variables within the economy. Our model sheds light on the improvement of the traditional DSGE model by introducing a housing market, financial frictions and household heterogeneities into the original NCW/DSGE model. What is more, the FHSAM gives special attention to emerging market economies, making it more suitable for DSGE modelling in emerging market economies, in which studies using dynamic expectation models are still at a preliminary stage.

Appendix

To demonstrate the solution to the dynamic model, the second-order approximation[14] generated by MATLAB Dynare is demonstrated in this appendix. By definition discussed in Eq. 9.1, the second-order approximation to the dynamic system denoted by state representation y_t can be written as

$$\begin{aligned} y_t = y^* + 0.5\Delta^2 + Ay_{t-1}^d + Bu_t + 0.5C(y_{t-1}^d \otimes y_{t-1}^d) \\ + 0.5D(u_t \otimes u_t) + E(y_{t-1}^d \otimes u_t) \end{aligned} \tag{12.1}$$

where y^* is the steady-state value of y, Δ^2 represents the shift effect of the variance of future innovations, and y_t^d is the deviation from the steady-state value, $y_t^d = y_t - y^*$.

According to Dynare, the decision rules represented by matrices A, B, C, Δ^2, D, and E are stored in the oo_.dr struct of the MATLAB file. More specifically, matrix A is stored in oo_.dr.ghx. For the full model specified for China, is a 51×19 matrix shown as:

[14] For simplicity, only second-order approximation is illustrated, as the first order approximation, $y_t = y^* - Ay_{t-1}^d + Bu_t$, is the reduced form of higher order approximations.

$$A = \begin{bmatrix} -0.1161 & 0.0095 & 0.3538 & -0.1702 & \dots & -1.1222 & 0.1131 & 0.0613 & -1.5890 \\ -0.0023 & -0.1840 & 0.0589 & 0.1064 & \dots & 0.8889 & -0.0891 & 0.0430 & 1.6212 \\ -0.0175 & 0.0016 & 0.0227 & -0.0092 & \dots & 0.3948 & 0.1047 & 0.0076 & -0.2885 \\ \vdots & \vdots & \vdots & \vdots & \ddots & \vdots & \vdots & \vdots & \vdots \\ -0.4919 & 0.0676 & 0.0140 & -0.3843 & \dots & -4.2624 & 5.7385 & 0.1140 & 3.5719 \\ -0.0038 & -0.0050 & -0.0041 & -0.0378 & \dots & -0.0277 & 0.0247 & 0.0163 & -0.0206 \end{bmatrix} \tag{12.2}$$

Matrix B is stored in oo_.dr.ghu, and is 51×5 written as

$$B = \begin{bmatrix} -3.5074 & -3.4463 & 0.3660 & -0.0779 & 2.2583 \\ 0.6841 & 1.2488 & -0.1132 & 0.0202 & 2.3042 \\ 0.0746 & -0.1606 & 0.0315 & 0.0091 & -1.0041 \\ \vdots & \vdots & \vdots & \vdots & \vdots \\ -3.9307 & -1.3347 & 0.1949 & -0.0853 & 5.0765 \\ 0.0698 & -0.5228 & 0.0473 & -0.0015 & 0.0292 \end{bmatrix} \tag{12.3}$$

Similarly, matrix C is stored in oo_.dr.ghxx, Δ^2 in oo_.dr.ghs2, D in oo_.dr.ghuu, and finally E in oo_.dr.ghxu.

References

1. Iacoviello, M., & Neri, S. (2010). Housing market spillovers: Evidence from an estimated DSGE model. *American Economic Journal: Macroeconomics*, *2*(2), 125–164.
2. Bin, L. (2004). Recent development of the research of monetary policy rules. *Journal of Finance*, *2*, 2–28.
3. Bin, L. (2008). Development and application of the DSGE model for monetary policy analysis in China. *Journal of Financial Research*, *10*, 4–24.
4. Chen, W., & Xu, B. (2009). Bank lending and economic fluctuations in China: 1993–2005. *China Economic Quarterly*, *3*, 1–11.
5. Xi, J., & He, Y. (2010). The welfare losses of China's monetary policy and the selection of intermediate target: A New Keynesian DSGE model. *Journal of Finance and Economics*, *36*(2), 89–98.
6. Luo, W., & Wu, Y. (2012). Macroeconomic effects of house property tax reform and house price movement: A simulation analysis based on DSGE model. *Journal of Financial Research*, *5*, 3–28.
7. Bernanke, B., Gertler, M., & Gilchrist, S. (1999). The financial accelerator in a quantitative business cycle framework. *Handbook of Macroeconomics*, *1*, 1341–1393.

8. Smets, F., & Wouters, R. (2007). Shocks and frictions in US business cycles: A Bayesian DSGE approach. *The American Economic Review*, *97*(3), 586–606.
9. Christiano, L. J., Motto, R., & Rostagno, M. (2010). *Financial factors in economic fluctuations* (European Central Bank Working Papers No. 1192).
10. Peiris, S. J., Saxegaard, M., & Anand, R. (2010). *An estimated model with macrofinancial linkages for India* (IMF Working Papers No. 1021).
11. Gabriel, V., Levine, P., Pearlman, J., & Yang, B. (2010). *An estimated DSGE model of the Indian economy* (Universidade do Minho Working Papers No. 29).
12. Messenger, J. C., Lee, S., & McCann, D. (2007). *Working time around the world: Trends in working hours, laws and policies in a global comparative perspective*. London and Geneva: Routledge and ILO.
13. Clark, R. (2004). India working: Essays on society and economy. *Journal of Asian Economics*, *15*(2), 253–278.
14. Spector, P. E., Cooper, C. L., Poelmans, S., Allen, T. D., O'Driscoll, M., Sanchez, J. I., et al. (2004). A cross-national comparative study of work-family stressors, working hours, and well-being: China and Latin America versus the Anglo world. *Personnel Psychology*, *57*(1), 119–142.
15. Hu, Z. F., & Khan, M. S. (1997). Why is China growing so fast? *IMF Staff Papers*, *44*(1), 103–131.
16. Wong, K., Fu, D., Li, C. Y., & Song, H. X. (2007). Rural migrant workers in urban China: Living a marginalised life. *International Journal of Social Welfare*, *16*(1), 32–40.
17. Bouakez, H., Cardia, E., & Ruge-Murcia, F. J. (2005). Habit formation and the persistence of monetary shocks. *International Journal of Social Welfare*, *52*(6), 1073–1088.
18. Bouakez, H., & Kano, T. (2006). Learning-by-doing or habit formation? *Journal of Monetary Economics*, *9*(3), 508–524.
19. Smets, F., & Wouters, R. (2005). Comparing shocks and frictions in US and Euro area business cycles: A Bayesian DSGE approach. *Journal of Applied Econometrics*, *20*(2), 161–183.
20. Chowdhury, I., Hoffmann, M., & Schabert, A. (2006). Inflation dynamics and the cost channel of monetary transmission. *European Economic Review*, *50*(4), 995–1016.
21. Cabezon, E. (2014). *Working capital, financial frictions and monetary policy in Brazil* (University of North Carolina Economics Working Papers No. 11).

PART V

Summary

CHAPTER 13

Conclusion and Discussion

13.1 Conclusion

This book attempts to review the development of dynamic macroeconomic modelling and to build new DSGE models, FHSAM, with the financial and the housing markets and the social stratification to capture the characteristics of the economic dynamics and relationships among different economic agents in emerging market economies, represented by Brazil, India and China. This research accounts for the missing social category structure of emerging market economies in the relevant literature, and gives emphasis on the financial and the housing markets in these economies. The results of empirical analysis are consistent with the observed data of the target economies and our theoretical hypotheses.

As shown in the previous chapters, the model economy of the FHSAM exhibits good consistence with the stylized facts and the theoretical hypotheses. This consistence can be demonstrated in terms of correlations between economic variables and of standard deviations of economic variables, as shown in Tables 13.1 and 13.2. Additionally, there is a good consistence in terms of impulse responses. To better indicate such consistence, we summarize the comparison between model results[1] and hypotheses of impulse

[1] Here, we demonstrate the results produced by the full model specified for China. The results generated by the full model specified for Brazil and India are similar as we have shown in the previous chapter.

D. L. Jia, *Dynamic Macroeconomic Models in Emerging Market Economies*,
https://doi.org/10.1007/978-981-15-4588-7_13

Table 13.1 The statistical features of our models: correlations

Correlations	*Theoretical hypotheses*	*Stylized facts*	*Model output*		
			Basic	*Advanced*	*Full*
Consum., GDP	Positive	0.7389	0.9598	0.7852	0.7315
Inv., GDP	Positive	0.7234	0.9676	0.7210	0.7296
Wage, GDP	Positive	0.6460	0.9576	0.5842	0.6119
Inflation, GDP	Positive	0.6413	–	0.6646	0.6523
Consum., Inv.	Positive	0.5994	0.9078	0.4981	0.5418
p_h, GDP	Positive	0.5624	–	0.8255	0.7971
p_h, Consum.	Positive	0.4132	–	0.5096	0.4460
p_h, Inv.	Positive	0.6332	–	0.7887	0.6840
p_h, Llh	Positive	0.6263	–	0.7386	0.7245
Llh, GDP	Positive	0.7145	–	0.7578	0.7551

Table 13.2 The statistical features of our models: standard deviations

Stdev.	*Stylized facts*	*Model output*		
		Basic	*Advanced*	*Full*
Consumption	0.017293	0.007610	0.015114	0.016044
Investment	0.045452	0.014848	0.041103	0.041322
Inflation	0.018656	0.010786	0.013757	0.013923
GDP	0.030811	0.022000	0.026874	0.029844
Real interest	0.012772	0.000491	0.015481	0.015245
Real wages	0.033231	0.017620	0.046083	0.053277
Housing prices	0.093910	–	0.099408	0.098147

responses to productivity shocks in the non-housing market, $A_{c,t}$, and in the housing market, $A_{h,t}$, in Tables 13.3 and 13.4.

Tables 13.5 and 13.6 summarize the comparison between model results and the theoretical hypotheses in impulse responses to housing demand shocks and interest-rate shocks.

Based on these models, we can make accurate analysis and prediction of economic reactions in emerging market economies to policy changes. This would be useful for policymakers and researchers to suggest policies that correspond to the expected results. Our models give quantitative information about how a positive change of the interest rate can influence the overall economy. As we have shown in the empirical analysis, a 1% positive interest-rate hike causes a drop to the real GDP by about 0.28% in China, 0.30% in Brazil and 0.32% in India. Such interest-rate hike causes real investment in fixed physical assets to decrease by

Table 13.3 The consistence between theoretical hypotheses and the full model: impulse responses to productivity shocks

Economic variables	*Exogenous shock (positive)*	*Hypothesized response*	*Model output*
GDP_t	Productivity shock, $A_{c,t}$	Gradually rise to a new level	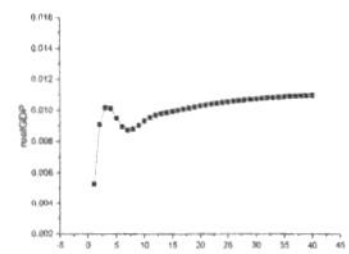
Investment	Productivity shock, $A_{c,t}$	Instantly rise and gradually descend to a new level	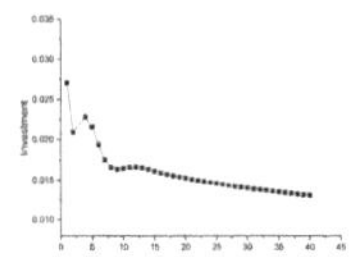
Consumption	Productivity shock, $A_{c,t}$	Gradually rise to a new level	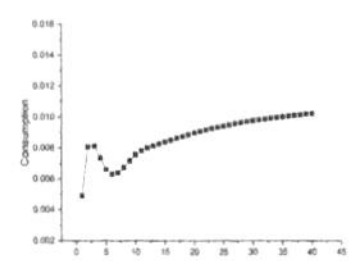
Real wage	Productivity shock, $A_{c,t}$	Gradually rise to a new level	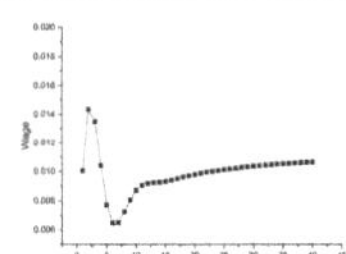
GDP_t	Productivity shock, $A_{h,t}$	Instantly small rise and gradually descend to a new level	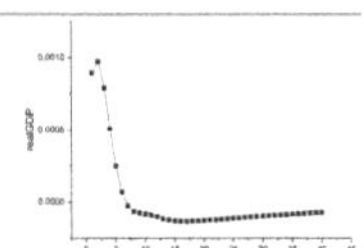
Investment	Productivity shock, $A_{h,t}$	Instantly small decrease and gradually rise to a new level	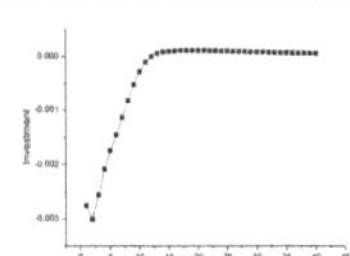
Consumption	Productivity shock, $A_{h,t}$	Instantly small increase and gradually descend to a new level	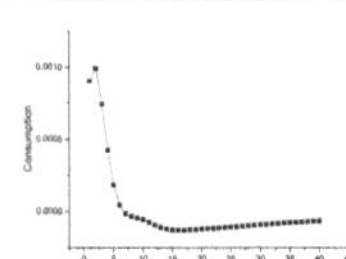
Real wages	Productivity shock, $A_{h,t}$	Instantly small increase and gradually descend to a new level	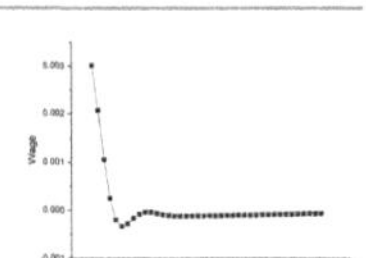

Table 13.4 The consistence between theoretical hypotheses and the full model: impulse responses to productivity shocks

Economic variables	*Exogenous shock (positive)*	*Hypothesized response*	*Model output*
Inflation	Productivity shock, $A_{c,t}$	Rise and then return to the original level	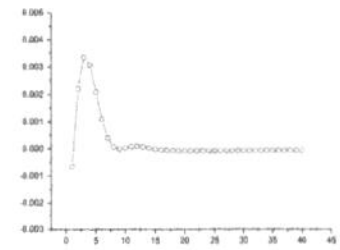
Real interest rate	Productivity shock, $A_{c,t}$	Instantly rise and gradually descend to the original level	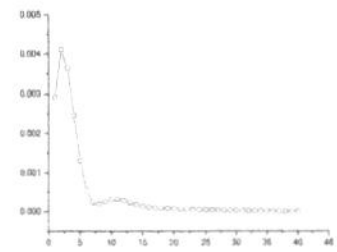
Real housing prices	Productivity shock, $A_{c,t}$	Gradually rise to a new level	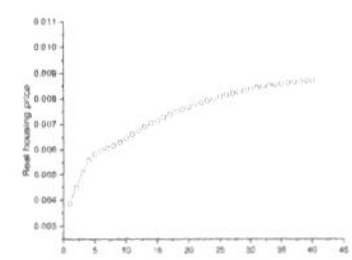
Inflation	Productivity shock, $A_{h,t}$	Instantly rise and gradually return to the original level	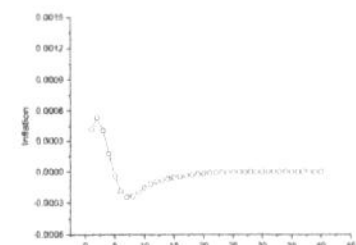
Real interest rate	Productivity shock, $A_{h,t}$	Instantly rise and gradually descend to the original level	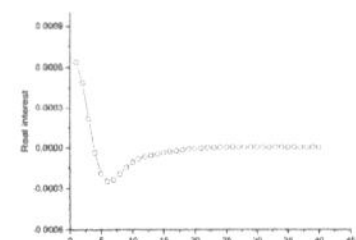
Real housing prices	Productivity shock, $A_{h,t}$	Instant drop and gradually return to a new level	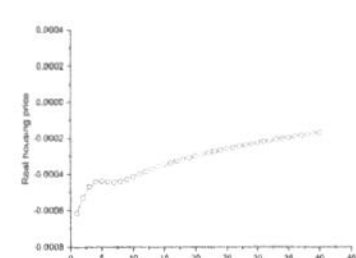

Table 13.5 The consistence between theoretical hypotheses and the full model: impulse responses to housing demand and interest-rate shocks

Economic variables	*Exogenous shock (positive)*	*Hypothesized response*	*Model output*
GDP_t	Housing demand, j_t	Increase and then return to the original level	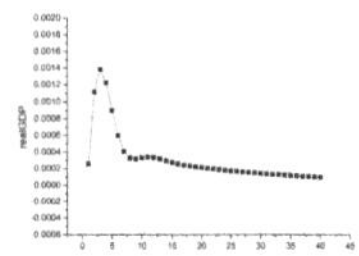
Investment	Housing demand, j_t	Instantly rise and gradually descend to the original level	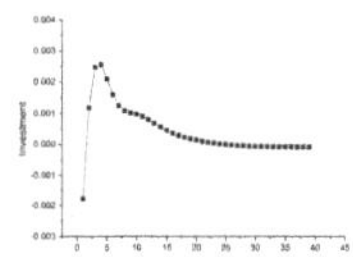
Consumption	Housing demand, j_t	Instantly increase and gradually descend to the original level	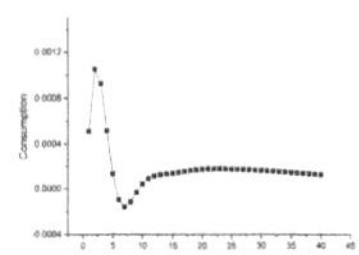
Real wages	Housing demand, j_t	Instantly increase and gradually descend to the original level	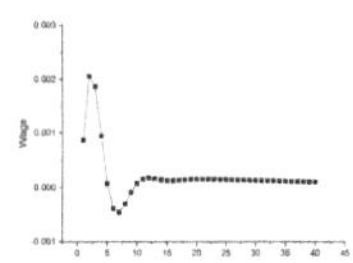
GDP_t	Interest rate, $e_{r,t}$	Sharply drop and gradually rise to the original level	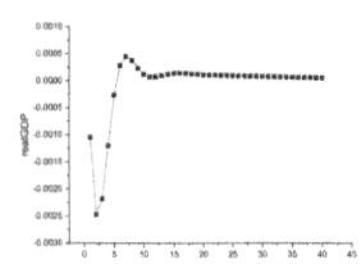
Investment	Interest rate, $e_{r,t}$	Sharply drop and gradually rise to the original level	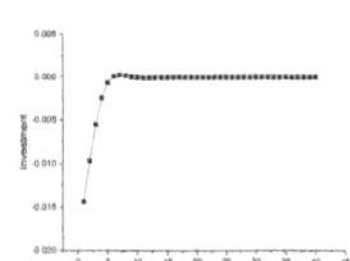
Consumption	Interest rate, $e_{r,t}$	Sharply drop and gradually rise to the original level	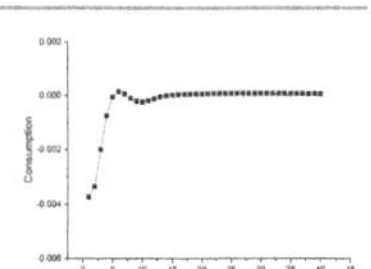
Real wages	Interest rate, $e_{r,t}$	Sharply drop and gradually rise to the original level	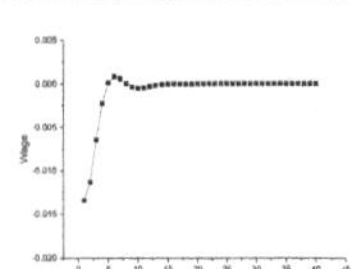

Table 13.6 The consistence between theoretical hypotheses and the full model: impulse responses to housing demand and interest rate shocks

Economic variables	*Exogenous shock (positive)*	*Hypothesized response*	*Model output*
Inflation	Housing demand, j_t	Gradually rise to the original level	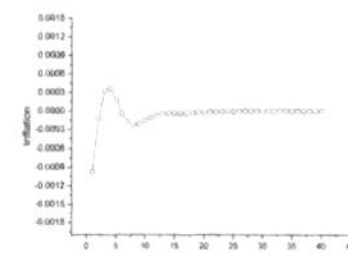
Real interest rate	Housing demand, j_t	Instantly rise and gradually descend to the original level	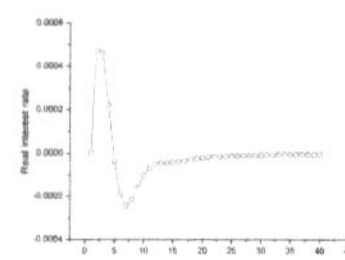
Real housing prices	Housing demand, j_t	Instantly increase and gradually descend to the original level	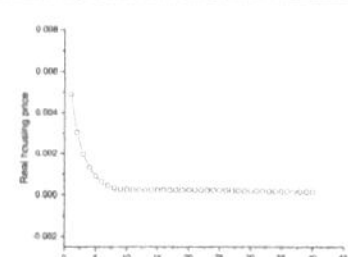
Inflation	Interest rate, $e_{r,t}$	Rise and then descend to the original level	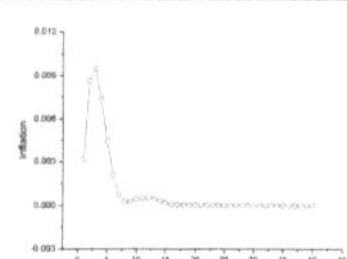
Real housing prices	Interest rate, $e_{r,t}$	Instantly sharp drop and gradually return to the original level	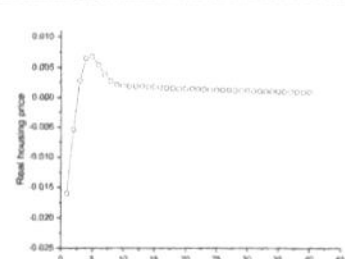

a larger amount: of about 1.50% in China, 1.60% in Brazil and 1.70% in India. Similarly, after such interest-rate change, consumption drops by about 0.40% and real household wage 1.40% in these three countries. Real housing prices are sensitive to monetary policy in that the change of the interest rate determines the willingness and capability of households to buy real estate assets. Our model indicates that a 1% positive real interest-rate hike is typically followed by a drop of about

1.60% in real housing prices. These results can give policymakers and market participants valuable information with accurate quantitative image. On the one hand, policymakers can use them to evaluate the predicted outcomes of decision on potential policy. On the other hand, market participants can use it to quantitatively analyse the market change to make better performance of their economic activities. Our models also indicate the important role played by collateral mortgages and financial frictions. As shown in the empirical analysis of the full model, we compare the model-generated impulse responses in two scenarios: with collateral mortgages and financial frictions and without them. The results demonstrate that collateral mortgages and financial frictions can give rise to material amplification effects on the overall economy to the original exogenous shocks. As shown in Figs. 12.56–12.61, collateral mortgages and financial frictions effects account for major differences in impulse responses of the economic variables to the interest-rate shocks. Under the mechanism with collateral mortgages and financial frictions, the impulse responses of real GDP, investment in fixed physical assets, consumption and wages are almost tripled than in the scenario without collateral mortgages and financial frictions. Collateral mortgages and financial frictions also play amplification role in the impulse responses of inflation and real housing prices: the difference between the drop of real housing prices after a 1% increase of the real interest rate with and without collateral mortgage and financial frictions is about 30% in China, Brazil and India. These findings are consistent with our theoretical hypotheses, economic intuition, stylized facts and results of previous DSGE modelling, indicating that the housing and the financial markets have become the major components of the overall economy not only in developed economies but also in the emerging ones. Therefore, more attention should be paid to these subjects in macroeconomics. Our model, both in terms of its theoretical innovation and empirical results, provides an attractive way to build dynamic macroeconomic models for emerging market economies with special consideration of unique economic and social features in these economies. The good consistence between model results and theoretical analysis shows the strong robustness of our model, indicating wide application of models of this kind in macroeconomic analysis in the emerging market economies.

13.2 The Potentials of FHSAM

As discussed in the theoretical framework of the FHSAM, this model is a closed economy model with focus on the dynamics and economic performance of the relevant economies. The connection between domestic and foreign economies is not included in this model. The DSGE models of this kind have been widely used in studying economies and have shown good results. The performance of good consistence between model results and stylized facts confirms such plausibility. But, like all other economic models, this model also has potential to be improved in the future. As far as we concerned, one of the most possible improvements of this model is to add import and export features into it, making this model an open economy model. Equipped with such feature, the new model should be able to quantify the dynamic connection between domestic and foreign agents and to accurately analyse the fluctuations of the exchange rate, which is a key variable in international trading and financial markets. Our model shows strong robustness and good consistence with our theoretical hypotheses and the stylized facts. It provides valuable information for macroeconomic analysis and policymaking. It also provides prototype DSGE models for emerging market economies with special consideration of economic and social features in these economies, based on which improvements can be conducted to refine the model economy and to incorporate more comprehensive economic features. The potential improvements of FHSAM are summarized as follows:

- Open economy model: FHSAM developed in this book is a closed economy framework. To extend its application in open economy cases, the original framework should be refined, incorporating foreign trade department in the model economy;
- Social stratification: More comprehensive structure in the housing sector can be introduced into the model economy, according to the actual condition in the target economy;
- Wage rigidities in the labour market: Adding wage rigidities in the labour market of different types of household into the model economy;
- More detailed description of the government: Behaviours other than public finance can be considered in the model economy as governmental agents are major market players in emerging market economies;

- Financial assets: In FHSAM, several types of financial assets are included: money, bond, deposit, mortgage, entrepreneur loan and real estate asset. To improve, more asset types such as stock and derivatives can be added, and financial contagion among financial assets can be modelled.

Glossary

NOTATIONS I: LINEAR ALGEBRA

Scalars A scalar is defined as a quantity that is completely described by its magnitude, without any direction. Italic symbols are used for scalars, for example $x_1, x_2...$

Vector A vector, y, is defined as a column of scalars, for example

$$y = \begin{bmatrix} y_1 \\ y_2 \\ . \\ . \\ . \\ y_n \end{bmatrix} \tag{1}$$

in which y_i for all integer $i, 0 \leq i \leq n$, are scalars. By definition, y is a $1 \times n$ vector. The inner product of a pair of n dimensional vectors, y and z, is

$$y'z = [y_1, y_2, ..., y_n] \begin{bmatrix} z_1 \\ z_2 \\ . \\ . \\ . \\ z_n \end{bmatrix} = \sum_{i=1}^{n} y_i z_i \tag{2}$$

D. L. Jia, *Dynamic Macroeconomic Models in Emerging Market Economies*,
https://doi.org/10.1007/978-981-15-4588-7

where y' denotes the matrix transposition of y. Therefore, matrix multiplication is defined as the product of two matrices, p and q, and is written as

$$pq = \begin{bmatrix} p_{11} & \cdots & p_{1m} \\ p_{21} & \cdots & p_{2m} \\ \cdot & \cdots & \cdot \\ \cdot & \cdots & \cdot \\ \cdot & \cdots & \cdot \\ p_{n1} & \cdots & p_{nm} \end{bmatrix} \begin{bmatrix} q_{11} & \cdots & q_{1l} \\ q_{21} & \cdots & q_{2l} \\ \cdot & \cdots & \cdot \\ \cdot & \cdots & \cdot \\ \cdot & \cdots & \cdot \\ q_{m1} & \cdots & q_{ml} \end{bmatrix} = w \tag{3}$$

where p is a $n \times m$ dimensional matrix, q $m \times l$, and w is a $n \times l$ dimensional matrix, each entry is

$$w_{ij} = \sum_{k=1}^{m} p_{ik} q_{kj} \tag{4}$$

NOTATIONS II: CONTROL THEORY & STATE SPACE

State vector Based on the definition of vector, a state vector, $\mathbf{x}_t$, represents the state of a system with n states at time t:

$$\mathbf{x}_t = \begin{bmatrix} x_1 \\ x_2 \\ \cdot \\ \cdot \\ \cdot \\ x_n \end{bmatrix} \tag{5}$$

Thus, $\mathbf{x}_t$ denotes the complete information of the system in a n dimensional state space at time t.

Multi-input multi-output, MIMO In a MIMO system, both input to and output of the system are multidimensional. A standard MIMO system can be written as

$$\begin{aligned} \dot{\mathbf{x}}_t &= A\mathbf{x}_t + B\mathbf{u}_t \\ \mathbf{y}_t &= C\mathbf{x}_t + D\mathbf{u}_t \end{aligned} \tag{6}$$

where $\mathbf{u}_t$ is the $p \times 1$ input (innovation) vector,[1] $\mathbf{y}_t$ the $q \times 1$ output vector, and $\dot{\mathbf{x}}_t$ the state deviation, capturing the dynamic evolution of the system.

[1] In a dynamic macroeconomic model, such input denotes the unexpected shocks to the model economy.

A is a $n \times n$ matrix, B a $n \times p$ matrix, C a $q \times n$ matrix, and D a $q \times p$ matrix, and $p, q > 1$. One thing that needs to be noted is that A is, by definition, a square matrix, which is diagonalizable:

$$\begin{aligned} A &= Q \Lambda Q^{-1} \\ \Lambda &= Q^{-1} A Q \end{aligned} \tag{7}$$

in which Λ is a diagonal matrix with eigenvalues of matrix A on its diagonal entries.

Linear time invariant, LTI A system denoted by Eq. 6 is LTI system when matrices A, B, C, and D are independent of time. Typically, the dynamic macroeconomic systems of NCM/DSGE type that are represented by the linear state space representation and the corresponding policy rules are in the LTI form.

Laplace transform It transforms signal in time domain to the one in the frequency domain

$$\begin{aligned} \mathcal{L}\{x_t\} &= \sum_{0}^{1} x_{(t)} e^{-st} dt \\ &= \hat{x}_{(s)} \end{aligned} \tag{8}$$

in which $x_{(t)}$ is the original signal in time domain and $\hat{x}_{(s)}$ is the transformed signal in the frequency domain. Applying Laplace transform in Eq. 6, we find the transformed MIMO in the frequency domain

$$\begin{aligned} \hat{\mathbf{x}}_{(s)} &= (SI - A)^{-1} B \hat{\mathbf{u}}_{(s)} \\ \hat{\mathbf{y}}_{(s)} &= [C(SI - A)^{-1} B + D] \hat{\mathbf{u}}_{(s)} \end{aligned} \tag{9}$$

where S is a scalar and I is the $n \times n$ identity matrix.

NOTATIONS III: PROBABILITY THEORY

Random variables A variable is random when its value is the function of the result of a statistical experiment. Its value is unknown until the realization of the statistical experiment. Italic symbols are used to denote random variables.

Random vectors According to the definition of vector, random vector is defined as a vector whose entries are random variables. We use italic uppercase symbols for random vectors.

Prior distribution and posterior distribution Prior (posterior) distribution is defined as a probability distribution of variables or parameters before (after) empirical information is obtained. In Bayesian inference, the unknown parameter is given a prior distribution and Bayes' Theorem combines this with the likelihood from the observed data to derive the posterior distribution.

Index

D. L. Jia, *Dynamic Macroeconomic Models in Emerging Market Economies*, https://doi.org/10.1007/978-981-15-4588-7

Q

R

S

T

U

W

The manufacturer's authorised representative in the EU is Springer Nature Customer Service Centre GmbH, Europaplatz 3, 69115 Heidelberg, Germany. If you have any concerns regarding our products, please contact ProductSafety@springernature.com

Printed and bound by CPI Group (UK) Ltd, Croydon, CR0 4YY
25/09/2026
02222902-0007